Salesmanship and Sales Force Management

This is the third of four volumes of articles selected from the *Harvard Business Review* for the series entitled The Business Administrator.

Salesmanship and Sales Force Management

Edited by Edward C. Bursk, Editor, Harvard Business Review, *and*
G. Scott Hutchison, Senior Associate Editor, Harvard Business Review

Harvard University Press, Cambridge, Massachusetts, 1971

Distributed in Great Britain by Oxford University Press, London

Library of Congress Catalog Card Number 78-150007
SBN 674-78530-4
Printed in the United States of America

Contents

Introduction

"Without a sale, nothing happens." With these five words, a sales engineer summed up the critical role the selling function has in modern commerce and industry.

His is, admittedly, a somewhat biased view, but the point is both refreshing and valid. It is refreshing in that it runs contrary to a large segment of management thinking which invariably starts at the other end of the production process with plant and facilities, conversion of raw materials into finished goods, and, finally, sales. Similarly, it is valid because without a sale there is no justification for servicing, shipping, warehousing, manufacturing, receiving, purchasing, and all the other business activities that comprise the process of producing something.

This is another way of saying that some business executives have been looking, perhaps, at their operations through the wrong end of the telescope. Certainly, few business subjects are more widely misunderstood than salesmanship. "Misconceptions range the whole way from the popular notion that successful salesmen are rare individuals who somehow have been born with natural qualities of glibness and smooth talk," says J. M. Hickerson, "to the equally errant idea that salesmanship is a science, a kind of push-button psychology, which anyone can practice if he is let in on the secrets."[1]

In the years since the early 1950s, when Hickerson expressed those thoughts, new developments in the problem of improving salesmanship have moved "the state of the art" in the direction of a far more scientific approach to *"salesmanship and sales force management."* Naturally, no compilation of articles on "new" developments can expect to remain new for very long. But a judicious selection of articles, which presents thoughtfully and accurately basic concepts that have stood the test of time, can be of considerable value to both the manager who is seeking to improve his skills and to the younger salesman who desires to learn more about the fundamental tools of his profession.

The editors of this book have made such a selection. Out of thirty-five articles on various aspects of the sales function, they have chosen nineteen *Harvard Business Review* best sellers which give a well-rounded picture of the theories, studies, and techniques that provide greater insight to the salesman in his front-line relationship with his customers and to the sales manager with his subordinates.

This series leads off with nine chapters devoted to the topic "The Development of Sales and Salesmen." Since "nothing happens" until a sale is made, the editors have chosen to introduce this first section with a discussion of "What Makes a Good Salesman." What counts more than experience, the authors explain, is a man's central characteristics of empathy and ego drive, which he must have in order to sell sucessfully. This chapter helps a manager to see that training can only succeed if selection succeeds.

Two of the chapters in this section present contrasting views on sales training. In one, the author advances the concept that role-playing, which forces learning by doing—practicing—rather than just talking, can be used with considerable success in developing a salesman's skill in handling face-to-face involvement with customers and prospects. In the other chapter, the authors contend that there are two distinct kinds of selling jobs: sales development and sales maintenance. Since these two jobs require different skills, management would do well to

1. See Chapter 7, below.

divide the sales force into two specialized groups. This way, the authors claim, the sales manager could raise field performance to new levels and pave the way for the development of many new accounts.

Other pertinent discussions covered within the "development" section include door-to-door selling, the pay of salesmen in relation to their actual contribution to the success of the business, a method for the scientific deployment of manpower in multi-line companies to achieve effective coverage and equitable territories, the instincts that produce a successful consumer-goods salesman, and a natural formula based on psychological principles for a successful sales presentation.

In the second part of the book, six chapters are included under the heading "The Role of the Sales Force Manager." The discussion begins, quite aptly, with the mandate "Sales Managers Must Manage." This is true, but how are they to understand what managing is? Vital to their understanding is a simplified concept of managing for sales managers stated in terms of day-to-day duties and responsibilities.

Another chapter reports on a detailed study of some fifty-four companies, which reveals that poor or mediocre performance at the vital contact point between the home office and the customer is widespread, and that it damages morale, weakens initiative, wastes salespower, and causes high turnover. In "Sales Management in the Field," the author analyzes the problem in helpful detail. He then suggests some methods for improving the situation, placing most of the responsibility for carrying them out on the top sales executive group in a company.

For the analytically minded field sales manager, there is a new sales tool, ROAM ("return on assets managed"), which can be valid for making decisions that affect either directly or indirectly the level of inventories or the range of accounts receivable committed.

Chapter 13, "Sales Power Through Planned Careers," based on a study of thirty large companies, reports on the growing recognition that effective sales manpower development requires that a whole range of activities be closely linked together into an integrated program called the "career path concept." The discussion describes the concept as it applies to both sales management and career salesmen in the leading companies that participated in the study.

The title of Chapter 14—"Get the Most Out of Your Sales Force"—is appropriate. By querying 1,029 sales executives on their practices and then matching the responses with indicators of high success, Derek A. Newton has derived a useful set of guidelines for each of four major kinds of selling activity: trade, missionary, technical, and new-business.

Rounding out the second part of the book is "How Many Salesmen Do You Need?" Managers usually try to resolve this problem by experience and seasoned judgment. This discussion should provide a sharper focus for the manager's thinking in approaching this persistent question.

The final section of the book is devoted to "The Relationship of Sales and Marketing" and includes four chapters selected especially to help top executives charged with these responsibilities.

"Behavioral Approach to Industrial Selling" reports on the successful experience of a major producer and marketer of specialized industrial materials and material systems in developing a companywide sales training program that integrates behavioral science concepts with selling. In describing the program the authors reveal how the program has led to the development of the company's human resources, greater organizational flexibility, and a market-oriented network of communication.

Since "without a sale there is no justification for . . . all the business activities . . . which comprise the process of producing something," a short chapter is devoted to the central point that while some companies use the "investment" approach in new product planning and brand promotion, almost none apply it in an area where, if anything, it is more needed and more likely to sharpen decision making. Edward C. Bursk, coeditor of this volume, presents a useful concept for analyzing certain kinds of marketing situations, particularly those where marketers depend on continuing patronage. In Chapter 17, "View Your Customers as Investments," he points out that there are various ways of investing time, money, and effort to increase the volume or profitability of customer patronage. "If the marketer compares them in explicit, quantitative terms," he concludes, "he will be more likely to make intelligent decisions."

"How to Rationalize Your Marketing Risks" pursues a similar theme of improving marketing decisions. In this chapter the author describes a logical, step-by-step process for measuring risks and evaluating probabilities and then deciding either not to go ahead or to go ahead, but on the basis of taking preventive action to minimize possible losses.

No volume compiled from *HBR* articles on the subject of selling and sales management would be complete without one written by Theodore Levitt. It is quite fitting, then, that the editors have chosen "The New Markets—Think Before You Leap" as the final selection for this book. "There can be a need, but no market; or a market, but no customer," Levitt says. Market forecasters who fail to understand these concepts have made spectacular miscalculations about the apparent opportunities; thus market plans must be tempered with common sense.

The editors of this volume (which has been printed from reproduction proofs of the *HBR*) have chosen articles that would mix the various sales and marketing ingredients in the correct proportions to achieve optimum results from *Salesmanship and Sales Force Management*.

E.C.B.
G.S.H.

The Relationship of Sales and Marketing

David Mayer and Herbert M. Greenberg

1 What Makes a Good Salesman

More than 35 years ago, the insurance industry embarked on an intensive program to solve the problem of costly, wasteful turnover among its agents. Estimates at that time indicated that there was a turnover of better than 50% within the first year and almost 80% within the first 3 years. After the expenditure of millions of dollars and 35 years of research, the turnover in the insurance industry remains approximately 50% within the first year and 80% within the first 3 years.

What is the cost of this turnover? Nearly incalculable. Consider:

- The substantial sums paid new salesmen as salary, draw on commission, expense accounts, and so on, which are wasted when those salesmen fail to sell.
- The staggering company costs, in time, money, and energy, of recruiting, selecting, training, and supervising men who inherently do not have the ability to succeed.
- The vast costs caused by lost sales, dropouts, reduced company reputation, poor morale, permanently burned territory, and the like.

What accounts for this expensive inefficiency? Basically this: companies have simply not known what makes one man able to sell and another not. As Robert N. McMurry has observed:

> "A very high proportion of those engaged in selling cannot sell. . . . If American sales efficiency is to be maximized and the appalling waste of money and manpower which exists today is to be minimized, a constructive analysis must be made of what selling really is and how its effectiveness can be enhanced. . . . We must look a good deal further — into the mysteries of personality and psychology — if we want real answers." [1]

It was the obvious need for a better method of sales selection that led us to embark on seven years of field research in this area. The article which follows is based on the insights we gained as to the basic characteristics necessary for a salesman to be able to sell successfully. Confirming the fact that we are on the right track is the predictive power of the selection instrument (battery of tests) that we developed out of the same research; see EXHIBIT I.

Two Essentials

Our basic theory is that a good salesman must have at least two basic qualities: empathy and ego drive.

Ability to Feel

Empathy, the important central ability to *feel* as the other fellow does in order to be able to sell him a product or service, must be possessed in large measure. Having empathy does not necessarily mean being sympathetic. One can know what the other fellow feels without agreeing with that feeling. But a salesman simply cannot sell well without the invaluable and irreplaceable ability to get a powerful feedback from his client through empathy.

A parallel might be drawn in this connection between the old antiaircraft weapons and the new heat-attracted missiles. With the old type

[1] "The Mystique of Super-Salesmanship," HBR March–April, 1961, p. 113.

EXHIBIT I. THREE EXAMPLES OF PREDICTIVE RESULTS FROM SELECTION INSTRUMENT BASED ON EMPATHY AND EGO-DRIVE

Number of men predicted for each group *		Data at end of (months)	Actual sales performance (number of men who reached each quarter of sales force)				Quit or fired
			Top half		Bottom half		
			Top/quarter	2nd/quarter	3rd/quarter	Bottom/quarter	
IN THE RETAIL AUTOMOBILE INDUSTRY							
A	34	6 mos.	17	13	1	0	3
		18	19	9	0	0	6
B	49	6	9	23	8	2	7
		18	10	19	8	0	12
C	60	6	0	9	20	14	17
		18	0	2	21	8	29
D	52	6	0	0	10	18	24
		18	0	0	9	7	36
IN THE INSURANCE INDUSTRY							
A	22	6 mos.	13	4	1	0	4
		14	13	4	0	0	5
B	55	6	7	23	11	2	12
		14	11	20	7	1	16
C	56	6	1	5	19	12	19
		14	1	4	11	5	35
D	48	6	0	0	4	10	34
		14	0	0	3	4	41
IN THE MUTUAL FUNDS INDUSTRY							
A	11	6 mos.	5	4	1	0	1
B	20	6	4	9	3	0	4
C	49	6	0	4	15	12	18
D	34	6	0	1	7	10	16

* Predictions made on basis of test, without seeing men or any records:
A means outstanding, top potential as a salesman, almost certain to succeed with high productivity.
B means recommended, good productivity, and can sometimes be designated as developable into an *A*.
C means not recommended, even though a C can under the right circumstances edge into becoming a low B.
D means absolutely not recommended; the applicant concerned has virtually no possibility of success.

of ballistic weapon, the gunner would take aim at an airplane, correcting as best he could for windage and driftage, and then fire. If the shell missed by just a few inches because of a slight error in calculation or because the plane took evasive action, the miss might just as well have been by hundreds of yards for all the good it did.

This is the salesman with poor empathy. He aims at the target as best he can and proceeds along his sales track; but if his target — the customer — fails to perform as predicted, the sale is missed.

On the other hand, the new missiles, if they are anywhere near the target, become attracted to the heat of the target's engine, and regardless of its evasive action, they finally home in and hit their mark.

This is the salesman with good empathy. He senses the reactions of the customer and is able to adjust to these reactions. He is not simply bound by a prepared sales track, but he functions in terms of the real interaction between himself and the customer. Sensing what the customer is feeling, he is able to change pace, double back on his track, and make whatever creative modifications might be necessary to home in on the target and close the sale.

Need to Conquer

The second of the basic qualities absolutely needed by a good salesman is a particular kind of *ego drive* which makes him want and need to make the sale in a personal or ego way, not merely for the money to be gained. His feeling must be that he *has* to make the sale; the customer is there to help him fulfill his personal need. In effect, to the top salesman, the sale — the conquest — provides a powerful means of enhancing his ego. His self-picture improves dramatically by virtue of conquest, and diminishes with failure.

Because of the nature of all selling, the salesman will fail to sell more often than he will succeed. Thus, since failure tends to diminish his self-picture, his ego cannot be so weak that the poor self-picture continues for too long a time. Rather, the failure must act as a trigger — as a motivation toward greater efforts — which with success will bring the ego enhancement he seeks. A subtle balance must be found between (a) an ego partially weakened in precisely the right way to need a great deal of enhancement (the sale) and (b) an ego sufficiently strong to be motivated by failure but not to be shattered by it.

The salesman's empathy, coupled with his intense ego drive, enables him to home in on the target effectively and make the sale. He has the drive, the need to make the sale, and his empathy gives him the connecting tool with which to do it.

Synergistic Effects

In this discussion of the relationship of empathy and ego drive to successful selling, we will treat these dynamic factors as separate characteristics. Indeed, they are separate in that someone can have a great deal of empathy and any level of ego drive — extremely strong to extremely weak. Someone with poor empathy can also have any level of ego drive. Yet, as determinants of sales ability, empathy and ego drive act on and, in fact, reinforce each other.

The person with strong ego drive has maximum motivation to fully utilize whatever empathy he possesses. Needing the sale, he is not likely to let his empathy spill over and become sympathy. His ego need for the conquest is not likely to allow him to side with the customer; instead, it spurs him on to use his knowledge of the customer fully to make the sale.

On the other hand, the person with little or no ego drive is hardly likely to use his empathy in a persuasive manner. He understands people and may know perfectly well what things he might say to close the sale effectively, but his understanding is apt to become sympathy. If he does not need the conquest, his very knowledge of the real needs of the potential customer may tell him that the customer in fact should not buy. Since he does not need the sale in an inner personal sense, he then may not persuade the customer to buy. So we frequently say in our evaluations of potential salesmen, "This man has fine empathy, but he is not likely to use it persuasively — he will not use it to close."

Thus, there is a dynamic relationship beween empathy and ego drive. It takes a combination of the two, each working to reinforce the other — each enabling the other to be fully utilized — to make the successful salesman.

Need for Balance

It calls for a very special, balanced ego to need the sale intensely and yet allow the salesman to look closely at the customer and fully benefit from an empathic perception of the customer's reactions and needs.

Thus, there are a number of possible permutations of empathy and drive. A man may have a high degree of both empathy and drive (*ED*), or little of either (*ed*), or two kinds of combinations in between (*Ed* and *eD*). For example:

ED — A salesman who has a great deal of both empathy and strong inner sales drive will be at or near the top of the sales force.

Ed — A salesman with fine empathy but too little drive may be a splendid person but will be unable to close his deals effectively. This is the "nice guy." Everyone likes him, and from all appearances he should turn out to be one of the best men on the force. He somehow "doesn't make it." People end up liking him, but buying from the company down the street. He is often hired because he does have such fine personal qualities. Yet his closing ability is weak. He will get along with the customer, understand him, and bring him near the close; but he does not have that inner hunger to move the customer that final one foot to the actual sale. It is this last element of the sale — the close — which empathy alone cannot achieve, and where the assertive quality of ego drive becomes the all-important essential.

eD — A salesman with much drive but too little empathy will bulldoze his way through to some sales, but he will miss a great many and will hurt his employer through his lack of understanding of people.

ed — A salesman without much empathy or drive should not actually be a salesman, although a great many present salesmen fall into this group. An employer would avoid much grief by finding this out in advance, before so much effort is spent in trying to hire, train, and spoon-feed a man who does not have within him the basic dynamics to be successful.

Failure of Tests

Since the selection of top salesmen is potentially of such enormous value, why, it might be asked, has there been so little success to date in developing methods to preselect effectively?

For at least 50 years, psychologists have been working very hard in the area of testing. Almost every aspect of human personality, behavior, attitude, and ability has at one time or another come under the scrutiny of the tester. There have been some notable successes in testing, most especially perhaps in the IQ and mechanical-ability areas. Of late, personality testing, especially with the increasing use of projective techniques, has gained a certain level of sophistication. The area which has been to date most barren of real scientific success has been aptitude testing, where the aptitude consists of personality dynamics rather than simple mechanical abilities.

Four Reasons

The ability to sell, an exceedingly human and totally nonmechanical aptitude, has resisted attempts to measure it effectively. The reasons for this failure up until now are many, but there appear to be four basic causes for sales aptitude test failure.

1. *Tests have been looking for interest, not ability.* The concept that a man's interest is equatable to his ability is perhaps the single largest cause of test failure. Thus, tests have been developed through asking questions of successful salesmen or successful people in other fields, with the assumption that if an applicant expresses the same kind of interest pattern as an established salesman, he too will be a successful salesman.

This assumption is wrong on its face. Psychologically, interest does not equal aptitude. Even if someone is interested in exactly the same specific things as Mickey Mantle or Willie Mays, this of course does not in any way indicate the possession of a similar baseball skill. Equally, the fact that an individual might have the same interest pattern as a successful salesman does not mean that he can sell. Even if he wants to sell, it does not mean that he *can* sell.

2. *Tests have been eminently "fakable."* When an individual is applying for a job, he obviously will attempt to tell the potential employer whatever he thinks the employer wants to hear. Given a certain amount of intelligence, the applicant will know that he should say he would "rather be a salesman than a librarian," regardless of his real preference. He knows that he should say he would "rather be with people than at home reading a good book," that he "prefers talking to a P.T.A. group to listening to good music," or that he would "rather lead a group discussion than be a forest ranger."

There are manuals on the market on how to beat sales aptitude tests, but, even without such a manual, the average intelligent person can quickly see what is sought and then give the tester what the tester wants. Thus, the tests may simply succeed in negatively screening those who are so unintelligent that they are unable to see the particular response pattern sought. In other words, since they are too dull to fake, they may be screened out. The perceptive interviewer, however, is likely to notice this kind of stupidity even more quickly than the tests do, and he can probably do a better job of this negative screening than the average fakable test.

3. *Tests have favored group conformity, not individual creativity.* Recent critics of psychological testing decry the testers who are seeking conformity and the standardized ways in which they judge applicants for sales and other occupations. This criticism is all too valid. The creative thinker, the impulsive free spirit, the original, imaginative, hard-driving individual is often screened out by tests which demand rigid adherence to convention — an adherence, in fact, that borders on a passive acceptance of authority, a fear of anything that might in any way upset the applecart of bureaucratic order. Paradoxically, this fearful, cautious, authoritarian conformist, although he might make a good civil servant, or even a fair controller or paperwork administrative executive, would never make a successful salesman.

Many of these tests not only fail to select good salesmen, but they may actually screen out the really top producers because of their creativity, impulsiveness, or originality — characteristics which most tests downgrade as strangeness or weakness. We discovered a situation of this type recently in working with a client:

> A company in the Southwest embarked on an intensive recruiting effort for salesmen. We began receiving the tests of a number of applicants. These tests all appeared to follow a certain pattern. The men were not quite recommendable, and all for about the same reason — a definite lack of ego drive. For the most part, they had some empathy, and without exception they had good verbal ability, but none had the intense inner need for the sale that we look for in a productive salesman.

After about 20 such tests came through our office, we questioned the sales manager as to what criteria he was using for screening the men who took the test. We found that before he gave the men our test, he had them take the sales aptitude test which had been developed by his company some years before. Those men who scored high on that test were given our test.

We had previously analyzed that company's test and found it to be a fairly good verbal abilities measure, and to some extent a measure of intelligence and insight. Men with strong ego drive could not as a rule score near the top of that test. And so the very men with the quality we were seeking — strong ego drive — were actually screened out. We then asked the sales manager not to use that test but to screen only for credit reference and general appearance, and to give our test to those who passed this simple screening. After that we began seeing the expected number of "A" and "B" recommendable applicants — about one man in every five.

4. *Tests have tried to isolate fractional traits rather than to reveal the whole dynamics of the man.* Most personality and aptitude tests are totally traitological in their construction and approach. They see personality as a series or "bundle" of piecemeal traits. Thus, someone may be high in "sociability" while being low in "self-sufficiency" and "dominance." Someone else may be high in "personal relations," but low in "co-operativeness." Somehow, the whole (or the *Gestalt*) gets lost. The dynamic interaction that is personality, as viewed by most modern-day psychologists, is buried in a series of fractionalized, mathematically separable traits.

Thus, it is said that the salesman, somewhat like the Boy Scout, should be very "sociable," "dominant," "friendly," "responsible," "honest," and "loyal." The totality — the dynamics within the person that will permit him to sell successfully — is really lost sight of. Clearly, someone may be "sociable," "responsible," and so on, but still be a very poor salesman.

In our research we attempted to bypass traits and to go directly to the central dynamisms that we believed were basic to sales ability: empathy and ego drive. By seeking these deeper, more central, characteristics, we immediately reduced the possibility of faking, since the respondent would find it extremely difficult to determine what *in fact* was being sought. Needless to say, the importance of interest as a variable has been reduced sharply, and the conformity factor has been completely subordinated to the basic central characteristics being measured. Thus, rather than starting with the question, "How do salesmen collectively answer certain items?" we began with the question, "What makes a really fine salesman?" and then, "How do you discover these human characteristics?"

This use of central dynamics rather than traits, with its corollary implications, has produced what we believe to be a positive method of predicting sales success that is advanced beyond what has been done to date.

Fallacy of Experience

Many sales executives feel that the type of selling in their industry (and even in their particular company) is somehow completely special and unique. This is true to an extent. There is no question that a data-processing equipment salesman needs somewhat different training and background than does an automobile salesman. Differences in requirements are obvious, and whether or not the applicant meets the special qualifications for a particular job can easily be seen in the applicant's biography or readily measured. What is not so easily seen, however, are the basic sales dynamics we have been discussing, which permit an individual to sell successfully, almost regardless of what he is selling.

To date, we have gained experience with more than 7,000 salesmen of tangibles as well as intangibles, in wholesale as well as retail selling, big-ticket and little-ticket items. And the dynamics of success remain approximately the same in all cases. Sales ability is fundamental, more so than the product being sold. Long before he comes to know the product, mostly during his childhood and growing-up experience, the future successful salesman is developing the human qualities essential for selling. Thus, when emphasis is placed on experience, and experience counts more than such essentials as empathy and drive, what is accomplished can only be called the *inbreeding of mediocrity*.

We have found that the experienced person who is pirated from a competitor is most often piratable simply because he is not succeeding well with that competitor. He feels that somehow he can magically do better with the new company. This is rarely true. He remains what he is, mediocre, or worse. What companies need is a greater willingness to seek individuals with basic sales potential in the general marketplace. Experience is more or less easily gained, but real sales ability is not at all so easily gained.

Among butchers, coal miners, steelworkers, and even the unemployed there are many — *perhaps one in ten* — who, whether they themselves know it or not, possess ability to be an "A," top-producing salesman; and at least one in five would be on a "B" or better level for most types of selling. Many of these are potentially far better salesmen than some who have accumulated many years of experience. The case of "Big Jim," as we shall call him, is a good example:

All we knew about Jim at first was that he had walked into the showroom of one of our automobile clients in response to its ad and had taken our test. We reported that he was the only "A" in the group, and strongly recommended that he be hired. There was shocked silence at the other end of the telephone. We were then told that his test had been included as a joke.

As it was described to us, he had ambled into the showroom one morning wearing dungarees, an old polo shirt, and sneakers. He had then gone on to proclaim, "I sure do hanker to sell them there cars." The dealer had included his test just to get a laugh, or perhaps to see if we were sufficiently alert to weed him out. The man had never sold a car or anything else in his life, and had neither the appearance nor the background which would indicate that he ever could sell anything.

Today he is one of the dealer's best salesmen. Soon after he started working, he "hankered to see that there Seattle World's Fair," and sold enough cars in the first week of the month to give him money to get there and spend two weeks. On his return he made enough money in the last week of the month to equal the staff's monthly average.

Obviously, most men down from the hills wearing dungarees and sneakers are not going to be top salesmen. Some, however, may be, and their lack of experience in no way reduces the possibility that they have the inner dynamics of which fine top producers are made. It is equally obvious that a great many men who present a fine appearance, a "good front," do not turn out to be top salesmen. The real question — and always the first question — is, "Does this man have the basic inner dynamics to sell successfully?"

Background Blindness

Putting emphasis on experience often works in another way to reduce sales effectiveness. A company grows used to seeing its men in various job "slots," in certain departments, limited to special kinds of experience. Such men may be doing a satisfactory job where they are. But it frequently happens that the blind habit of "special experience" has kept the company from using the man in a more effective and appropriate way. For instance:

A western company in the leasing business wanted us to evaluate a branch employing 42 men to determine why there had been a mediocre level of sales activity, why there had been some difficulties among the men, and whether some of the 42 should possibly be let go. After looking at the test of each man, we did an "X ray" of the branch; that is, following the table of organization, we evaluated the staff, department by department, especially in terms of who was working with, over, and under whom, pointing out the strengths and weaknesses of each department.

Virtually all the men on the staff were found to be worth keeping on, but a good third were suggested for job shifts to other departments. Thus, the man with greatest sales ability, together with a great deal of managerial ability (by no means the same thing), was found in the accounting department. But that job did not completely satisfy him. He has since become the new branch sales manager, a more appropriate use of his considerable abilities.

One of the older men, though rated an adequate "B" salesman, was evaluated as an "A" office manager. He had good empathy, but not the strongest ego drive, which was why he was a "B" rather than an "A" salesman. But on the managerial side, he had the ability to handle details, relatively rare for a salesman; he was able to delegate authority and make decisions fairly rapidly and well. These qualities, plus his good empathy, gave him excellent potential as a manager, but not as sales manager, for his only moderate drive would have hurt him in the latter position. As office-administrative manager, the position he was moved up into, he has performed solidly.

The former office-administrative manager, a man well able to handle details reliably and responsibly, but with little empathy (and thus unable to deal understandingly with his office staff), was moved laterally into the accounting department, an area in which he had had some previous experience, and where he could carefully deal with and manage details rather than people.

Thus, what counts more than experience is the man's basic inner abilities. Each present employee, as well as each new applicant, should be placed in the area where he can be most creative and productive.

Role of Training

The steelworker, the coal miner, the displaced textile worker, or for that matter even "Big Jim," regardless of how much real sales ability each possesses, cannot suddenly start selling insurance, mutual funds, electronics equipment, or automobiles. Each one will need training. Companies have spent very large sums of money in developing effective training programs. When they are working with a man with potential, these training programs can and do bring out this potential and develop an excellent salesman. Without sound training, even "A" level salesmen are seriously limited.

Yet how often have men gone through long and expensive training programs only to fail totally when put out into the field? When this happens, the trainer, and perhaps the training program itself, is blamed, and sometimes even discarded. But most often it is neither the trainer nor the training program that is at fault; rather it is the fact that they were given the impossible task of turning a sow's ear into a silk purse. The most skilled diamond polisher, given a piece of coal, can only succeed in creating a highly polished piece of coal; but given the roughest type of uncut diamond, he can indeed turn it into the most precious stone. Here is a case in point:

About three years ago, a company in the Northeast installed an especially fine training program, in which a great deal of money was invested. At the end of two years, the results of this program were appraised. It was found that sales had not increased beyond what might normally be expected in that industry during that period of time. The investment in the training program seemed to have been a total waste. The entire training program was therefore dropped. Six months later, we were asked by management to test and evaluate the present sales force and to try to determine why the training program, so highly recommended, had failed so badly.

The reason was immediately apparent. Out of a sales force of 18 men, there was only one rating "A," and his sales actually had improved after the training program. Two other men were "B" level salesmen, and they too had improved to some extent with training. The remaining 15 men were "C" and "D" salesmen who should not have been selling in the first place. They simply did not have the potential of good salesmen. They were rigid, opinionated, and for the most part seriously lacking in empathy. This type of man rarely responds to training, no matter how thoroughgoing the program. This was an obvious case of trying to make silk purses out of 15 assorted sow's ears.

The role of training is clear. It is vital. In today's highly competitive market it is most important to bring every employee up to his maximum potential of productivity. Efficiency in training, using the best of modern methods, is necessary to do this. But training can succeed only if selection succeeds. Good raw silk must be provided first, before the training department can be expected to produce the silk purses. Just as few manufacturers would allow their products to be produced on the basis of rough estimates of size and weight, but would demand scientific control of these basic characteristics, so too must the process of selection be made more scientific and accurate.

The role of the salesman is so vital to the success of a company that it is amazing to these writers how little stress industry has placed on selecting the best raw material. To sell effectively in the U.S. market of today, a salesman needs to have empathy. To sell effectively in the foreign market, crossing cultural lines, requires even more empathy. And marketing goods and services anywhere calls for a great deal of ego drive. The U.S. Department of Commerce recently stated that American industry has no problem with its production. Its main problem is distribution. Effective salesmen are the key to distribution, and proper selection is the key to finding, using, and profiting from salesmen of good quality.

Conclusion

Industry must improve its ability to select top salesmen. Failure to date has stemmed from such errors as: the belief that interest equals aptitude; the fakability of aptitude tests; the crippling emphasis on conformity rather than creativity; and the subdivision of a man into piecemeal traits, rather than understanding him as a whole person. Experience appears to be less important than a man's possession of the two central characteristics of empathy and ego drive, which he must have to permit him to sell successfully. Training can only succeed when the raw material is present.

Selecting men with empathy and ego drive should contribute in some degree to helping industry meet one of its most pressing problems: reducing the high cost of turnover and selecting genuinely better salesmen.

Kenneth R. Davis

2 Are Your Salesmen Paid Too Much?

◖ Why is there so much reluctance on the part of management to make downward adjustments in the level of earnings of salesmen?

◖ Is this a genuine management problem?

◖ Under what conditions is it likely to develop?

◖ Is there a general apathy on the part of management when it comes to analyzing the level of salesmen's compensation?

◖ How do you cope with the problem when it is present?

Only one out of thirty-five conferees at a recent marketing management conference believed it feasible to lower the level of salesmen's earnings. Yet most of the participants acknowledged that situations often develop where salesmen earn incomes beyond their worth.

Ever-Present Problem

The problem of salesmen's compensation has always been troublesome to management. One difficulty has been how to maximize incentive while maintaining control over the salesman's activities. Another has been how to appraise the salesman's contribution toward company goals in comparison with that of other personnel. Even determining the relative merit and compensation of men within the sales force has had its pitfalls.

Business conferences dealing with sales management problems have usually included several panels or papers on *methods* of compensating salesmen but no discussion of how to determine *how much* they should be paid. Similarly, trade paper and professional journal articles have been chiefly devoted to discussing ways in which compensation plans have, or have not, been developed to meet particular needs. The typical article presents the pros and cons of commission versus salary versus some combination plan, and cites the experiences of individual firms. But little, if anything, is said about the actual *level* of sales force compensation.

It is not hard to understand why there has been such preoccupation with methods. There exists in this area of sales management considerable operating history which companies are willing to reveal. Certainly the many ramifications of different compensation plans have made interesting material for discussion purposes. And without doubt the method of compensating the salesmen is an important managerial problem. Furthermore, there is often an implicit relationship between a new method of compensation and the salesmen's level of earnings.

Nevertheless, the issues surrounding the determination of an appropriate level of compensation for the sales force warrant greater attention than they have been given. In spite of repeated appeals for lowering distribution costs, how many firms have critically reviewed their cost of personal selling as a step toward this broader goal? Can the ineffectiveness of sales personnel, complained of by many sales managers, be attributed to an inappropriate level of salesmen's earnings? [1]

Full and realistic analysis of the level of salesmen's compensation may of course reveal that the earnings of salesmen should be raised instead

[1] See Edward C. Bursk, "Thinking Ahead: Drift to No-Pressure Selling," HBR September–October 1956, p. 25.

of lowered. There are undoubtedly times when a higher level of compensation will be called for. This may be because it attracts better salesmen or because it provides the basis for greater incentive. In either case it is wise to pay the higher price. But such a need rarely goes unnoticed or unexamined, whereas overcompensation often is accepted with little or no questioning. Hence this discussion will be cast in terms of taking action to correct situations where compensation is too high, though the analysis made here could be applied to any situation in which the level of compensation is out of line.

Conditions of Overcompensation

The specific concern here is with overcompensation of salesmen relative to other salesmen, not to others in the labor force — engineers, carpenters, doctors, accountants, or bellhops.

Whether salesmen *generally* are overpaid or not may be important for the economy as a whole, but it is completely irrelevant for the *individual* company, which must pay a certain amount of money to get the kind of salesmen it needs in the light of the competitive manpower market. Rather the question is whether or not Company A is paying more than it has to under the circumstances. Thus, if Company A's salesmen are earning more than Company B's when both companies are operating under the same conditions and with the same degree of selling effectiveness, then presumably Company A's salesmen are being overcompensated.

There are four main reasons why so many companies allow overcompensation to develop:

- Outright uncertainty as to the salesmen's worth — perhaps the most important.
- Fear that salesmen have become indispensable in their territories.
- Top management lethargy or apathy in the area of wage administration.
- Sales managers' bias in favor of high rewards for their sales people.

Each of these conditions will be examined in some detail. Then an actual case will be presented to illustrate the points involved, and certain procedures to be followed in lowering the level of salesmen's earnings will be suggested.

Uncertainty as to Worth

The worth of salesmen depends both on what they produce and on what they cost — in short, on sales results per dollar of compensation. To appraise this value it is necessary to know both the productivity of the salesmen and the true cost of their services.

Determining Productivity

Despite the increasing gains that have resulted from the use of scientific methods in establishing market potentials, quotas, and supervision of salesmen, there remains a large element of guesswork in determining a salesman's productivity. The combined effects of advertising, product changes, and price shifts frequently cloud the picture of why sales have materialized. Moreover, the impact of personal selling, as is the case with advertising, is often deferred, thereby limiting the opportunity to relate effort and results. And of course there always exists that most significant unknown, changing business conditions.

Indicative of the difficulty encountered in measuring a salesman's productivity is the absence of job evaluation systems for salesmen. The National Industrial Conference Board has recognized this shortcoming as follows:

> "Few companies have thought to answer the question 'How much?' by trying to evaluate the over-all importance of the sales job in relation to other jobs in the company. While the use of job evaluation principles to determine salaries and wages is found in many industries, job evaluation techniques have rarely been applied to selling positions." [2]

Sales management's hesitancy in applying job evaluation procedures stems from a variety of sources:

¶ A major stumbling block is the nature of selling. In general, sales managers are likely to feel that the intangible aspects of a salesman's job exempt it from any systematic comparison with other jobs in the company.

¶ Another part of the explanation is found in the type of personnel that head today's sales organizations. Many sales managers have come up through the selling ranks and so have had little administrative experience. They may possess outstanding leadership traits, but their chief value — and it is indeed a very important one — is a knowledge of the market. Having been salesmen, they feel that they are capable of judging the strong and the weak men in their sales force. They see no reason to supplement their subjective judgments with more objective measures of productivity.

[2] "Determining Salesmen's Base Pay: A Role of Job Evaluation," *Studies in Personnel Policy No. 98*, p. 1.

¶ As companies have grown, the work of sales managers has been supplemented by staff personnel who have assumed the responsibility for administering more objective merit rating systems. This staff assistance does not usually develop, however, until the number of salesmen has become sizable. Since 75% of today's sales organizations have less than 30 salesmen, few firms have developed adequate procedures for measuring the productivity of their salesmen.

¶ The small number of people to be rated reduces the incentive to introduce job evaluation procedures and apply them carefully. It is one thing to establish a job evaluation system for a factory where there are a thousand production workers and another to establish a similar system for the company sales force which may number only ten or twenty men.

¶ Finally, when it comes to representing their position in the sales organization, salesmen are adept at selling themselves just as they are at selling the products or services of their firm. They often bargain persuasively and effectively for their compensation, leaving management in the position of a "satisfied customer" but not knowing exactly what it has bought.

This does not mean that it is impossible to apply or adapt regular job evaluation procedures to salesmen, but simply that to do so presents difficulties and most companies fail to try to overcome them.

Comparing Cost

Not only is it difficult to determine the productivity of salesmen, but it is also difficult to obtain useful information on what the cost of a salesman should be. How does a firm know what the going rate of pay is for salesmen?

Broad gauges such as turnover may indicate that the pay scale is out of line. But turnover rates reflect a variety of conditions, only one of which may be the level of compensation; only in extreme cases will turnover in the sales force tell the whole story. Other guides to appropriate levels of salesmen's compensation are word-of-mouth reports, but these are often biased and represent too small a sample on which to base decisions. The individuality of selling assignments makes it especially difficult for companies to gather data on the incomes of salesmen selling the same product under the same circumstances. Accordingly, about the only place to look for guidance would seem to be the more generalized surveys like the following:

¶ In July 1947 the National Industrial Conference Board published a comprehensive study of salesmen's compensation. This report is entitled *Salesmen's Compensation Plans*, but includes a section on earnings. Data on earnings cover 410 companies for the years 1945 and 1946. Somewhat smaller studies have been released by the NICB in its monthly publication, *Management Record*, in March 1948, March 1949, and April 1950.

The NICB has also made a very worthwhile contribution in a study, *Determining Salesmen's Base Pay, A Role of Job Evaluation*, published in 1948. While this report does not cover data on salesmen's earnings, it does include several companies' experience with job evaluation procedures and reviews problems of job evaluation as applied to salesmen.

More recently, June 1956, the NICB has released a study, *Measuring Salesmen's Performance*. This study indirectly approaches the problem of appraising the level of salesmen's earnings by focusing attention on the problem of measuring their productivity. It does not treat the question of cost as reflected in earning levels, however.

¶ The Dartnell Corporation has analyzed the level of salesmen's compensation periodically since 1929. The most recent study was released in 1953 and covered salesmen's earnings in 380 companies for the period October 1, 1951 to October 1, 1952. Other surveys have been made for the years 1929, 1933, 1940, 1943, 1945, 1947, 1949, 1950, and 1951. This represents the most sustained effort by any organization to present the trend in the level of salesmen's earnings.

¶ Under the direction of Professor Harry R. Tosdal of the Harvard University Graduate School of Business Administration, National Sales Executives, Inc., has made a complete and comprehensive survey of salesmen's compensation. Data presented in this survey cover the operating experience of 1,022 companies with 1,254 sales forces for the years 1948 and 1949. The report was released in 1951 in pamphlet form and later was incorporated in Professor Tosdal's two-volume study, *Salesmen's Compensation*, published in 1953 by the Division of Research, Harvard Business School.

¶ The *Current Population Reports* published by the United States Government Bureau of the Census include periodic studies of the level of earnings among sales workers. Data representing three broad industry classifications — manufacturers, wholesalers, and retailers — are broken down by salesmen. Statistics are also available for two narrower industry classifications, agents and brokers for insurance and real estate firms.

While these government reports are of limited value in appraising the level of compensation of a particular company's sales force, they are helpful in detecting changes in relative position. Thus, if the trend in a given company is rising faster than is the level of manufacturers' salesmen's incomes shown by the Census, then it should be looked at closely to see if it is out of line.

¶ Certain trade associations whose membership is large and whose leadership is vested in personnel who are especially concerned about distribution problems — not the general run of trade associations — have made useful surveys of the level of salesmen's compensation in member firms. To the extent that such trade association material is available, it is likely to be more closely related to the firm's operating experience than the data available through the previously cited sources.

¶ Management consulting firms often gather data on salesmen's earnings, but on a confidential basis. These firms will, however, undertake tailor-made surveys for individual companies and are frequently called on when the delicate question of level of salesmen's compensation is under consideration. They are likely to represent the individual firm's best source for comparable company compensation figures.

Do the sporadic studies of these various organizations provide statistical data that can be used in determining what a salesman should cost a company? The answer is hardly an unqualified *yes.* Most of these surveys cover so many types of firms that it is impossible to obtain from them a large enough sample of firms selling like products under like conditions. For example, in a national survey of over 1,000 firms it was reported that the average income of office equipment salesmen in 37 firms ranged from $2,000 to $11,000. What does this mean to a specific manufacturer of, say, typewriters?

The fact remains that there is a role for such surveys. Indeed, they have to be used for all they can contribute. But their limitations do help to explain why the level of salesmen's income is open to a wide range of interpretation and why management does not know whether the cost of its salesmen is in line or not.

Fear of Salesmen

In some companies, a salesman operates under a minimum amount of supervision. As a result, he assumes a certain autonomy in his day-to-day activities. He develops the feeling of "property rights" over his customers. His technical and personal skills are his chief assets, and through them he controls his territory. If he is successful, his customers look on him as their benefactor, and their allegiance is to him rather than to the company.

Once this relationship is built up, the salesman is a sort of monopolist, controlling the supply of customers in his territory. The company is reluctant to take strong action for fear he will leave and take his customers with him. As a result he may exact an unusually large income.

Such a situation develops only when other selling methods such as advertising are not significant in the company's marketing mix. It is particularly prevalent where compensation is paid on a straight commission basis. It is also often found when brokers, manufacturer's agents, or sales agents are used, and it is more likely to be a characteristic of the small firm than the large firm.

Many companies have found that, when it comes to a test, no individual salesman is as indispensable as they thought. But the general attitude persists — "Why court possible trouble?"

Management Lethargy

While many managers will openly acknowledge their fear of salesmen as a cause of overcompensation, they are not as likely to be aware of another important cause — their own lethargy.

Changing Conditions

Under today's dynamic marketing conditions, management may fail to adjust the level of salesmen's compensation in accord with changing selling conditions. Thus, as new markets or new products or new marketing techniques evolve, the role of the salesman may not be interpreted, or reinterpreted, correctly.

For example, as a company increases the use of advertising, the value of its salesmen may diminish; yet often no move is made to take advantage of the fact that a new type of man is called for — paid by a different method and at a lower level. The same kind of situation is created when salesmen start out with a small company on straight commission and remain on that basis despite the fact that, as the company grows larger, selling conditions become entirely different.

Management's failure to adjust to new operating conditions is in part a reflection of the difficulties encountered in changing a salesman's method of compensation. A salesman's income is usually geared to the territory in which he sells. As changes develop in the market potential of his territory, adjusting his compensation calls for new territory lines, and, except where salesmen are operating under a straight salary, this is a complicated task. Only as time goes on and the burden of salesmen's salaries becomes more and more obvious, does management take action.

Speaking of the situation shortly after the outbreak of war in Korea, James C. Olsen, partner in the management consulting firm of Booz, Allen & Hamilton, observed:

"If a salesman's increase in income since Korea is much greater percentagewise than the increase in consumer prices, these companies probably have failed to 'move the fence back' in setting quotas, and have failed to recognize that it is now easier to sell a dollar of volume than it was a year ago.

"The concept to bear in mind is one that has long been adopted in the shop. Companies pay for a fair day's work. If, because of the change in the nature of job performance through introduction of a new method, the task becomes easier, the rate per piece produced or dollar sold is correspondingly reduced. Nothing here should be construed to mean that salesmen should not be rewarded for extraordinary effort. But they should not be permitted to cash in on major upswings . . . not of their own making. Since the profits of these companies are good, many of them will be inclined to live with this out-of-line pay situation. But they should be careful not to spoil their salesmen for the future."

While Mr. Olsen's comments refer to the conditions arising out of the Korean War, it does not take such an unusual event as a war to have salesmen's earnings get out of line. Thus, recent shifts of population to the West Coast and of manufacturing facilities to the South have materially affected the territory potentials of consumer and industrial goods salesmen. The post-World War II period of expanding markets throughout the country has undoubtedly caused salesmen's earnings to rise inordinately high in some companies because managements have not made appropriate adjustments.

Moving Slowly

Another sign of management lethargy is the tendency to accept traditional methods of compensation in an industry despite the fact that the firm may not be typical of that industry. When commissions of a given per cent have been paid by firms in an industry for many years, salesmen and sales managers come to accept them as inviolable. If commission percentages are held constant, it is necessary for management to turn to territorial changes to alter levels of income. This may be difficult to do if customer-salesman relationships are important.

Finally, management may not scrutinize salesmen's costs as closely as other personnel costs. Sales force budgets are more flexible and subject to the personal interpretations and evaluations of the sales manager. Although systematic procedures for wage bargaining are the rule in dealing with factory personnel, and to a lesser extent with clerical personnel, they are the exception in dealing with salesmen. For one thing, less than 5% of today's outside salesmen are unionized.

Perhaps this tendency to move slowly in adjusting the level of salesmen's earnings reflects the distinctive character of the salesman's job more than management inefficiency. This is no reason, however, for management not to constantly appraise the level of salesmen's earnings in the light of the firm's marketing mix as well as market conditions.

Sales Managers' Bias

In a few companies the sales manager may have a bias favoring his men, even at the expense of the company. This may stem from past experience as a salesman, or it may reflect a natural attempt to maintain high morale. Just such a situation prevailed in one furniture company. This company had 35 manufacturer's agents, none of whom earned less than $25,000, with the top performer having an income of over $100,000. When the sales manager was asked if he did not think that this was excessive, he replied, "Well, I was a salesman once, and I worked hard for my pay — so do these men."

Bias may also develop out of a natural philosophy of sales managers — i.e., that the way to make money is to spend money. This attitude is reflected in the following statements by sales executives:

¶ "The cheapest salesman who ever worked for me was a man in the soft drink business who in four years averaged a little over $200,000 a year — twice as much as the president of the company."

¶ "Remember when you set up your compensation plan that the salesman has to make enough money to live decently and to save something at the same time. He has to present an appearance that properly represents your company. He does not make a good impression when he walks around in a threadbare suit."

¶ "I would try to see how much I could pay my salesmen, not how little I could pay them. I would suggest that you try to get your company to have the reputation of having the highest paid salesmen in its industry."

¶ "We are strongly in favor of rewards for merit and results and have tried to line up our recompense to salesmen in this manner. Therefore, the more our salesmen would earn, the more profit the firm would make, and we can't see how any company could go broke doing that. If the man's earnings are out of proportion, this might be caused by mistaken judgment in the original setup — at which time, perhaps, the reward for additional business was placed on too high a plane."

¶ "Even with the proper recompense of a salesman, it is possible that he may make more than the sales manager. We do not consider this an altogether undesirable situation, because we have a yardstick for the salesman's work; and if he does make more than the sales manager, we know definitely that he is increasing the profit of the company that much more."

Statements of this sort are not unusual. The tendency is to think that sales volume is the measure of salesmen's worth. But that is not a very precise yardstick. Even though the margin on increased sales may be enough to carry increased compensation, why pay more than is needed? Management does not stop looking for more economical production processes just because it has machines that are currently operating efficiently.

A Case Study

Now let us see how all this worked out in an actual case (with name and description necessarily altered).

Background Facts

The Dooley Company, which manufactured shoes, was well known in the trade and had had over 50 years of successful operation.

The firm's sales force consisted of 30 men, all paid on a straight commission basis, which happened to be the typical method of compensating salesmen in this particular industry. Over the years the salesmen had enjoyed a great deal of independence; supervision from the home office had been at a minimum. The sales force was made up of men who had had considerable experience either in selling shoes in retail stores or for manufacturers, and several of them had been representing the Dooley company for 20 to 30 years.

In 1953 the average net income of salesmen in the organization was $16,810. Earnings ranged from $6,967 to $31,594. For the past six years the average earnings had been $17,996. It was generally conceded in the trade that salesmen in this firm were among the highest paid in the industry.

In the 1930's, Dooley had inaugurated a national advertising program and had since developed national brand recognition for its shoes. It was spending approximately $750,000 for advertising and promotion. Not only had the firm undertaken to presell its merchandise, but like a number of other shoe manufacturers it had gradually built up a chain of leased departments and shoe stores. The company salesmen called on these "controlled" accounts, selling them the line as they sold any other retail outlet, although they received a smaller commission on this business and in addition were required to assume more responsibility for merchandising the line in the store. Over one-quarter of the company's production went to these outlets.

These factors had secured a strong position in the consumer market for Dooley, and in the opinion of company management had changed the salesmen's selling conditions. Moreover, while Dooley had initially needed the flexible expense of a straight commission — as was essential for many small shoe manufacturers — the company was no longer small and was not as limited financially.

Use of Surveys

Considering these factors, Dooley management wanted to determine what salesmen in similar selling situations were being paid. Accordingly, it turned to the available sources only to find that no survey was specifically applicable to shoe salesmen. Government and trade association sources were completely barren of useful information. However, it was possible to compile the data presented in Exhibit 1 from three general surveys.

It seemed clear from the general survey figures that the Dooley salesmen were earning much more than comparable salesmen — almost twice as much, in fact. Fortunately the management was not satisfied that it had an accurate enough

Exhibit i. Comparative incomes of salesmen allied to the shoe industry

National Industrial Conference Board Survey (1946)	27 textile and textile products manufacturers	Dooley Company
Net earnings of top salesmen	$18,750	$27,895
Net earnings of average salesmen	7,750	13,748
Net earnings of bottom salesmen	4,250	6,855
National Sales Executives Survey (1948–1949)	24 clothing and footwear manufacturers	Dooley Company
Net earnings of top salesmen	$16,300	$30,482
Net earnings of average salesmen	7,500	16,978
Net earnings of bottom salesmen	4,500	8,388
Dartnell Corporation Survey (1952)	4 clothing manufacturers	Dooley Company
Net earnings of top salesmen	$22,000	$32,656
Net earnings of average salesmen	9,000	16,537
Net earnings of bottom salesmen	7,500	10,698

guide, so it had a special survey made of its closest competitors in the footwear industry. The results are shown in Exhibit ii.

When all the facts were in, it became apparent that Dooley was paying more for its salesmen than its competitors were for theirs, but not so much more as was suggested by the general surveys. Dooley's problems in trying to use generalized information on the earnings level of salesmen are undoubtedly typical. If the Dooley management had relied on the general surveys, it would have grossly underestimated shoe salesmen's level of compensation. Not until a tailor-made survey had been conducted among near competitors could a reasonable estimate be obtained of what Dooley salesmen should be earning.

Exhibit ii. Survey of shoe salesmen's compensation (1953)

	12 shoe manufacturers	Dooley Company
Net earnings of average top salesmen	$23,123	$31,594
Net earnings of average salesmen	12,047	16,810
Net earnings of average bottom salesmen	7,500	6,967

Underlying Conditions

Why did this situation of apparent overcompensation develop at Dooley? Many of the conditions cited earlier as causes of overcompensation were present:

• This firm, like most, had had no access to current data on the earnings level of shoe salesmen. Management in the firm had not seen fit to make a periodic review of the level of salesmen's earnings. With a sales force of only 30 men, it had not seen the need for a job evaluation system for salesmen, and it had set up only limited procedures for measuring the men's productivity. Sales management in the firm was hard pressed for time to develop a new compensation plan, new territories, and new supervisory procedures to the extent these changes were called for.

• Tradition in the industry had set the company's method of compensation despite the changed selling conditions. Thus, this firm had grown large and successful but was still using a method and a level of compensation applicable to the many smaller firms in the industry that were more dependent on their salesmen.

• Finally, there was an understandable desire on the part of the sales manager to avoid "rocking the boat." He was concerned about losing accounts and perhaps some of his star salesmen. He also felt that any downward adjustment in the compensation of his sales force should be carefully evaluated in terms of its effect on morale. At the same time, however, he was conscious of the need for a new compensation philosophy and, when the facts were available, he adopted a new plan based on a new lower level of earnings.

Action Taken

The Dooley management was wise enough to realize that, although statistical evidence indicated its salesmen were overcompensated, there were still some basic questions which would have to be resolved before it could reduce the level of earnings:

¶ On the one hand was the possibility that the marketing strategy of the firm would be furthered by having salesmen of higher caliber than competitors' salesmen, just for the sake of extra selling power. The conclusion was, however, that higher earnings were not attracting men who were that much more able or willing to work that much harder. In fact, it appeared that excessive earnings had led to a feeling of complacency rather than of incentive.

¶ On the other hand was the fact that national advertising and controlled distribution did a substantial part of the salesmen's job for them. Further, the established position of the Dooley firm made the job attractive in terms of stability of employment and earnings. To go below the competitive level might have unfortunate repercussions, but at least it seemed possible to get the kind of men needed at substantially less than Dooley had been paying.

After a very careful analysis of the salesmen's job, the Dooley management took as its goal the adoption of a level of earnings about equal to that paid by its close competitors who operated under substantially similar conditions.

Management Guides

The case study just presented does not do full justice to the depth of analysis preceding Dooley's decision to lower the level of salesmen's earnings. Especially slighted is the extreme care taken in moving toward its goal. The real success of such action hinges on the meticulous handling of details, and these are always unique to the individual company. About all that can be done here is to emphasize that every company which comes to a similar decision — i.e., that salesmen's earnings are too high — must figure out a way to carry through the decision in terms of its own particular organization. Perhaps it will be helpful, however, to suggest the general procedures management should follow.

Marketing Mix

The first step when contemplating a change in the earnings level of salesmen is an appraisal of the role of the salesman in the firm's marketing mix. Fundamentally, the firm's marketing program represents a mix of product and price and promotion. Any one of this trilogy can be altered to stimulate demand. If the choice is increased or decreased promotion, the two chief alternatives are advertising or personal selling expenditures. For each company, accordingly, management must determine how significant personal selling will be in the total sales formula. This will vary from firm to firm, according to product, company size, age, and financial resources, as well as price policies.

For every firm there will be at any given time an optimum combination of these factors that influence sales. Their relative significance will change from time to time — markedly so for some firms. For others a particular combination may prove effective for years. Within the mix it may be desirable to raise or lower the total amount spent on the field sales force. This, in turn, may take the form of a larger or smaller sales organization, or higher or lower paid salesmen, or some combination of these two. Thus, for example, one well-known company manufacturing major items for the home decided that the personal selling formula most productive for it would be based on a larger total sales organization made up of lower paid individuals.

Objective Data

It is imperative that management be on firm ground before lowering the earnings level of the sales force, both for its own sake in making a sound decision and for the sake of the effect on the salesmen. This again brings up the question of surveys of competitive earnings and job evaluation.

As mentioned previously, job evaluation has not been used extensively in the sales field. There is a definite split regarding its value. One leading authority on salesmen's compensation feels that the intangible aspects in sales work make the job evaluation procedures so difficult as to be impractical. Another, who is a consultant on wage administration to a leading electrical manufacturer, feels that job evaluation is the only realistic way to determine the level of salesmen's earnings. He reasons that comparative earnings data obtained from surveys are valueless because of the large degree of variation in the selling task from company to company.

A more realistic position is to accept both approaches, for each of them can make a worthwhile contribution in determining the appropriate level of earnings. Under certain circumstances, correctly designed surveys on the earnings level of salesmen can provide desirable bench-mark data. Where the firms in an industry are about the same size, employ a large number of salesmen, and the selling task is fairly standardized, survey data are likely to be of definite help. This is the case in such industries as meat products, pharmaceuticals, packaged and canned foods, petroleum products, and life insurance. In other industries, such as furniture and clothing, publishing, and industrial heating or power equipment, the contrary is true.

But most firms would benefit greatly by supplementing available survey data with a job evaluation study. Through such a study, job descriptions for salesmen and a systematic procedure for determining the relative importance of the sales job with other jobs in the organization would evolve. Such comparison at the very outset will throw considerable light on the question of whether the earnings level of men on the sales force is appropriate.

Using a double-barreled approach to analyze the level of salesmen's earnings has obvious merit when it comes to explaining to the sales organization why downward adjustments in earnings are in order. Comparative statistics of salesmen in other firms in the same industry, plus objective appraisal of the salesman's job relative to other jobs in the organization, present a good argument for a new lower level of earnings.

Management Support

The above steps are also essential if management itself is to be sold on the need for a new concept of salesmen's earnings.

Successful introduction of a lower pay scale for salesmen is unlikely if top management is not behind the move. This would seem to be self-evident. Yet too often some members of management are not completely convinced that the move is desirable and accordingly give it only token support. Such an attitude is understandable, for lowering income is in no case an enviable task.

If the new pay scale is warranted, however, management will recognize that its introduction is essential if the firm is to maintain its competitive position. No firm will permit an inordinately large advertising budget or excessive packaging costs to prevail. Similarly it should not incur excessive personal selling costs. It is certainly true that the latter involves the "human element" and, therefore, downward adjustment will always be more difficult. The remaining two procedures suggest how this adjustment can be more readily executed.

Selling the Salesmen

It is generally conceded that obtaining the views of the salesmen will speed adoption of any new compensation plan. This is even more essential when the objective is a lower level of earnings.

Often the implications of direct personal selling costs — higher prices or lower profits from which capital expansion may have to come — are so removed from the salesman's scene that he gives them little consideration in appraising the merits of the suggested change. If, however, the men can see the broad implications of inordinately high personal selling costs, they are at least a little more likely to accept the change. Obviously, any good salesman is going to try to sell management on not making the change; but if he sees that alternative opportunities are less attractive, he will not fight it so hard.

Softening the Blow

In any event, management will want to avoid impairing morale. No matter how logical or necessary the move, it is likely to stir up emotional resistance. However, this is an argument, not against making the change, but in favor of making it *carefully*. So management will want to do everything it can to soften the impact.

Thus, older men near retirement can be made exempt. Territorial realignment will enable the firm to reduce inequities in the earnings of individual men and to minimize the cut for those men hardest hit. In some cases management can combine territories and thereby increase a man's work load but not reduce his net earnings. Fringe benefits can be introduced. Stability of earnings can be incorporated in the change.

These types of efforts often necessitate a new method as well as a new level of compensation. And, indeed, it is probably true more often than is generally conceded that the introduction of a new compensation plan is part and parcel of a move to reduce selling costs.

Conclusion

There is a real need for sales managers to take a longer and harder look at the problems surrounding the *level* of compensation of salesmen, as well as the problems of *method* of compensation. It would seem that through increased efforts to measure salesmen's productivity and determine more precisely their normal earnings level, many firms would improve the effectiveness of their sales force and at the same time reduce selling costs.

To realize these goals, there must be a willingness to think imaginatively and critically when it comes to the question of the level of salesmen's compensation. It is not easy for management to pause in the hustle of getting additional sales long enough to examine its position in the light of underlying conditions. But the effort may pay off — whether the outcome shows that selling effectiveness is suffering because of too low a level of earnings for salesmen or that, as so easily can happen, money is being wasted by overcompensation.

John M. Frey

3 Missing Ingredient in Sales Training

◖ Businessmen have now generally accepted low-pressure selling as the best way to sell industrial goods to supposedly rational purchasers, and it is increasingly applied to the sale of consumer goods as the public becomes more sophisticated in budgeting and buying.

◖ Sometimes labeled the *customer-problem approach*, or the *"you" sale*, low-pressure selling focuses on how the company's products can help fulfill the needs and wants of the customer. The customer or prospect holds the center of the stage, and all efforts are directed at attempting to understand him and to sincerely help him solve his problems.

◖ This approach seems to me to be completely sound and valid. Even if it were not the preferred method from the standpoint of effectiveness — and I am convinced the only exceptions are ones of degree — it still would have to be used because today's generation of salesmen just will not countenance the old slam-bang and sometimes tricky methods of the past.

◖ But this modern kind of selling is more difficult to do, more difficult to learn, and the training program is correspondingly more acute. In fact, it calls for one particular element that previous selling did not need and most present-day training does not provide. It is my purpose here to show what this missing ingredient is, why it is important, and how it can be secured.

The nub of the problem was pointed out by Edward C. Bursk in what was the earliest full-scale analysis and still is perhaps the clearest exposition of low-pressure selling:

"It is relatively easy to teach high-pressure techniques. Because the essence of that approach is that the prospect submits to something imposed on him from without, it is possible to standardize the sales presentation — to formulate it in the home office and show the salesmen how to do it. The opposite is the case with low-pressure selling. Although of course something can be prepared in the way of suggested openings, possible answers to objections, and so on, any hint of a 'canned' sales talk, learned and repeated from memory, will ruin a low-pressure approach completely."[1]

Carrying this idea further, it is clear that the salesman must relate himself to the customer in such a way that he can understand the customer's needs and wants. Not only must the salesman be able to communicate his ideas and beliefs to the prospect, but it is vital that he develop the ability to understand what the prospect is attempting, explicitly and implicitly, to communicate to him. To understand these difficult problems of two-way communication in face-to-face relationships, the salesman must develop a frame of reference about human nature and behavior that will allow him to evaluate and learn effective lessons from his experience. In essence, he needs to develop his human relations skills.

Before exploring this line of thought, however, I must recognize and deal with two ques-

[1] Edward C. Bursk, "Low-Pressure Selling," HBR Winter 1947, pp. 239–240.

tions that are likely to occur to the reader who is familiar with current sales training literature and practices:

(1) What you say is all well and good, but don't present-day sales training courses encompass an approach similar to that found in a plethora of books and literature on successful selling, psychology in selling, how to influence people, secrets of closing sales, and even tested selling sentences?

(2) What is the difference between these viewpoints and this so-called need for human relations that you are talking about?

Such questions express a healthy skepticism. In the answers to them, however, lies the very core of my feeling of disturbance with the present general status of sales training.

Current Programs

It is obvious that the actual sales training programs employed by various companies differ widely, and that anything like full discussion of the myriads of practices would be impossible. At the same time, the goals of many of our top sales trainers in effect are synthesized in the *Handbook of Sales Training* compiled by the National Society of Sales Training Executives.[2] To a considerable extent the viewpoint expressed in this book does represent the general climate of present opinion (although actual performance undoubtedly lags behind).

In establishing a program for sales training, the *Handbook* states that once the general objectives of the program have been determined, it is necessary to decide who needs to be trained, what the subjects should be, and how the job can best be done. In connection with the selection of subjects, here is an illuminating excerpt:

"An analysis of this problem reveals the following facts:

New Salesmen Need

1. Facts about the company; its history, policies, standards, and so forth.
2. Facts about their products.
3. Instructions on how to use company systems and procedures.
4. Fundamentals of selling their specific product.
5. Attitude, or morale training.

Regular Salesmen Need

1. All facts needed by new salesmen, plus:
2. Facts on any changes in policies, systems, and procedures.
3. Facts about new products.
4. Advance facts on company advertising, promotions, and other sales plans.

Promotable Salesmen Need

1. Detailed facts on company systems, policies, and procedures.
2. Knowledge of the over-all methods of company merchandising and operation.
3. Knowledge of how to supervise and lead others.
4. Knowledge of how to assume and discharge responsibility.
5. Attitude, or morale training.

Supervisors Need

1. All of the facts and skills needed by others.
2. Ability to train others.
3. Ability to organize and lead.
4. Ability to analyze and plan.
5. Ability to evaluate and follow up.

"If these four groups of salesmen are helped by the sales trainer or sales training director to get the facts and information they need quickly and completely, the training job will be well done."[3]

Neglect of Salesmanship

For our purposes here, the most important fact to note in this list of recommended subjects is that there appears to be relatively little emphasis on the subject of salesmanship itself. Techniques and methods of selling are presumably included in the agenda for new salesmen under the item "Fundamentals of selling their specific product," but it is clear that the major task of the sales trainer is to indoctrinate newcomers as to company history, products, proper attitude, and so on, and to advise regular salesmen and other personnel about policy changes, new product developments, promotional campaigns, and other pertinent information.

Recently, there has been a growing objection to the lack of time spent in formal sales training programs on the subject of salesmanship. For example, Ray C. Brewster has decried the fact that, in the case of the companies he has observed, usually as much as 75% of the training time is applied to imparting information on company products, policies, routines, and similar topics.[4] In fairness to the authors of the *Handbook*, it should be noted that they stress the importance of continuous field (or on-the-job) training, and here the subject of salesmanship does receive more attention. Even so, there is doubt

[2] *Handbook of Sales Training* (New York, Prentice-Hall, Inc., Third Edition, 1951).

[3] Ibid., pp. 116–117.

[4] Ray C. Brewster, "More Psychology in Selling," HBR July–August 1953, p. 91.

whether it receives *enough* emphasis in view of its importance in low-pressure selling.

Sales Formulas

Now let us turn to the question of how the time that *is* devoted to salesmanship training is used. What does management typically try to teach about (1) basic guidelines to be used in making a sale, and (2) rules for personal behavior and selling techniques?

Basic Guidelines

Outlines for guiding the course of a sale are inevitably based on the accumulated experience of the writer or trainer involved. Because of different personal experiences, as well as the varying nature of the specific products involved, these recommended approaches are all somewhat different, and are couched in dissimilar terminology. Yet, for all the different verbiage involved, these basic selling formulas have many similarities:

- The progression of steps in making a sale that is advocated in the training manual of one national consumer goods manufacturer is as follows: getting attention, arousing interest, creating desire, and securing action.

- A national industrial goods manufacturer describes the selling process as a succession of three steps: (a) the sales approach, (b) the intermediate steps, and (c) the close, including the follow-through. Using still other terminology, this same company describes the steps as being: (a) problem isolated, (b) recommendation made, (c) recommendation sold, and (d) action (i.e., the order).

- Ray C. Brewster states that "the natural formula for persuasive presentation" involves four steps: (1) show openers and establish mental accord, (2) declare your hand and tie in the product; (3) prove the openers; (4) show-down and close.[5]

In a slightly different category we find other broad selling formulas that assume different viewpoints and ways of looking at the selling problem. Three in particular are worth mentioning here.

(1) In his plea for more psychology in selling, Brewster states: "One of our chief problems in selling is to be realistic in appraising the customer, in trying to understand his mind."[6] To accomplish this, he advocates that salesmen follow three rules, or psychological check points: (a) tune in on the buyer's wave length; (b) head right, see things as the buyer does; and (c) avoid "interference" by staying tuned in.

(2) In the third of a series of five articles for *Sales Management*[7] the late president of Amercoat Corporation, Alan E. Turner, stresses the effectiveness of preplanning as a selling technique. He advocates the building of a "prospect analysis chart" in which the following five factors that influence each individual selling problem are listed: (a) group influence on buying decisions; (b) job influence; (c) buyer's attitude; (d) buyer's knowledge; and (e) buying habits.

(3) Several companies have recently inaugurated a breakdown of their customers into personality trait categories: e.g., extrovert or introvert. Though the broad selling framework remains unchanged, the rules for behavior and the techniques of presentation within this framework vary according to the personality classification.

Rules and Techniques

Many books have been written and a lot of training stress has been laid on rules and techniques of personal behavior for successful salesmen. The following book titles are typical: *Successful Salesmanship*; *The Essentials of Selling*; *Successful Selling*; *Tested Sentences that Sell*; and *How to Make People Like You* (not forgetting, of course, *How to Win Friends and Influence People*). The general orientation toward salesmanship is aptly illustrated in Chapter 10 of the *Handbook of Sales Training*, "Training in Effective Speaking," which deals generally with the importance of effective speech, vocabulary building, the proper use of the voice, and the mechanics of speaking. In stressing the need for word planning and word selection, it states:

> "A straight line is not always the shortest path to the sale. Just as in our daily contacts we must use diplomacy and care in what we say, so in our selling contacts we must use finesse in order to reach our objective . . . . In talking with prospects (whom we should always try to make feel important), we must use words that have the right connotation or implication. For instance, we may refer to a prospect as 'pressed for funds,' but not as 'broke'; as 'lenient,' but not 'lax'; as 'careful,' but never 'stingy' . . . ."[8]

Another example is "The Little Blue Book" which the *Handbook* advocates giving to sales-

[5] Ibid., p. 97.
[6] Ibid., p. 95.
[7] Alan E. Turner, "Wanted: More Creative Selling for Products Sold to Industry," *Sales Management*, September 15, 1953, p. 40.
[8] *Handbook*, op. cit., pp. 178–190.

men. Here the following two groups of thoughts are featured:

I. *Five Steps to a More Effective Personality*

1. Learn to like people.
2. Have a friendly smile.
3. Be generous with honest praise.
4. Listen! . . . people like good listeners.
5. Talk in terms of "you," not "I."

II. *Seven Ways to Become More Persuasive*

1. Learn to "agree before you disagree."
2. Don't argue . . . if you win, you lose.
3. When you are wrong . . . don't be afraid to say so!
4. Try to understand the other fellow's viewpoint.
5. Use showmanship in your selling.
6. Ask questions that make it easy for the other fellow to say "yes."
7. Don't knock — it destroys confidence.

Limited Usefulness

How helpful are such methods and techniques of salesmanship to the salesman?

Let us take the basic guidelines first. Clearly, a broad outline of an effective progression of steps is advantageous. New salesmen need such guidance and direction, and many regular salesmen need frequent reminders. Based as they are on a diagnosis of past success, these guidelines provide a highly beneficial framework around which the salesman can orient his thinking.

However, guidelines are generalizations only. Of necessity, they have extremely limited usefulness to an individual salesman facing particular problems in a specific situation. Therefore, it has been the natural tendency for writers and trainers to expand on the basic selling formulas. The salesman is entreated to focus his attention on the customer — his needs, his wants, and his characteristics. If the theory of low-pressure selling is accepted, it would seem that awareness of such factors would be exceptionally valuable to him.

Thus, the salesman receives added direction, over and above the basic selling framework. But his training still falls short for two reasons:

(1) He is told what he should do, but not how to do it. For instance, take Brewster's three psychological check points: (a) tune in on the buyer's wave length; (b) head right and see things as the buyer does; and (c) avoid "interference" by staying tuned in. As factors or principles to keep in mind, these are fine. But just how does a salesman apply them to a concrete situation?

(2) The viewpoints and principles are, if not properly understood or interpreted, potentially dangerous. For instance, Turner's predetermined generalizations concerning the attitude, knowledge, and habits of buyers are not likely to fit any one individual buyer or circumstance. Consequently, any actions based on these assumptions are likely to produce a situation where the "map" does not fit the "territory." Similarly, the behavior that seems appropriate to the prospect's personality trait classification might lead the salesman into left field!

A single-valued orientation, based on such terms as "introvert" or "extrovert," "rational" or "emotional," does not take into consideration the actual complexity of human situations, does not recognize that behavioral skill involves maintaining a balance between many interrelated factors. Thus it may even be theorized that if the salesman's actions, based on a one-dimensional personality trait breakdown, lead to any unexpected consequence, he will tend to feel insecure. To respond to this feeling of inadequacy he will be inclined to continue his original approach in an attempt to maintain his "self" concept. Consequently, he will find it difficult either to act or to analyze his actions effectively.

Now let us take the rules and techniques — the injunctions about word planning and selection, the five ways to do this and the seven ways to do that, and so on. I believe that there is reason to be deeply worried not only about the usefulness of this type of sales training but about the basic tenet on which it is built. The entire approach apparently proceeds on the assumption that manipulation of the customer is necessary and good. Thus, the *Handbook of Sales Training* states that "as salesmen acquire manipulative skills, technical facts, related knowledge, attitudes, ideas, and other controls of personal conduct and job performance, they are learning."[9] I question whether application of "manipulative skills" is compatible with the sincerity of the customer-problem approach. If it means "leadership," perhaps it is. If it means deliberately using certain word combinations or behavior mannerisms to get prescribed reactions, it is not — and, in this form, I do not think it is likely to be very successful, anyway.

Actually, these "success" rules do not, in themselves, force the use of manipulative behavior. They are commonly interpreted that way, however, and are used as a vehicle to achieve that purpose in all too many sales training courses.

Aside from questioning the basic purpose of rules of behavior, we must look at another problem. Do such rules provide the salesman with

[9] Ibid., p. 98.

any real understanding of the difficult and complex task with which he is faced? This is the human relations problem. It centers around the development of a person's skill in relating himself to, and handling his face-to-face involvement with, other people.

Rules for behavior do not develop this skill. Telling the salesman that he should plan and select words that are tactful and diplomatic does not develop this skill. Giving him a "Little Blue Book" on human relations does not develop this skill either.

Actually, I believe that the authors of the *Handbook* realize this. In concluding the section on effective speaking, they state:

> "Each selling sentence must carry a full sales load. It can. The task requires a study of words, of course, but more important, it requires a knowledge of people — a study of behavior patterns and human reactions. Skill in the use of the right selling words is an ACQUIRED ability, proving again that there is no such thing as a born salesman." [10]

Yet, having recognized this, the *Handbook* authors let their training recommendations stop short. They give no recommendation as to *how* the needed ability can be acquired or developed. They imply that the salesman should not expect to develop it overnight, but that if he flounders around long enough in the sea of human activity and interaction he is likely to learn something.

New Ingredient

What *can* be done to develop a salesman's skill in relating himself to and handling his face-to-face involvement with other people? Certainly, plain old-fashioned "experience" is necessary and helpful, but it is a long-term proposition; also many people do not learn effective or useful lessons from their experience. If this learning process can somehow be speeded up through training, it most certainly should be explored.

Basic Approach

First of all, I believe that sales trainers must rid themselves of a "rules for behavior" orientation. In its place must be substituted an effective *method* or *frame of reference* for looking at behavior and at the factors affecting behavior. Training should naturally be concerned with the personality traits and characteristics of individuals and groups, but it should not be preoccupied with them. Rather, it should center around the problems of communication.

What should a salesman understand about the communication process that will help his selling efforts? He should understand what the process of communication entails; the complex social context in which it occurs; the difficulties that are likely to arise; the difference between statements of feeling and statements of content; the context in which words are spoken. Further, he should be aware that different people are bringing to each situation different assumptions, perceptions, and feelings based on their personal experience and "self" concept; that these assumptions, perceptions, and feelings are constantly interacting with his own; that he is intellectually, emotionally, and very personally involved in most situations; that recognition and acceptance of responsibility for this involvement are vital.

If such factors are understood by the salesman, he will be able to increase his skill in understanding people and in handling his face-to-face involvements. He will be able to increase his sales power accordingly.

But can such matters be taught to salesmen? Difficulty stems from two sources. First, in talking about the human relations problem, it is surprisingly easy (and natural) for the trainer to draw conclusions on the basis of his own past experience, and from these conclusions to generalize about principles, theories, rules, and techniques for behavior. This would complete the circle in which we have been traveling, however, and leave us at the starting point — at being dissatisfied with the usefulness of rules for behavior. To avoid this trap, sales trainers could well borrow a concept from the field of supervisory training:

> "We have to stop telling supervisors how they should behave and what their attitudes should be. . . . Let us remember that our new objective is to assist people in learning from their own experience. We are no longer trying to change them; we are giving them the opportunity to change themselves, if they wish, by reflecting upon and re-evaluating their own experience. . . . We are not interpreting their own experience *for them*; we are not telling them *our* personal experience. Instead, *we are allowing them to examine and re-evaluate their own experience.*" [11]

Working within such a conceptual scheme, Roethlisberger proposes three ways in which the

[10] Ibid., pp. 181–182.

[11] F. J. Roethlisberger, "Training Supervisors in Human Relations," HBR September 1951, p. 51.

trainer can facilitate the process of self-learning: (1) helping people to recognize the attitudes they bring to experience; (2) helping people to ask better questions of experience; and (3) providing them with a useful way of thinking about matters of human behavior so that they can make better observations about themselves and their relations to others.

A second difficulty, of course, is that knowledge of human relations concepts is not enough to solve the salesman's problem. Theories have a strange way of collapsing in the thick of face-to-face involvement. Talking *about* people is not tantamount to talking *with* people. A sound training program must also help the salesman in action.

Case Method Inadequate

To meet the difficulties mentioned, the case method of instruction has been proposed. Many human relations clinicians advocate this approach, having found it in actual practice to be a highly successful vehicle for instruction and learning. However, the case method has several serious limitations:

(1) Case study, by its very nature, can do relatively little in the translation of theory to practice. Its chief virtue is that it enables the student, through analysis, diagnosis, and discussion, to develop an effective way of looking at human behavior. This is important, but it is not the critical need.

(2) Several practical difficulties arise in using the case method outside the confines of educational institutions. In business the element of "time" looms large. The preponderant majority of cases require the student to do some preparation if the ensuing discussion is to be productive. Where is the necessary time for study to come from?

And, even if the time can be arranged, there remains the problem of motivating salesmen to put in sufficient study effort. If we are considering new young salesmen in an organized training-indoctrination course, such problems are minor. But they are major in the case of on-the-job training for regular salesmen who possess a wide diversity of experience, capabilities, and educational background.

(3) Any company attempting the case method would find itself somewhat of a pioneer, with little or no realistic, ready-made case material concerning applicable selling situations. The time, expense, and general difficulties involved in building up an adequate store of such case material are appreciable.

Closely related to the case method approach is the use of recorded selling conversations as the basis for discussion. A number of companies have experimented with this approach, and, according to my information, most of them have been well satisfied with the results. But although recorded selling conversations require less preparation time than written cases, they are subject to the first and third limitations just described.

Role-Playing

The most promising approach, I believe, centers around the use of role-playing. This is essentially a self-explanatory term. In sales training role-playing puts one man acting as a buyer, another as a salesman. Many variations are possible. For instance, the "buyer" can be told to act as he himself personally feels. Or he can be given a few basic "facts" about himself, or even a relatively complete characterization to portray. As for the "salesman," he can be given many, few, or no facts about the "buyer." Each instructor will naturally want to adopt the particular variation that suits his own personal preference and situation.

To illustrate what a company can do with role-playing, here is the experience of a firm employing a fairly large salesforce in a highly competitive industry:

In the beginning the salesmen — particularly the older, more experienced ones — were skeptical of the value of this role-playing. Agreement was finally reached, however, to experiment with the plan on an informal basis in one department. At first the salesman acting the part of the "buyer" played the role as he himself felt. The acting was somewhat stilted. The players were rather embarrassed, and a number of jokes and humorous comments were made. The ensuing discussions were restrained and brief.

But soon the atmosphere changed. The initial embarrassment was gone. The participating salesmen began to get deeply involved in what they were doing. So did the observing salesmen. The formal discussions waxed hot and heavy, continuing in informal groups for days afterward. One salesman suggested acting out the part of a real buyer whom he had recently come in contact with. This was done, and it worked out very well.

At times the discussions wandered. At times they got out of hand. But for the most part they were remarkably beneficial. The salesmen gradually became more consciously aware of the assumptions, perceptions, and feelings that they were bringing to a particular situation, and of how these feelings and attitudes were inextricably interwoven into their relationship with a buyer. They also became more perceptive of the feelings and emotions of a buyer.

And they began to recognize the nature — and consequences — of the term "involvement."

In the particular situation of the company making this experiment the problem of price negotiation has continually loomed large. Quite naturally, therefore, the bargaining process arose in almost every role-playing situation. Initially, the natural tendency of the discussions was to focus on the "best" method of bargaining with a buyer — a natural error in this day of "how-to-sell" books. Consequently, a strong effort was made to guide the discussions away from a "right-wrong" basis to a "what happened" basis, which was found to be far more profitable.

In general, then, it would seem that role-playing can be used with considerable success. One great advantage of the method is that it forces learning by doing — practicing — rather than just talking. The men cannot say, for instance, that they should be tactful; they must *be* tactful. Role-playing allows the players (and observers) to learn from their own experience, in a sheltered atmosphere. Because the men are not "playing for keeps," they are free to experiment. At the same time, role-playing gets the players close enough to an actual situation so that they become excited and concerned about it.

Note that, in addition, role-playing is relatively practical. In contrast to the case method of instruction, it does not require prior preparation on the part of the salesmen, nor does it require the development of case material.

Caveats

Role-playing is not an easy form of training. It requires thought, effort, and careful planning on the part of the trainer. And, as with the case method and recorded selling conversations, he must orient his thinking and training to foster a spirit of inquiry rather than of judgment. The emphasis must be on "what has happened" rather than on "was it good or bad." It must be on "how was this accomplished" rather than on "was this done in a right or wrong way." Even after this emphasis has once been gained, it is extremely difficult to keep. It is surprisingly easy to lapse into a situation where the trainer *tells* the salesman. The temptation is to do what one well-known sales consulting organization does with its recorded and filmed dramatized cases (according to the brochure):

"The minute the dramatized case has been presented, discussion is likely to start spontaneously; for every salesman in the room has his decided views on what was done by the salesman in the playlet and what he should have done. The meeting comes alive.

"Differences of opinion about the right answers are aired in friendly but spirited debate. Interest is keyed up to a high pitch. The men in the group are thinking — and their thinking is centered on how to sell your products.

"When the discussion has gone far enough, the leader plays the reverse side of the record which reports the decision on each question of a committee, or 'jury,' together with a re-enactment of critical points in the case. Finally, the leader summarizes the essential conclusions and distributes a short text or take-home piece."

I grant and heartily support the thesis that it is highly beneficial to stimulate mental activity on the part of the salesmen. But to channel this activity into a right-wrong discussion of various questions (that apparently have predetermined answers) misses the whole complex problem with which the study of human relations is concerned.

Conclusion

There are, of course, other very practical problems in setting up a sound training program. Management must be persuaded that the need exists, and salesman acceptance must be gained. Human relations must be meshed with the other very necessary elements in sales training, and limited time allocated accordingly. Continued training must face up to the problem of geographic dispersion, and to the ability and willingness of field supervisors to undertake the task. Moreover, the trainers themselves — whether they be professional or field management personnel — must be grounded in the fundamentals of human relations.

Although knowledge in the human relations field has developed a great deal in the past 25 years, company practice has lagged sadly behind.

Perhaps it is because there is still so much to be done in the area of the factory that little or no attention has been paid to the field of sales. Or perhaps it is due to the fact that the study of human relations has all too often been associated solely with superior-subordinate relationships. In any case, I believe that salesmen stand to gain as much from the effective practice of human relations skills as any other group in the company — possibly more. Role-playing as described here is a means to that end. It is not yet a perfected idea, but it is a step forward.

George N. Kahn and Abraham Shuchman

4 Specialize Your Salesmen!

The 1960's promise to be a period of more intense competition than current managements have yet experienced. The signals are now clearly discernible:

- A rising flood of new products and imports.
- A growing saturation of markets for older products.
- An increasing invasion of markets by firms formerly regarded as noncompetitive.
- The spread of automation with its enormous output potential.

These trends emphasize a compelling need for marketing programs that will assure new account development for existing products and maximum efforts for new products, despite massive onslaughts by competitors for whom new customers and new markets are also an urgent necessity. If recent experience is a reliable indicator, managers seeking a hard-hitting program for market development will focus on advertising and other impersonal methods of sales promotion.

For many firms, however, and particularly for firms selling industrial products or selling consumer goods through distributors, the central role has been and will continue to be played by personal selling. Unfortunately, personal selling, aside from the provision of increased staff support, continues to be organized almost exactly as it was a generation ago in the days of the drummer. Territories, products, and sometimes (but not often) customers are the main divisions in current sales organization. Virtually no attempt has been made to organize personal selling on the basis of the task to be performed.

Why has specialization in personal selling stopped with territories, products, and customers? Why has little effort been made to increase the productivity of personal selling by applying one of the basic principals of mass production — specialization by task? The failure arises from a number of misconceptions or badly digested knowledge on the part of top management about the work that field salesmen are asked to perform, and about the requirements for accomplishing this work. Management seems not to have perceived that:

◖ Salesmen are called on to do not one but two very different jobs.

◖ The performance of each of these jobs involves different problems and techniques.

◖ The personnel requirements for satisfactory performance of each of these jobs are very different.

◖ The difficulties of reorganizing for specialization in the two jobs may be more than compensated for in improved sales performance.

In sum, top management has been overlooking an opportunity to raise field performance to levels never before achievable, and consequently an opportunity to develop a promotional weapon that could achieve new account development on an unprecedented scale.

Salesman's Two Jobs

First of all, while many executives may sense, or be vaguely aware of, the underlying principle, they do not comprehend the extent or the real nature of it: that in almost every company, and for almost every product, the work of a field salesman breaks down into two distinct jobs — (a) *sales development* and (b) *sales maintenance.*

On the one hand, the field salesman must service and cultivate existing customers. He must preserve and, if possible, expand the volume of business these customers do with his firm by maintaining and building on the favorable attitudes which already exist. He is engaged in a holding operation. The objective of sales maintenance is the *creation of sales* from people who already are customers, and whose habits and patterns of thought are already conducive to such sales.

On the other hand, the field salesman is expected to obtain new customers for his firm as well. He must convince companies that are not now using his firm's products to adopt them. To do this, he must eliminate and alter either the unfavorable or the indifferent attitudes and habits that are a part of the potential customer he is facing. He is engaged in a conversion operation. The objective of sales development is not so much the creation of sales as the *creation of customers* out of people who do not at the moment view his company favorably, and who are undoubtedly resistant to change.

Since these two jobs put such different requirements on a man, charging a field salesman with both creating sales and creating customers can only result in his undertaking the task he prefers to the detriment of the task he dislikes. The usual result is that among field salesmen, sales maintenance activity drives out sales development activity.

Why? Simply because the latter task is more difficult for the salesman to endure. None of us likes to enter and work in an unfriendly atmosphere in which rebuffs and even lack of common courtesy often prevail, in which we are given no recognition or status, and in which the probabilities of achieving one's objectives, despite the expenditure of considerable effort, are small. But this is exactly the situation faced by a salesman when he is engaged in sales development! As the social scientist would put it, he is a *change agent* in such a situation, and frequently faces a very hostile environment.

On the contrary, most of us prefer to go where we are known and where we know who is who, where we are treated with respect and accepted as an equal, and where the probabilities of achieving our goals without undue exertion are high. This is the situation faced by a salesman when he is engaged in sales *maintenance*, and, being only human, he will prefer to concentrate on the task of sales maintenance and avoid the task of sales development.

Creating Customers

However, failure to create new customers is due only in part to the reluctance of salesmen to devote themselves to this onerous task. Even when salesmen make a real effort, most of them cannot perform the task satisfactorily. The reason is simply that most field men possess neither the temperament nor the skills which the job requires.

As noted earlier, developing new accounts requires the reshaping of the prospective buyers' attitudes, habits, and patterns of thought. Essentially, this is a highly creative task requiring considerable time, talent, resourcefulness, and ingenuity. The talents needed by a development salesman can best be outlined by discussing the succession of stages through which the salesman must work to create a customer:

(1) To start with, the development salesman must identify those firms in his territory which are worthwhile for him to attempt to convert, and identify the influential executive in each. He must secure access to these executives for himself, and in many cases for his firm's technical specialists, under conditions which will assure him attention. This signifies that the development salesman must be an analyst as well as a talented tactician who understands that he must approach an executive in terms of the executive's company rather than in terms of the salesman's product.

(2) The development salesman must establish with these executives a relationship in which he is perceived as a source of possible help in solving company problems. To achieve this, the development salesman must be capable of understanding his prospects to the degree that he can communicate both his appreciation of their problems and an image of himself as a source of help in solving such problems.

(3) He must motivate prospects to change by helping them become aware of a need for change. He must be able to develop an appetite in the prospect when he is not hungry, by fostering a constructive discontent with things as they are. Since prospects, generally, are satisfied with their present behavior, he must disturb prospects' satisfaction with the status quo.

To accomplish this, he must have the talent and ability to create a situation in which each prospect *can learn for himself*, rather than be told or shown that he has problems and needs which can be better solved and satisfied.

(4) He must transform a readiness to change into an actual change in behavior. This transformation, the keystone of the entire development process, requires that the salesman be able to arouse in prospects the intention to change as well as the conviction that the suggested change is appropriate. It means, as well, that the development salesman must encourage and support prospects while they deliberate the change and try to put it into practice.

(5) However, securing an initial order or even a short sequence of orders does not signal, as too many marketers seem to believe, the end of the development process. Making a sale is not equivalent to creating a customer. The prospect may still very quickly become — with little provocation — a tenant of the inactive customer file. Consequently, the development salesman's job remains unfinished. He must still convert his prospect's action into habit. The salesman's final goal, therefore, is to stabilize the change he has created.

To do this, the development salesman must have sufficient awareness to reinforce his prospect's conviction that the innovation is wise by providing as much reassurance as possible. He must be capable of generating for his prospect both the experiences and the information which emphasize the advantages of the innovation.

Maintaining Sales

Once the purchase of the salesman's product has become habitual, the strategic objective of the development process has been achieved. The work of sales development is finished and that of sales maintenance begins. When the prospect has been converted to a customer, then the motives and objectives of the seller shift. Keeping the customer and making him a better customer are now a salesman's goals. His aim is to preserve and build on the foundation of confidence and acceptance established in the development process.

What the maintenance salesman seeks, therefore, is not change but *constancy*. His selling strategy is defensive rather than offensive. His selling tactics must be designed, not to break through established positions, but to make his own position entrenched and secure, impregnable to the assaults of competitors. In maintaining and strengthening customer loyalty and preference, the maintenance salesman starts from a well-prepared and propitious vantage point. He not only possesses much vital information but is supported and aided, in addition, by many forces in his customer's psychological and organizational environment:

(1) He knows directly or has been thoroughly briefed about the customer's operations, organization, and personnel.

(2) Even if he has not done the development work himself, he has ready access to key executives and is perceived as a source of help.

(3) He derives advantage from his customer's conservatism and inertia, from his customer's characteristic fear of and resistance to change, and from his customer's feelings of comfort and security, engendered by the knowledge that the salesman's product and firm perform well.

(4) He is aided by his customer's reluctance to seek a new supplier as long as the present one is doing an acceptable job. This is due, at least in part, to the knowledge that such a search and accommodation to a new product is costly in time, money, effort, and psychological strain and tension.

Thus, the conditions and circumstances under which the maintenance salesman works are far different and far more favorable than those under which the development salesman works. The principal task of the maintenance salesman is to keep his customers content with and happy in their relationship with his firm. It is to preserve and deepen his customers' satisfaction with the status quo. This satisfaction lasts for a time, after the intensive development work that produced it. But it is like a fire. It is lit; it burns; it is warm. It needs fuel. It does not last forever unless it is fed, regularly and carefully. The fire can be made to burn even more brightly through the use of two additives — friendliness and personal attention. Maintenance salesmen must have the happy ability to inject humor and warmth into the customer's business life.

Customer Service

The basic fuel for the fire of customer loyalty, however, is service. It is making the customer's work less difficult by being helpful and useful in improving his job performance. It is aiding him to solve his problems and assisting him to move toward the promotion of greater profits that is his goal. It is, in other words, doing such an effective job *for* the buyer that he himself wants to and actually helps the salesman to do an effective job *with* him.

For the *industrial* maintenance salesman this means that he must know the applications of his product better than do the customer's own technicians. He must know not only every conceivable use — and limitation — of his product, but the engineering behind it and the possibilities of complementary and competing products. He must understand his customer's processes and operations so well that he knows precisely where his product can and cannot be used as well as how it must be used in order to yield maximum benefit.

The maintenance salesman working among *distributors* and *dealers* has similar needs. This means that he must be intimately acquainted, not only with the general practices and problems of the trades to which he is selling, but also with the specific practices and problems of each customer. Moreover, he must be able to spot weaknesses and wastes in these practices, come up with practical suggestions for eliminating them, and help provide the skills needed to accomplish this elimination.

But comprehensive knowledge of products, processes, and trades is only one requirement for success in maintenance selling. In addition, the maintenance salesman must be the communicator of cogent and important market information and a crossbreeder of ideas. For industrial products he must be able to keep abreast of technological developments that can affect both his own and his customer's markets. He must be able to evaluate the impact on his customer's markets of these developments as well as of trends in competing industries.

Similarly, the salesman working in intermediate markets must be able to supply information about what is being sold by whom, how it is being sold, and who is doing the buying. Beyond this, he must be able to serve as an exchange medium for merchandising and promotional ideas. He must be alert to novel ideas and approaches used effectively by creative and pioneering jobbers or dealers and must take these to other distributors or dealers.

The Big Difference

Maintenance and development salesmen both need such talents as facilitate the acquisition, analysis, use, and communication of information. However, while they both must be able to apply these talents and skills to the products, markets, and operations of the customer company, the development salesman must be able to apply them under much more difficult conditions to an audience with very different attitudes.

The ability to obtain and communicate information about customer products, markets, and operations is, in most instances, sufficient for success in maintenance selling. It is by no means a sufficient condition for success in development work. On the contrary, the *sine qua non* of success in new account development is the ability to obtain, understand, and use information about the prospect himself; about his needs, fears, aspirations, and perceptions; about his prejudices, loyalties, ambitions, and enthusiasms.

The really critical abilities are the faculties to acquire, understand, and use not "technical" information or objective facts, as is the case for maintenance selling, but psychological information or subjective facts; and, equally important, to communicate and bring about effective communication between others. The crucial talents and skills of the development salesman are qualities that a maintenance salesman requires only to a very limited extent and perhaps not at all — such traits as empathy, a sharp "third ear," introspective skill, and superior intelligence.

There are other talents and skills which a development salesman must have and a maintenance salesman need not have. The former must be a creative strategist, a tactician capable of designing and implementing original, effective sales approaches and sales presentations — "custom-tailored" for each prospect and for each person influencing the purchase. He must be able to mobilize and exploit skills, knowledge, and ideas of technical and missionary specialists. As a result, the development salesman is required to be alert and active, with an inventive imagination, and a sensitivity to or feel for the appropriate deed and the appropriate time. He requires resourcefulness, ingenuity, much tact and skill in interrogation, and the administrative skills needed to plan, organize, coordinate, direct, and control the work of others.

Born, Not Trained

Thus, there are real and very substantial differences between the talents and skills which determine success in development selling and those which determine success in maintenance selling. But this fact in itself, although interesting, is certainly no revelation to some marketing managers. *What is really significant* (and has not been apparent to managers, however) *is that most of the qualities needed for successful development selling cannot be acquired.*

No amount of training can provide these qualities if a man does not possess them. A man has them or he does not. If he has them, training can develop and strengthen them; it can improve their use. But if he does not have them, training will not give them to him. Clearly, an adult who is not empathic, introspective, or sensitive to subtleties of expression cannot be taught to be so.

We have no means for increasing an adult's intelligence, imagination, resourcefulness, or ingenuity. Training can provide information, skills, and technical competence; but training, in the usual sense in which this word is used, cannot enable a person to develop new and different personality and character traits. This is what would be required in order to make most salesmen real development salesmen.

To make matters worse, adults who possess, in both the appropriate degree and combination, the qualities necessary for successful development selling are scarce. Moreover, these people are in such great demand in other occupations that only a relatively few are ever recruited into selling. How can strong market or sales development be obtained in the face of a severe shortage of field personnel competent to perform the task?

Strong Market Development

Any solution, to be genuinely effective, must satisfy two conditions. First, it must assure that new account development cannot be treated as a peripheral assignment to be attended to only if and when sales maintenance responsibilities permit. Secondly, the solution must ensure that the talents and skills of every field salesman are used to best advantage. No man should be used for a job which can be performed by another of lesser talent and skill.

As noted earlier, there is a "Gresham's Law" of personal selling: when a salesman has a choice between routine sales maintenance activities and sales development activities requiring creativity, ingenuity, and resourcefulness, he will tend to give precedence to sales maintenance. Therefore, if sales development is to take place as a sustained and all-out effort, it is necessary to assign the task to salesmen who are prohibited from engaging in sales maintenance and are rewarded only for developing new accounts; in other words, to set up a specialized development task force within or auxiliary to the field sales department.

Specialization by task of the field sales force is a solution which also satisfies the second condition — using to best advantage the talents and skills of every field salesman. Men who possess the qualities necessary for development work can be relieved of maintenance work which does not require full use of their rare and valuable capabilities. Similarly, salesmen who are effective in sales maintenance but lack the traits needed for new account development can be relieved of the need for "putting in" time and effort at the latter job. This time and this effort are largely wasted in such activity, but they can and would bring results in sales maintenance. Specialization will effectively barricade the avenues now used by salesmen to escape from the demanding tasks of strong market development and will ensure all-out effort.

Furthermore, specialization should eliminate much of the very great waste which now typifies personal selling, by making possible more efficient utilization of manpower resources. In particular, it should eliminate the very high costs which are incurred when men with the gifts required for performance of the vital, difficult, and trying assignment of sales development are given responsibility for sales maintenance which they can do almost without half-trying, while other men who are not sufficiently gifted to develop markets but who can perform sales maintenance skillfully are, nevertheless, called on to work at development and are unhappy while doing it. Thus, specialization by task assures both that adequate attention is given to market development and that more efficient and fuller use is made of available talents and skills.

Without question, therefore, it can result in a significant increase in the productivity of personal selling.

New Products

For firms seeking to introduce new products, market development is, of course, of paramount importance. Ineffectively organized sales forces are unable to make the benefits of their new products highly visible. As a consequence, many new products fail to succeed, not because they offer no valuable benefits, but because these benefits are not communicated.

A good example is new materials and components which substitute for something already used. To fabricators and distributors, the greatest benefit of any product is the opportunity afforded for obtaining increased sales volume and penetrating new markets without great cost in money or effort.

The success or failure of such development jobs rides on the ability of the firm's salesmen to demonstrate that (1) a high and active level of demand for the new product already exists among the prospect's current and potential customers, and (2) the salesmen's firm is successfully creating and will continue to create an expanding demand for the product in the markets which the prospect serves and would like to serve.

A flow of orders usually impresses even the most skeptical and suspicious fabricator or distributor — particularly when it includes orders from customers to whom the prospect has previously been unable to sell. However, the inertia, doubt, and skepticism of some distributors and fabricators run so deep that even a flow of profitable orders cannot convince them that a change to the new product is desirable.

Specialization by development salesmen can be used to establish conditions that may lead *ultimately* to this conviction. Only the most unperceptive prospect is not "shaken up" after being repeatedly confronted by the question: "Well, if you don't buy the product to fill this order from your customer, what do you want me to do, take it to your competitor?"

Securing buying action in this way does not create a customer, for the prospect's attitudes remain unchanged and his fears and anxieties are not relieved. But attitude change can follow rather than precede behavior change. The prospect may find, in other words, that "it's not so bad as I had thought. In fact this outfit is really doing a job for me." Only specialized development salesmen can spend the time and the sustained effort and create the impression needed to produce this conclusion.

In the development of markets for new products, missionary selling is essential. It must, however, be missionary selling that is aimed at the specific goal of generating orders from prospects' customers and not merely detail work which aims only at the general goals of creating good will or easing the way for prospects' salesmen. Unfortunately, few firms introducing new products seem to understand that the impact of such missionary work is generally far greater than can be obtained from verbal or pictorial descriptions of the product's benefits or from vicariously experienced success stories, no matter how elaborate and how dramatic the frame in which these are embedded. No selling aid has the potency of a flow of orders in sweeping away the objections and stilling the doubts of the fabricators and distributors. Development salesmen, specializing in creating a flow of orders, are the most potent tool available for new market development in this area.

Since most firms introduce new products only periodically, their need for development selling in general may be only sporadic. For such firms, specialization by task of their own field force can be too costly and wasteful. However, this does not mean that these companies cannot obtain the benefits of specialization. Organizations consisting of specialists in every phase of market development (including development selling) exist and their services can, of course, be purchased for more or less extended but definite periods of time. It is possible, therefore, for firms to obtain specialization by task even if they cannot economically support twin sales forces of their own: they can secure this specialization by employing *periodically* an auxiliary market development task force.

Service Industries

In some industries, development selling is already specialized — for example, in firms rendering professional services, in the giant-size firms of the construction industry, and in the architectural, engineering, and factoring firms where responsibility for new account development is carried by high-echelon executives.

Such executives have the savoir-faire necessary for successful development work. However, these executives often lack the talents and skills needed to locate and contact worthwhile prospects. More often, they simply lack the time needed for the study and the design of effective first-stage strategy and tactics. Yet this is an essential element in the development salesman's job. In either case, the result is the same. The executives perform very well indeed when invited to make a presentation, but they have serious difficulty in obtaining invitations from enough worthwhile prospects.

Aware of this difficulty, some of the leading architectural, engineering, and contracting firms have begun to specialize *within* the development process by hiring men whose sole job is to "flush out" valuable prospects, establish contact with them, and procure an invitation for a presentation by the firm. The difficulty such companies have encountered, however, has been in finding salesmen with the unique talents and skills needed, and the desire to accomplish this very difficult and psychologically strenuous phase of development work. To obtain such personnel, some firms have, as an experiment, incorporated within their organizations (as a kind of subsidiary) a firm of development specialists.

Few professional service firms have, as yet, had the perspicacity or courage to undertake the experiment described. The principal benefit, which brings in its wake a number of others, is that increased specialization permits a much more efficient use of the firm's most limited and valuable resource: the time and talents of top executives. These executives no longer spend a great deal of time hopping from city to city in the hope, often fruitless, of ferreting out a project which is being planned. The job is now done for them by specialists, following each project to the point where professional advice and skill should be introduced, and arranging for presentations by executives.

As a result, executives in the firms which are experimenting have found that they can concentrate on the stages of the development process in which they are most proficient, while others who are singularly proficient in "opening" the process assume that responsibility. Above all, increased specialization has brought, in most cases, a continuous and heavy flow of invited presentations to desirable clients.

Problems of Specialization

Although specialization of the field sales force by task holds great potential for increasing the efficiency of personal selling, there are difficulties which must be overcome if this potential is to be realized. For example, the inauguration of twin sales forces raises problems of coordination, morale, and control just as does the splitting up of any other job.

One such problem is that of achieving a transition from development to maintenance selling which is smooth and does not disturb the customer-supplier relationship. This requires, of course, a close and harmonious working relationship between the two salesmen for a period during which they call on the customer together in order to set the stage for the transfer of responsibility. The customer must not get the feeling that he is being shunted aside. If anything, he must be assured that he will be getting even better service and attention than he received before.

Another problem is the impact of specialization on the attitudes of the men whose activities are now restricted to maintenance selling. By the very nature of their qualifications and their task, these men cannot and should not be rewarded as well, or be permitted as much freedom of action, as development salesmen. Some bitterness and antagonism will without doubt arise, and will have to be especially allayed when customers are being transferred.

A third problem sometimes appears when specialization is achieved through the use of an auxiliary task force rather than the restructuring of the company's own field sales department. Some sales managers, because they feel themselves threatened by the new vitality which specialization gives to their sales operation, will attempt to sabotage the innovation.

Finally, it is not easy to establish standards of performance for development salesmen. As we have seen, the development process often requires considerable time before there is a payoff. Therefore, a salesman may readily have extended periods in which his output of new accounts is nil or abysmally low. He may, nevertheless, be doing such a highly effective job that his output will soar eventually. It is difficult to determine during this period of low output, however, whether or not the salesman's performance is adequate. And it is difficult in general to establish monthly or even quarterly quotas that can be used as a reliable measure of performance.

As a result, specialization requires a change in top-management attitudes about personal selling organization and about the costs and performance of development work if it is to be effective.

Attitude Barriers

The failure of more firms to employ the techniques of specialization is difficult to understand. Discussions with executives of many industries have led us to conclude, however, that there are at least three explanations. To overcome them requires a major change in management attitudes. They are:

(1) *An inability to relieve salesmen of their maintenance responsibilities so that they can concentrate on development selling.* Top management will have to recognize that the field salesman *is* required to do two different jobs, and that these two jobs require men with different personalities and skills. In effect, it must be willing to look closely at the old bogey of twin sales forces without old prejudices. Of course it is going to be more difficult to supervise two sets of salesmen. It is going to require, in all probability, a higher dollar outlay. And of course it is going to be difficult to upset company organization and traditional ways. But the final increase in efficiency and tactical power will more than compensate for all such problems by an increase in sales and customer satisfaction.

(2) *The dearth of manpower capable and knowledgeable enough to be effective in developing orders for the new products among the accounts of prospective customers.* Given the current scarcity of sales personnel qualified for development selling, management will have to change its tactics in order to attract the best men. Recruiting, selection and training programs, and other procedures will have to be revised to make appraisal of a candidate's qualifications for development work paramount and to focus training on the development of these qualities to their best degree. Compensation plans must recognize both the importance and the scarcity of development salesmen — you have to pay the top man to get the top job done.

The sad and bleak truth is, however, that field selling, while still regarded in most quarters as an honorable vocation, is on the whole no longer looked on as a desirable vocation. Moreover, the reasons for this low status are rooted so deeply in our mid-century culture that little, if anything, can be done to alter the fact. Even the promise of relatively high incomes will apparently not suffice to attract an abundance of manpower with the potential for development selling. Many firms — and, unfortunately, very frequently those which need effective sales development most — will not find it feasible to recruit both a maintenance and a development sales force. These firms will have to obtain the benefits of specialization by hiring auxiliary market development task forces.

(3) *The* idée fixe *prevalent among executives that personal selling costs are fully and completely current operating expenses which must be met entirely by some predetermined proportion of current income.* The biggest single obstacle to greater productivity in personal selling through specialization by task is the insistence by management that for any accounting period the cost of personal selling should not exceed some arbitrary percentage of sales. Such a restriction may not impair sales maintenance (though even this is doubtful), but it virtually makes impossible effective sales development.

Maximum sales development simply cannot be obtained efficiently if management demands that income from it exceed its cost period by period. Development expenditure is not an operating cost, but a capital investment ranking among the most important that a firm can make. The only factor that makes production facilities worth anything more than their "knockdown" or auction value is the existence of profitable customers for the goods these facilities can produce. The most valuable asset of a firm is its pool of customers, and if development selling is to succeed, it must be viewed as a capital investment in developing this pool.

In short, expenditures for sales development have precisely the same characteristics as expenditures for product development. Both are investments, not current operating expenses. And for neither can it be expected that the payoff comes in the same period as the expenditure. While this idea is generally recognized for product development expenditures, as yet it is rarely recognized for sales development expenditures.

Conclusion

The application of specialization by task to personal selling can provide an opportunity to raise field performance to levels never before achievable, and consequently an opportunity to develop a promotional weapon that could achieve new account development on an unprecedented scale. Such specialization must focus around the fact that the work of a field salesman is really two distinct jobs: sales development and sales maintenance.

The objective of sales maintenance is the creation of sales from people who already are customers, and whose habits and patterns of thought are already conducive to such sales. The objective of sales development is not merely the creation of sales, but the creation of customers out of people who do not at the moment view the company or its products favorably, and who are undoubtedly resistant to change.

In effect, these two jobs require men of different calibre and sentiments. Maintenance and development salesmen both need talents which facilitate the acquisition, analysis, use, and communication of technical information. However, the development salesman must, in addition, have the ability to obtain, understand, and use information about his prospects' needs, fears, aspirations, perceptions, prejudices, loyalties, ambitions, and enthusiasms. One might call this key quality *social perceptiveness*, and what is really significant is that it cannot be acquired or taught.

As a result of the scarcity of such talented men in personal selling, the best method for ensuring thorough new account development with the best use of all selling talent available is to have salesmen specialize in the maintenance or development jobs, and try not to do both.

This specialization will undoubtedly create problems that will require careful management attention. But the rewards of specialization will more than offset the difficulties of transition periods between salesmen, rivalries between the two sales forces, and the development of performance standards.

This last point raises a crucial issue in the acceptance of specialization in personal selling: *top-management attitude.* If executives are to avail themselves of the opportunity for improving the efficiency of personal selling that is available, they must free themselves from traditional thinking. Management will have to change its hiring and training programs so that they stress finding the men who have the qualities for development selling.

Even more importantly, management must recognize that development selling cannot be expected to bear the immediate fruits of sales maintenance. It must come to recognize that expenditures for market development are the close and supporting kin to product development expenditures. Management must be ready to invest in the market in the same way as it invests in plant and equipment or research and development. It must recognize that creating and using a specialized development sales force is just such an investment in the future of the company.

Victor P. Buell

5 Door-to-Door Selling

Most manufacturers are giving closer attention to their distribution methods today than they have at any time in the past 15 years. With competition on the upswing, they are examining alternative methods of moving and selling their products to the consumer. One of the alternatives falling under the scrutiny of many is door-to-door selling — the method of selling merchandise by salesmen who make personal calls at a prospect's residence or place of work.

Suppose a manufacturer, having observed that other companies make successful use of door-to-door distribution, is considering the advisability of employing it for his own company. In order to make sure that any decision he makes is a sound one, he should answer four questions:

- Is there any chance of profitable volume?
- What are the major problems?
- What are the major advantages?
- Is my product the "right kind"?

Volume and Profit

How much chance does the company have to build profitable volume? A direct answer is next to impossible because of the unwillingness of most door-to-door distributors to give out their profit and cost figures. There are some indications that this can be a highly profitable way to do business; there are other indications that it is a good way to lose your shirt.

But if the company considering such a move has the right product and is aware of and prepared to meet the inevitable problems connected with door-to-door selling, it may do very well. Avon Products is a good example. Last year this cosmetics company, which sells exclusively door-to-door, had a net profit before taxes of nearly $7 million — more than three times that of such competitors as Helena Rubenstein and Lehn & Fink (Dorothy Gray, Tussy, etc.), both of whom distribute through retail stores.

Many authorities believe the same picture would show up if we could examine the books of other companies where the door-to-door salesman is not just the strongest, but in some cases the *only*, link in the distribution chain. Some of the larger companies, of course, do publish their figures; and though relatively few companies selling primarily door-to-door have become large, enough have done so — and profitably — to attest to the fact that door-to-door selling should not be discounted by consumer-goods manufacturers. Recent sales and earnings of some publicly held companies distributing primarily by door-to-door methods are shown in EXHIBIT 1 (on the next page).

A five-year look (1948–1952) at the earnings of such publicly held companies indicates — with the exception of the apparel companies — a generally good return on sales and a good-to-excellent return on invested capital. The annual reports for 1953 that are now available indicate no change in the pattern.

EXHIBIT I. ANNUAL SALES AND EARNINGS OF SOME PUBLICLY HELD COMPANIES EMPLOYING DOOR-TO-DOOR DISTRIBUTION

Company	*Sales*	*Net income before taxes*
Stanley Home Products, Inc. (brushes and household cleaning aids)	$57,701,162	$7,298,287
Avon Products, Inc.* (cosmetics)	47,033,052	6,963,337
Fuller Brush Company (brushes, cosmetics, household cleaning aids)	44,641,277	3,681,200
Electrolux Corporation * (vacuum cleaners)	†	4,210,024
Fashion Frocks, Inc. (dresses and other apparel)	21,178,891	1,286,698
Real Silk Hosiery Mills, Inc.* (hosiery and apparel)	8,739,813	96,131‡
Beauty Counselors, Inc. (cosmetics)	4,998,042	691,585
The Process Corporation (greeting cards)	2,035,051	144,176

* 1953 figures.
† Not reported.
‡ Excluding reserve adjustments.
NOTE: Figures are for 1952 unless otherwise noted.

Two more examples of companies that successfully plunged into door-to-door distribution in recent years are Saladmaster (vegetable shredders and cooking utensils), which reputedly has run its volume from scratch up to $9 million in six years, and Nutrilite Products (vitamin food supplements), which increased its sales from $60 thousand in 1946 to $12 million last year.

By and large the companies (or divisions of companies) selling primarily door-to-door can be classified as small to medium in size. However, in addition to the relatively small number of large companies that publish their figures, several privately held companies manufacturing silverware, cooking utensils, home furnishings, and wearing apparel are reported to have sales between $2 million and $15 million yearly.

One of the most successful enterprises — the C. H. & C. W. Stuart companies of Newark, New York — has approximately 20 subsidiaries and divisions all selling door-to-door. (They have found that once sales volume of a subsidiary begins to level off, it is usually more profitable to develop a new subsidiary company than it is to try to increase sales further.) Sales of these individual subsidiaries are reported to run from a few hundred thousand dollars up to as high as $14 million annually. Each subsidiary carries one major product line. Items sold include such varied products as nursery stock, cosmetics, silverware, jewelry, and china.

Over-All Trends

What has been the trend in the volume of door-to-door sales, and in the number and kind of companies which engage in this method of distribution?

Department of Commerce figures show a sales volume for direct selling organizations of $634,763,000 as of 1948 (a slight drop from 1939). If this amount increased at the same rate as did total retail sales volume between 1948 and 1953, direct selling organizations would have accounted for close to a billion dollars in sales in 1953.

Some observers are far more liberal in their estimates. One recent article referred to door-to-door selling as a $7-billion industry in 1948. A still more recently published estimate placed the current sales volume at $10 billion. If these figures could be believed, door-to-door selling would account for between 5½% and 6% of total retail sales in the United States.

In partial explanation of the enormous gap between these estimates is the fact that the more conservative Bureau of the Census figures do not include the considerable amount of door-to-door selling done by individuals or retail stores (as contrasted with crews of canvassers operating out of a sales headquarters); while the other figures go to the extreme of including milkmen, insurance agents, and cookie-selling Girl Scouts.

Reliable trade-association estimates are in between but closer to the Department of Commerce figures; they run from $1 billion to $4 billion. Something in this range is probably nearest the truth, at least for consumer goods sold door-to-door by manufacturers or their distributive organizations. The reluctance of door-to-door people (both individually and through their trade associations) to be any more informative is perfectly understandable, in view of the continuous attempts that have been made by retailers year after year in community after community to legislate the door-to-door selling companies out of business.

Recent Developments

Trade sources estimate that the total number of companies using door-to-door methods has declined from a high of 4,500 in 1930 to between 3,000 and 3,500 today, with no essential change in the total number since 1950. The exception to this is the door-to-door distributor, who is usually a local businessman engaged purely in buying and selling; the National Association of House to House Installment Companies reports an increase in this type of distributing business in recent years.

Also, it is likely that the drop in the total number of companies using door-to-door selling is accounted for mostly by casualties in the relatively large group of small firms depending entirely on low-caliber, "transient" salesmen rather than by any appreciable loss among the more outstanding companies that have at least a core of better-organized and better-trained salesmen.

As a matter of fact, there are some very strong points in the general picture, which make up for any loss in total number of companies. Particularly strong at the present time is the trend to selling through "home parties," whereby a housewife arranges for a demonstration to a group of her friends, with refreshments, and receives a merchandise prize for the sales made (and also, usually, for the number present who volunteer to give similar parties). Also increasing in popularity is the so-called "club" plan, common in selling big-ticket items such as silverware and chinaware. In this plan the customer receives additional merchandise free or at discount for each friend she gets to join the "X" Company Club (one joins by buying merchandise). Each new member is entitled to similar privileges for getting her friends to join, and so on ad infinitum.

As with companies using other types of distribution, there are companies going into business and out of business most of the time. Here are some of the recent developments in particular industries:

Because of the relatively narrow margins and competitive pricing practices of the apparel industry, apparel companies selling door-to-door have been particularly hard hit in recent years. Some of the foundation garment companies too have been experiencing unprofitable operations, and several hosiery companies have been fighting to stay out of the red.

Companies making pots and pans have also had hard going because of the influx of manufacturers into the field after World War II in an effort to put to use some of their facilities which had been taken off war work. Nevertheless, some old-timers such as Wearever Aluminum are still going strong.

Silverware and fine china have been on the increase lately among products distributed door-to-door. Companies selling them have opened up a whole new market among middle and lower income families who have been able and willing for the first time to invest in such nonnecessities. Salesmanship and reasonable installment payments have done the trick.

An increasing number of cosmetics companies, encouraged by the success of Avon Products, have been experimenting with door-to-door methods. A recent study indicated that in the last few years cosmetics sold door-to-door tripled their share of total cosmetics sales, going from 5½% to 16% in 1952. Nursery products (shrubs, rose bushes, etc.) have also continued strong, as have brushes, vacuum cleaners, and a variety of kitchen specialties. Many of these products are sold through the "party" method.

As for companies that have gone from door-to-door into retail store distribution, few have done so with success. One outstanding exception is the Dazey Corporation of St. Louis, which switched its can-opener business to retail store distribution some years ago. Dazey can openers and other kitchen specialties are now found in almost every retail hardware department.

Some companies try to use both distribution channels. The Hoover Company developed one of the most famous trade names in vacuum cleaners via door-to-door methods combined with department store demonstrations. For a time after World War II, Hoover relied principally on the retail store for its distribution but added door-to-door selling again when it saw some of its competitors, such as Electrolux, shoot ahead through reliance on the direct method.

Wearever Aluminum, which originally sold its products only through door-to-door methods, today also sells through retail stores; this is one of the outstanding examples of a manufacturer who has been able to distribute successfully through both channels while using the same trade-mark. Also, Singer Sewing Machine Company, which built its business through house-to-house methods, in recent years has added company-owned retail outlets; these help to develop prospects, who are then followed up in the home if the sale is not made at the retail store.

But this combination of retail store with door-to-door distribution is not automatically successful. Both Real Silk and Fuller Brush experimented with company-owned retail outlets as supplements to their direct methods, but gave them up after brief and unsuccessful trials.

For a broadly classified list of the types of companies engaging in door-to-door selling, see EXHIBIT II. This list is generally considered comprehensive, and it takes in several groups that do not fall within the Bureau of the Census classification.

Major Problems

Impressive as are some of the statistics just cited, an objective look at the major problems of selling directly to the consumer is in order before the management of a company goes on to look at the possible advantages and decide whether the time has come to scrap its present distribution system and adopt door-to-door selling instead.

Many manufacturers' sales executives selling consumer products through wholesale channels or direct to retailers have never experienced some of the problems common to door-to-door sales executives. Even where similarities exist, differences in emphasis are great. These problems are well known to every door-to-door sales executive but they are rarely discussed "on the outside." The major issues faced in developing and directing a door-to-door sales organization are as follows:

1. Recruiting large numbers of salespeople.
2. High turnover rate among sales personnel.
3. High sales costs.
4. Control of a salesforce made up of "non-employees" and many part-time salespeople.
5. Local ordinances preventing or harassing door-to-door selling.
6. Need for highly aggressive sales management and promotion.
7. Damage to the company reputation through misrepresentation by sales personnel.

Let us take a closer look at these problems.

Recruiting Job

Sales managing a door-to-door organization is first and foremost a constant job of recruiting salespeople.

Salesforces of from 2,000 to 5,000 salesmen are common for companies selling door-to-door on a national scale. Some companies have as many as 80,000 persons representing them at any one time.

Door-to-door companies have always obtained

EXHIBIT II. CLASSES OF COMPANIES USING DOOR-TO-DOOR SELLING

Reference book publishers. One trade association official estimates 90% of all encyclopedias and other reference books are sold door-to-door.

Magazine publishers. Door-to-door selling has been for years, and still remains, an important source of subscription business.

Tea and coffee route companies. These are primarily packaged food specialty houses — usually featuring their branded tea or coffee — that sell by truck-route salesmen who call at their customers' homes about every two weeks. Some of them have added other lines, such as apparel and household articles. Jewell Tea and Grand Union are two of the oldest and best known of these companies. Both of them have added chain supermarket operations in which their sales have far outstripped their door-to-door operations.

Milk and bread route companies. Most milk for home consumption is delivered to the householder by driver salesmen who try to increase the variety of milk products bought by their customers and who vie with other companies for new families on the truck route. Many cities have one or more bread companies that sell through truck-route salesmen calling on the householder two to three times weekly. Omar Incorporated, operating in the Midwest, with 1953 sales of $37,009,336, is a well-known firm in this field.

Door-to-door distributors. These are companies established solely for the purpose of distributing products purchased from manufacturers. Most are local or regional in their coverage, although a few, such as the L. B. Price Mercantile Company and the Senak Company, distribute in many sections of the country. They usually carry a wide variety of products in the personal and home furnishings fields, such as cooking utensils, silverware, blankets, bedspreads, clocks, jewelry, wearing apparel, and so forth. Some carry an exclusive line for one manufacturer. Most of these organizations sell on a credit basis (with small weekly collections — about $1.25 per week) to families making up the lower fourth of the national income scale.

Some of the products sold by these organizations are nationally known brands, but most of them are unadvertised brands, often developed especially for the distributive organization. Manufacturers who distribute through these channels have found that their entire approach toward pricing, packaging, and sales contacts must be altered to fit their special needs.

Retailers and dealers. These include a great variety of retail stores and dealers who may use door-to-door salesmen in addition to their floor salesmen to solicit business or follow up leads obtained in the retail outlet. Examples of products sometimes sold this way are home appliances, heating and air conditioning equipment, automobile tires and accessories, storm windows, insulation, roofing, and floor coverings.

Manufacturers. The manufacturer develops his own door-to-door sales organization to distribute one or more of his product lines. He may or may not also distribute through other channels. As a rule, if he does use another channel of distribution, he will not use the same brand name for his door-to-door line and the line distributed through the other channel.

their sales volume principally from large numbers of people selling a small volume each. While it is probable that most companies really do not prefer it this way, the fact is that relatively few salespeople are capable of making sizable sales and incomes in this type of selling. When they do make good incomes, they often are promoted to supervisory work or they leave for other types of sales jobs. The result is that most companies have a few salespeople making good-to-excellent yearly sales and earnings, but many people making small sales and earnings.

Using the figures of several well-known companies whose sales volume and average number of salespersons are known, we find that average annual volume per salesperson runs from a low of $230 in one company to a high of $3,500 in another. By applying the percentage of commission known to be paid by these companies, we find that average annual gross earnings for their salesmen vary from a low of $92 to a high of $700 — and salesmen must pay their own expenses out of their earnings! (Companies with higher averages are definite — and often outstanding — exceptions.) This is hardly a level of earnings to attract droves of recruits — though it must be remembered that most door-to-door salespeople are part-time workers in the capacity of agents or dealers rather than employees of the company.

Recruiting was relatively easy when many of today's most successful companies using door-to-door distribution got their start — during the 1920's and 1930's when unemployment of several millions of the nation's work force was commonplace. However, high employment conditions that existed after 1940 made recruiting of salespeople extremely difficult and expensive. That is why so many companies have been forced to resort primarily to part-time salespeople — housewives, men with other positions who need to supplement their income, and older persons on social security or pensions.

Turnover Problem

Manufacturers who use regular distribution methods would be aghast at turnover rates of door-to-door salesforces. Turnover up to 300% a year is not unusual. The primary reasons for this appear to be nonselective recruiting, straight commission form of compensation, distaste for door-to-door selling, and inadequate training and direction.

Because of the difficulty in obtaining people willing to sell door-to-door, these companies cannot afford the luxury of careful screening. The recruiting job tends to be one of convincing persons to try door-to-door selling rather than selecting the best applicants from those available. Standards of individual companies vary widely in this respect, but, generally speaking, screening involves nothing more than weeding out only the more obviously unqualified. Consequently, many persons unsuited to door-to-door selling are persuaded to try it and as a result leave their new jobs quickly.

Straight commission compensation is almost universal, although some companies add bonuses based on specified volume performance. Although this form of compensation offers opportunity for earnings tied directly to the ability and energy of the individual salesman, it does not add to stability of the salesforce. It also probably contributes to the lack of selectivity in recruiting, because of the notion held by some sales supervisors that little is lost in trying out a questionable recruit since he is paid only on the basis of his sales volume.

Few people really like to sell door-to-door. Many who take it up do so as a means to an end rather than through preference for this type of work. They may accept a door-to-door job to tide them over a period of unemployment. If otherwise employed, they may sell for a specific purpose such as to earn money to pay for unusual doctor bills or for Christmas expenses. After the need for extra money is gone, the salesperson quits.

Of course the opposite happens sometimes, and people who start selling door-to-door, expecting to remain at it only temporarily, like the work and are so successful they continue with it, sometimes giving up another position to sell full-time. Actually, such persons have been the source of most full-time salespeople in this field, at least during recent years. Nevertheless, the ones who are successful and remain are few compared with those who become dissatisfied and quit.

Because the field supervisor must spend so much time in recruiting (and often in doing personal selling himself), little time is left for sales training. In spite of the fact that selling has been developed to a high art by door-to-door companies (some of this country's outstanding sales and business executives got their basic selling know-how from door-to-door selling), the size of the salesforce that field supervisors must oversee makes it impossible for everyone to get adequate training. Training is often reduced to the supervisor's working with the few salespeople who have shown better-than-average results on their own.

And, of course, in companies that recruit and supervise by mail, personal sales training is nonexistent. Therefore, some people who might succeed with proper training quit before they ever taste success.

Sales Costs

Although to the casual observer it might appear that door-to-door distribution costs would be lower than those of retail store distribution, the reverse is usually true. For one thing, commissions paid to salesmen often equal or exceed markups taken by retailers. But the big difference, and not a readily apparent one, is that manufacturers selling door-to-door are faced with higher selling expenses, above and beyond salesmen's commissions, than are those distributing through retailers.

Large-scale recruitment, training, and high turnover rates are of course major cost factors. While these are partially absorbed by field managers, they result in higher commission rates to the managers and so actually increase the company's costs. In addition, there frequently are high development and turnover costs in the field supervisory force itself, as well as the cost of maintaining numerous branch offices.

Classified advertising costs are usually borne directly by the manufacturer. He must also bear the cost of record-keeping for a large salesforce with a high turnover rate. Also, he must provide selling equipment and samples for his salesforce, which may be counted in the thousands. True, some companies charge the salesperson a nominal price for the equipment (usually payable in installments from his earnings), but many others provide it entirely free. Either way this is a costly item, because handling and shipping in the quantities required is expensive, and it must be of relatively good quality for the salesperson to be able to back up the claims he makes for the product.

Order handling and shipping expenses are another important cost factor. One well-known manufacturer with both door-to-door and retail store distribution ships about 25,000 orders per week in his door-to-door operation compared to a few hundred shipments weekly to his retail store accounts. The office, warehousing, and shipping force number several hundred people in the door-to-door operation compared to a few score in the retail operation.

Where credit is extended to thousands of consumers on a time-payment basis, the credit department must obviously be heavily staffed as compared to that of the manufacturer extending the usual credit terms to a few hundred wholesalers or retailers. The cost of the larger capital investment needed to maintain a time-payment plan must also be considered.

Another sizable cost is the high-powered promotion needed to keep all the part-time salespeople busy making calls. Increasing use of premiums as buying incentives has created another item of expense.

Distribution costs vary widely for different types of products whether sold door-to-door or through retail channels. Furthermore, they vary for retail distribution according to whether the manufacturer is selling to chains or whether he is going direct to the retailer or selling to wholesalers. The amount of advertising required can also be a major variant.

The breakdown of distribution costs for one company selling door-to-door is shown below:

Distribution costs	*Per cent of retail selling price*
Salesmen's commission	40%
Field supervision (managers' commissions, branch expenses)	7
Administrative and other overhead (sales management, clerical, shipping, promotion, selling equipment, credit, etc.)	13
Total	60%

This case is presented as an illustration only. Distribution costs as a percentage of selling price may be greater or less than 60%. Furthermore, cost breakdowns vary widely with kinds of business conducted. For example, some door-to-door companies pay their salesmen commissions of only 20%. Some recruit only by mail and therefore have little or no field supervision expense. However, when the percentage of costs in one item goes down, it usually happens that percentages in other items go up correspondingly, so that for the same type of product they add up to approximately the same total percentage of retail selling price.

Control of Salesforce

Manufacturers who are accustomed to selling through the more usual channels of distribution and who have had a reasonable degree of control over their salesmen will be in for some surprises if they try a door-to-door salesforce. They will find they have little control over their salespeople. There are two basic reasons for this lack of control:

(1) A large number of part-time salespeople are not primarily dependent on their door-to-door jobs for their income. They are relatively independent and do not respond to close supervision and direction. Even full-time salesmen tend to be independent because of the ease with which they can switch to another company.

(2) The other reason is a legal one. Because of the high turnover, large salesforce, and already high sales costs, it is necessary in door-to-door distribution to avoid such additional costs as federal Social Security taxes, unemployment taxes, and federal withholding (income) taxes. In order to avoid these taxes, and record-keeping costs incident thereto, it is necessary to have salespeople qualify as independent agents rather than as employees of the company.

Although legal interpretations vary, the primary distinction is that an independent agent is not subject to detailed direction from the company. He must be free to work when, where, and how he chooses. So the degree of control the company can legally exercise is limited largely to suggestion and to the use of examples of the most successful sales methods followed by others.

Local Ordinances

Door-to-door salesmen for years have been faced with harassment in the form of municipal legislation, usually sponsored by local retailers who wanted to eliminate outside competition.

The door-to-door sellers for a long time had the United States Supreme Court and many state supreme courts on their side. Then in 1951 our highest federal court refused to review — and therefore in effect upheld — a lower court's decision that the so-called "Green River" ordinance was constitutional. This ordinance, in brief, makes it a misdemeanor to call at a home to solicit business unless invited to do so by the resident of the home.

At first the Supreme Court's decision appeared to be a severe blow to door-to-door selling, but concerted action by companies engaged in it and their several trade associations has been effective in preventing the spread of this ordinance. This action has taken the form of education and pressure at the local level whenever the "Green River" or a similar ordinance is introduced.

As a matter of fact, ordinances probably have little effect on holding down total door-to-door sales when considered on a national basis. However, a manufacturer entering door-to-door distribution will find the variety of ordinances in numerous localities to be, at best, a distinct nuisance. He must be aware of them and should provide for competent legal advice to minimize possible trouble from this source.

Sales Management

In many manufacturing companies sales management has tended to shift in recent years from the inspirational to the factual approach. As more and more emphasis has been placed on scientific sales management with corresponding attention to such factors as better selection and training of salesmen and concentration of effort on high-potential accounts, the type of sales manager who is strong on inspiration has been gradually disappearing.

Not so with door-to-door sales management. The door-to-door sales manager, while requiring the same intelligence and business sense as any good sales leader, must also be strong in inspirational techniques and capable of stimulating large groups of people through the spoken and written word.

He must stimulate his field aids to recruit new salespeople constantly and effectively. Also, by his own efforts and through his chain of command, he must inspire his thousands of salespeople to get out and make selling calls. Assuming the product is right and the house-to-house selling approach is right, sales management's job in door-to-door selling boils down to motivating more people to make more calls.

No door-to-door sales organization has ever saturated its market; no company has ever been able to recruit a sales organization large enough to make regular calls on more than a small percentage of potential users. For practical purposes, the market for most companies selling door-to-door today is "unlimited." That is why sales management's emphasis must be on getting more people to make more sales calls on more prospects. As the president of one company with sales of $10 million and 2,500 salesmen remarked, "If we could only get 25,000 salesmen, we would do a $100-million volume."

Sales managers of established sales organizations which for years have called primarily on established accounts have no conception of the emphasis door-to-door selling places on such fundamental sales techniques as the approach, creating interest, creating desire, the use of benefits, the handling of objections, and the close.

Misrepresentation

The problem of misrepresentation of the facts about its products is one faced by even the most reputable and careful door-to-door companies. Some of this is the result of personal dishonesty on the part of the salesman, but most is caused by his unintentional exaggeration of the product's qualities and benefits while pressing for an immediate order.

Dissatisfied customers tend to hold the manufacturer responsible rather than the salesperson (irrespective of the fact, of which they are probably unaware, that the salesman may have purchased the merchandise from the manufacturer and resold it to the customer on his own terms).

Manufacturers selling door-to-door find it necessary to establish liberal adjustment policies in order to preserve consumer goodwill. If a company is entering door-to-door distribution, such policies should be decided in advance instead of after goodwill has already been lost.

Major Advantages

Now, if management feels it can cope with the problems that may be encountered, it is time to consider the brighter side of the picture — the plus factors that may make the effort worth while. The major advantages are:

1. Personal selling direct to the customer, without middlemen.
2. Relative ease in getting acceptance and distribution for a new product.
3. Flexible direct sales costs.
4. Relative lack of competition.
5. Strength in time of depression.

Let us look at these factors in order.

Personal Selling

The dearth of personal selling on the part of retail store salesclerks is pretty widely accepted by now as a "sad-but-truism." The sales manager frustrated by this condition can appreciate the value of direct contact with the consumer by salesmen trained to present product advantages.

Door-to-door selling provides the means of making a forceful sales presentation — and product demonstration if the product or a miniature sample of it can be carried — direct to the prospect. This is particularly advantageous when an unknown product is being sold or a product has qualities superior to competitors' though not readily apparent without explanation.

Experience has shown that consumers in their own homes usually will listen to a complete sales presentation, once the salesman gets inside the home and overcomes any initial resistance (or distrust). The attention of the same consumer in stores can usually be held only briefly even though the retail clerk is competent to give a good demonstration. This may be due to the relaxed feeling people have at home or the inherent courtesy shown to a guest. In any case, the salesman is able to give his complete sales story and is given time to try to overcome buying objections. And he can usually try for several closes. As a result, door-to-door salesmen have a good record of sales per demonstration given.

The value of the personal presentation is further emphasized when one considers the number of other brands with which the manufacturer's product must compete on the retail shelf. For example, think of cosmetics displays in department stores and drugstores, where the profusion of well-advertised and well-merchandised competing brands is sometimes so great that the customer is confused and her buying impulse virtually paralyzed.

The increasing trend to self-service and self-selection in retailing is making door-to-door distribution, for many product lines, the one remaining method where personal salesmanship can be emphasized.

New Distribution

One of the big questions for a manufacturer of a new product or an unknown brand is: How will I get retailers to stock my product? More and more, retailers are insisting that consumer demand for a product exist before they will give it space on their shelves. This usually means sizable advertising expenditures to create that demand.

The company without sufficient capital to invest in creating demand well ahead of sales, or unwilling to risk such investment, has door-to-door distribution as an alternative. The door-to-door salesman creates a desire for the product with each sale. He is familiarizing consumers with the brand name every time he makes a call. (At least one company which has distributed its branded product both through retail channels and by door-to-door methods found its retail sales increased in markets where it added door-to-door distribution.)

Since the door-to-door salesman must create the sale to get paid himself, income to the manufacturer is immediate. On the other hand, it should be pointed out that expanding a door-to-door salesforce from market to market is a slow process if the manufacturer is building his own salesforce.

Several companies that distribute exclusively by door-to-door methods do media advertising. They find it not only helps salesmen gain the housewife's confidence but is an aid in recruiting the salesmen in the first place. However, most companies have not used media advertising until after they have become well established. In door-to-door distribution, media advertising is an auxiliary, not a necessity.

Flexible Costs

Tied in with the above advantage is the fact that direct-selling costs tend to parallel sales volume in door-to-door distribution more closely than they do in other forms of distribution.

Most manufacturers selling through the usual channels find it necessary or desirable to give their salesmen a salary, or a drawing account, as a basic part of their compensation program, and additional compensation in the form of incentives. Also, they usually reimburse their salesmen for traveling expenses. Payment by salary means not only an increased initial investment when a new salesforce is being built but also relatively fixed direct-sales costs during periods of fluctuating sales volume, in contrast with the straight commission paid to most door-to-door salesmen. Of course, the commission type of compensation has offsetting disadvantages of its own, as noted earlier, but it does mean less commitment and less investment of funds.

Short-Cutting Competition

Most products sold through retail channels have much competition. Even after the manufacturer is successful in getting the retailer to stock his product, it has to compete for the consumer's attention with similar brands.

People outside the door-to-door sales field find it difficult to understand that competition is relatively unimportant to the door-to-door distributor. There are several reasons for this relative freedom from competition:

(1) The salesman, once in the house, is facilitated in demonstrating his product's advantages by the fact that competitors' products are not present for comparison there.

(2) As manufacturers know, brand loyalty is hard to obtain and is often only precariously held from the time of one purchase to the next. A salesman in the home usually has little trouble convincing a prospect at least to try his brand if its general quality and features appear to approximate competitors' brands.

(3) Relatively few door-to-door companies are selling similar items in the same area. Indeed, as mentioned earlier, the coverage of potential prospects by any one company is extremely limited. Therefore, door-to-door companies rarely think of other door-to-door companies selling similar products as competitors, except as competitors for available sales personnel.

(4) Many items sold door-to-door are not yet in the "consumer demand" stage. For them a need and want must be created. Once desire is aroused, the salesman can usually close his sale then and there before competitive products have a chance to interest the prospective buyer.

Stable Volume

Advocates of door-to-door selling have long maintained that their sales volume suffers the least in times of depressed business activity. They believe that when a depression brings unemployment, more people are willing to try door-to-door selling, and consequently more sales result. Although each salesman may sell less, this is offset by the larger size of the salesforce. Also, when customers are staying away from retail stores, it is an important advantage to be able to go to them directly in their homes.

On the other hand, the higher distribution costs of the door-to-door method keep the product prices of many of these companies higher than the prices of similar items sold through the retail store. This becomes increasingly significant to the consumer in times of depressed incomes.

For about 15 years economic conditions have been so abnormal that it is impossible to prove or to disprove these observations conclusively. Nevertheless, several of today's largest and most successful door-to-door companies started their businesses, or expanded them, during the depression of the 1930's.

It should be noted that this advantage of strength during depression applies only to general business depressions when there is general unemployment and not to recessions within certain industries, such as the economy has experienced in recent years.

Elements of Success

With the possible problems and advantages in mind, management is ready to tackle the all-important question: Is my product the right kind for this distribution method?

The variety of products sold door-to-door is impressive. One has only to take a look at the products sold by companies with membership in the National Association of Direct Selling Companies to get an idea of their multiplicity:

> Included are chemicals, foods, dietary supplements, hygienic products, medicinal articles, toilet articles, cosmetics, children's wear, dresses, foundation garments, hosiery, jackets, knitwear, lingerie, neckties, raincoats, sanitary garments, shirts, shoes, sportswear, men's and women's suits and coats, uniforms, work garments, nursery stock (shrubs, plants, etc.), paints, books, greeting cards, cooking utensils, blankets, brushes, china, fire extinguishers, household furnishings, portraits and frames, roofing and siding, seeds, and vacuum cleaners.

In reviewing any list of elements that a successful door-to-door product line should contain, it is well to remember that there are successful companies selling products that do not meet *all* the standards. However, as in any business venture the more strong points a product has, the greater the chance of its success.

High Margin

Because of the inherently high costs of door-to-door distribution, it is essential that the product have a sufficient margin of gross profit to absorb these costs and still leave a satisfactory net profit. Companies currently selling door-to-door achieve this high margin in one of the following ways:

1. By offering products having low manufacturing and high distribution costs — as in the case of cosmetics, where manufacturers traditionally pay the costs of in-store clerks or demonstrators in addition to high advertising and packaging costs.

2. By offering products where price comparisons cannot easily be made with similar products sold in retail stores, which in turn can be accomplished by (a) adding special features to justify increased price; (b) promoting hidden quality features where quality is not apparent to the average consumer; and/or (c) offering products where the consumer is not usually aware of the "normal" retail price — e.g., household brushes, since they are neither standardized as to type and quality nor purchased frequently.

3. By selling on installment credit where the size of the regular weekly or monthly payment tends to be more important to the purchaser than the total cost of the item.

The importance of distribution cost as a percentage of selling price is illustrated by the fact that door-to-door sales organizations which buy from manufacturers usually sell their merchandise for from two and one-half to three times the price they pay the manufacturers.

Quality and Sales Appeal

Because most merchandise sold door-to-door must carry relatively high selling prices, it is essential that the delivered product be of good quality. A poor-quality product can very quickly spoil a whole territory for additional or repeat business. Furthermore, products sold on a time-payment basis must hold up well to eliminate any reneging on payments. The most effective prospect lists are ones developed from satisfied customers who are willing to introduce the salesmen to their friends.

As a general rule a product or product line must be such that the average salesman can make sales his first day in the field. This means the product line must have appeal to a large percentage of householders, or if it is a specialized line, prospective customers must be such that they can be quickly and easily located. The type and size of line to accomplish this can be determined only by field tests.

Average orders for door-to-door companies vary considerably according to the type of product sold. Average orders for brushes may run as low as $2; for apparel they may be $10; for vacuum cleaners, cooking utensils, and silverware, they may run over $100. Average sales of $40 to $50 made on the home-party basis (such as by Stanley Home Products) are common even for lines with low unit prices because of the number of people who buy at one party.

The frequency of sale and the size of the average order are important factors in the degree of interest the salesman will retain in his door-to-door selling job because he is paid on a straight-commission basis.

Other Characteristics

One of the big advantages offered by door-to-door selling is the personal demonstration.

Therefore, large or bulky items which cannot easily be carried around do not enjoy such an advantage, although this can sometimes be overcome by carrying a miniature sample or a part of the item that illustrates an important feature.

Another necessary characteristic of a product is ease of demonstration. Large-scale recruiting, lack of selectivity of salespeople, and high turnover preclude products which require long training for salesmen or salesmen with technical backgrounds.

Furthermore, the product should be of a size and type that can be delivered by the salesman. The costs of delivering to the customer, added to already high distribution costs, can have an important effect on company profits. In most of the more profitable companies, orders for the day or week are usually combined by the manufacturer and shipped to the salesman for individual delivery to the customer. Or the salesman may pick up orders from the branch office or warehouse.

Some door-to-door companies receive orders from the salesman and ship from the factory or warehouse directly to the customer c.o.d., parcel post, or express. Companies that must deliver in this manner as a rule are those with perishable products, such as nurseries or apparel companies where large inventories must be carried of various sizes, colors, and types of products. Increasing express, postal, and c.o.d. rates have created serious cost problems for many firms that must ship in this manner.

Summary

By reviewing these qualifications, one can readily see why products such as cosmetics, brushes, vacuum cleaners, silverware, china, and kitchenware have been unusually adaptable to successful door-to-door distribution and why it has been increasingly difficult to distribute such staple apparel items as hosiery and foundation garments door-to-door at a profit.

Undoubtedly, the most important factor in determining whether a product can be distributed successfully door-to-door is the gross profit margin. If it is a product for which distribution costs are not relatively high, there must be other very strong and compelling reasons for attempting door-to-door selling.

Specialty products have traditionally been ideal door-to-door items because of their high margins and need for good selling techniques. However, as they turned into staples, mass-distribution techniques with their attendant lower margins became more suitable methods of distribution. For example:

> The Real Silk Hosiery Mills enjoyed its dramatic and profitable growth in the early 1920's when silk hosiery was still a luxury available only to the wealthy woman. As it became a standard part of the wardrobe, prices and profit margins dropped. Volume increases to offset these lower margins could not be produced by door-to-door methods.

Again, although many staples are included in door-to-door lines, the items promoted most vigorously are not staples. Thus, the door-to-door cosmetics houses carry standard items, but they feature the special-formula preparations that are not usually bought except as a result of the selling techniques of the store demonstrator or the house-to-house saleslady. Similarly, while Fuller carries toothbrushes and other staple items, emphasis is on the many special brushes that are not usually found in stores.

Conclusion

There appears to be no reason for believing that door-to-door selling will achieve a major role in the American distribution system, or radically increase its present relatively small percentage of total retail sales. Along with mail-order selling and vending machines, it will probably continue as an adjunct to the principal method of consumer goods distribution — the retail store. But for this very reason it stands as an opportunity for the individual manufacturer to secure a special competitive advantage — if he has thought the question through and found the circumstances right.

Richard W. Stickney

6 Deploying Multi-Line Salesmen

The scientific deployment of one's sales manpower so as to achieve equitable territories is difficult enough in a single-line company. But it is even more difficult to achieve in a multi-line company which has sales representatives who handle more than one (if not every) product line.

There are several reasons for this:

◖ The geographic distribution of potential between product lines can and usually does differ substantially.

◖ Some companies, for one reason or another, have a practice of varying the number of product lines to be handled by their men in different areas of the country.

When either or both of these situations exist, the company is faced with a knotty problem if it wants to determine effective coverage and equitable territories. Fortunately, however, this problem is not without solution.

Initial Requirements

As in the case of a company selling a single product, a multi-line company must first possess or develop two things in order to achieve any sort of scientific basis for territorial determination — even before it gets to the problem of how to integrate single-line sales personnel with those who are handling more than one line. These two prerequisites are:

- The subdivision of the United States into geographical units or marketing areas.
- The determination of the potential of these geographical units by product line — either in terms of dollars or percentages.

The first prerequisite is necessary because the size and configuration of each marketing area results from the flow of trade which reflects the market influences of retail and wholesale outlets, topography, and transportation facilities. These are the very same factors which must be reflected in the definition of a sales territory, that is, if it is to be economically covered.

The second prerequisite is, of course, necessary because the use and application of geographical potentials — in one form or another — is a must if one hopes to achieve equitable territories and to equalize the selling effort between men. It is obvious that if the potential of a given territory is below the optimum, the salesman cannot use all of his time to advantage. Conversely, if there is too much potential in one territory, a single man cannot handle it all; therefore, the company loses sales.

If we assume that these two prerequisites are possessed by a multi-line company, there are a series of steps that, when followed systematically, will produce components which can be moved around like building blocks. Once these components are obtained, the developing of territories (whether they be for a single product or for several products) is accomplished simply by adding up these components, in any way one desires, until the equivalent of a whole or complete territory is reached.

After tentative territories have been developed on this basis for the entire country, common-sense judgment needs to be applied; the resulting territorial structure, of course, must be adjusted for such things as local or regional peculiarities that cannot be measured statistically.

This method of scientifically deploying salesmen and achieving equitable territories involves five relatively simple steps, which are outlined in the section that follows.

Five-Step Procedure

1. The initial step of this method involves the two prerequisites (knowledge concerning marketing areas and geographical potentials), since it entails determining what each marketing area should produce by product line.

If a company defines the word *potential* as the *anticipated volume it is to receive in a given year*, there is no problem. These figures are available and can be used directly. If, on the other hand, the word *potential* is defined as the *total available business*, the amount a given marketing area should produce must then be calculated; this is done by determining what percentage each marketing area potential figure is of the total United States potential, and then multiplying these percentages by the appropriate product line sales forecast.

The resultant figures are what each marketing area should produce for the product line in question. Such a determination is made necessary by the fact that the geographic distribution of potential between product lines can and does differ substantially.

2. The second step is to develop some sort of estimate of what one man *should* produce if he were to handle a given product line exclusively. This normal sales expectancy for each product line is, of course, nothing more than what is generally considered "standard sales performance." Naturally, it should differ by product line as a reflection of the differences in selling effort required to sell each line. Some typical differences are the number of calls required in order to make the average sale, the amount of technical assistance that has to be rendered, the amount of missionary work required, and so forth.

How is the normal sales expectancy per salesman determined? There are, in the main, two ways:

Method A. Divide the net billed sales for a given product line by the average number of men selling the product in question. Round the result off to a convenient figure.

Thus, if the net billed sales for a product line amount to $1,000,000 and four salesmen are, on the average, required to handle sales, the standard sales performance becomes $250,000 per man.

Method B. Determine what volume is required to pay a man an annual income satisfactory to the kind of man necessary to sell each line.

Let us assume that a salesman's direct expense cost is $15,000 per year and that the desired ratio of direct sales expense to sales is 5%. This means that the normal sales expectancy volume would be $300,000 — i.e., $15,000 ÷ 5% = $300,000.

3. The third step is to convert what each marketing area should produce by product line (results of Step #1) into equivalent manpower, using the above normal sales expectancy figures (results of Step #2). Thus, the formula for determining the equivalent manpower for each product line is:

$$\frac{\text{Marketing Area Potential}}{\text{Normal Sales Expectancy Volume}} = \text{Equivalent Manpower}$$

Carrying out this procedure, marketing area by marketing area and product line by product line, yields a table that looks like this:

	Product Line A	*Product Line B*	*Product Line C*	*Total*
Marketing Area #1	0.60	0.34	0.10	1.04
Marketing Area #2	0.40	0.34	0.13	0.87
Marketing Area #3	0.03	0.09	0.01	0.13
Total	1.03	0.77	0.24	2.04

For the entire United States (or one particular segment), the marketing areas are listed vertically and the product lines horizontally.

Opposite each marketing area and under each product line will be the equivalent manpower figures that were calculated in Step #3. They are expressed in fractions of men and represent the equivalent manpower needed, in terms of selling effort, to achieve the volume that each marketing area should produce by product line. The various equivalent manpower figures, regardless of product line, are comparable and may be used interchangeably because, as will be recalled, any deviations in selling effort required were reflected in Step #2.

4. The next step is to combine these various components, whether by marketing area or by product line, in any way one desires, until the equivalent of a whole or complete territory is reached, i.e., when the addition results in 1.00. For single-line coverage in a given area, the component figures in a given column are added vertically until a territory is reached. If, on the

other hand, multi-line coverage is sought, then the columns are added horizontally.

According to the example in the table, we can see that this general area should have two men as indicated by the lower right-hand figure of 2.04. What, however, are the possible alternative choices? There are, even in this simple example, two possibilities:

- The company can elect to have a single-line man cover Product Line A in all three marketing areas, with a second man covering Product Lines B and C in these same marketing areas.
- As an alternative, the company could have one man cover all three product lines in Marketing Area #1 and have another man cover all three product lines in Marketing Areas #2 and #3.

This technique of grouping either marketing areas or product lines into tentative territories — through knowledge of a company's equivalent manpower needs — greatly simplifies the task of scientifically deploying sales manpower. It not only results in effective coverage, but also helps to establish equality among the territories.

5. The final step in this process is to adjust the tentative territories (developed in Step #4) for the various special or administrative factors present in each. No doubt, there will be administrative and other factors present which are difficult to measure statistically, or which only apply to a given locality or region. Such adjustments may have to be made for competitive reasons, i.e., to reflect the effects of such things as proximity of competitors' plants, warehouses, or sales offices, or perhaps the number and deployment of their sales forces. And new account development, home office or national accounts, point of purchase versus point of use, and nonrepeat or windfall business may also require some adjustment to the tentative territorial structure, but should not basically alter the method or the results.

Conclusion

If this method for the scientific deployment of manpower is used as illustrated, and consideration given to each of the points outlined, a company should be able to develop sales territories which are determined and based on efficient deployment of selling effort. When periodic changes are required, regardless of whether they involve a change in the total number of sales personnel or a change in emphasis for a given product line, they can be accomplished with very little effort.[1]

[1] Readers who are experiencing problems, not in deploying salesmen, but in deciding on the optimum number to employ, may be interested in referring to Walter J. Semlow's "How Many Salesmen Do You Need?" HBR May–June 1959, p. 126. — *The Editors*

J. M. Hickerson

7 Successful Sales Techniques

IT MAY be true, as Robert A. Whitney, President of National Sales Executives, Inc., recently said, that salesmanship is an "American specialty." Certainly salesmanship typifies the competitive spirit of our economy; and if any one person symbolizes the difference between the capitalist and communist systems, it is probably the salesman. Yet few subjects in this country are more widely misunderstood. Misconceptions range the whole way from the popular notion that successful salesmen are rare individuals who somehow have been born with natural qualities of glibness and smooth talk to the equally errant idea that salesmanship is a science, a kind of push-button psychology which anyone can practice if he is let in on the secrets.

Sophisticated sales executives know differently. They are becoming increasingly selective in their employment and promotion policies, demanding salesmen with greater aptitude and ability. They are also becoming increasingly aware of the values and potentialities of training. Management's part in a salesman's development can be planned, positive. There are sound criteria for educating, leading, prodding, and inspiring an average young man with courage, initiative, and interest to become a better salesman.

Why should the selection and training of these men be left to luck or spur-of-the-moment inspiration any more than that of, say, accountants or industrial relations men? They represent the company personally to the public. Moreover, probably no function of the average company has traditionally — and deservedly — contributed so many men to top management as has sales. The bread-and-butter end of the business, it is also a first-class training ground for human relations, knowledge of consumer viewpoints, and understanding of the competitive picture.

Today business is good. To be sure, there are "soft spots" in the economy, but by and large the companies with reasonably good products to offer are able to sell them with comparatively little difficulty. In such circumstances, the need for aggressive, heads-up marketing policy is not so well recognized as it should be. *Most* firms are getting their share of the market. It may not be long, however, before production catches up again as it almost did in 1949 and early 1950. When this happens, the men will be separated from the boys, the professionals from the amateurs, so far as selling is concerned.

What is the difference between the approach of a good salesman and that of a mediocre or

AUTHOR'S NOTE: I wish to acknowledge the very great help of Mr. David W. Ewing in the preparation of this article.

poor one? What are the secrets of salesmanship? Certainly these are questions of great significance to the sales manager who seeks to increase the effectiveness of his force — and to the top-management team of which he is a part. Any attempt to answer such questions precisely would, of course, be doomed from the start. There *are* intangibles, there *are* mysteries of human interaction, and there *are*, furthermore, infinitely varied possibilities both of sales problems and of sales approaches. At the same time, the experience of successful salesmen does point up a number of definite object lessons which are of general application — if only to the extent that they indicate the fundamentals involved in meeting sales situations, rather than any ready-made techniques.

Accordingly, in this article I have attempted to take the experience of a number of successful salesmen and to present it in such a way that it will be useful to others. The cases discussed are drawn from a collection of 60 sales stories, contributed by men who are all leaders in their fields, which I had the privilege of editing last year under the title, *How I Made the Sale That Did the Most for Me.*[1] The stories are told by the men themselves; and while only a few of the 60 authors included in the book can be called upon here, it is my hope that the cases selected will serve to get across as much as possible of the pattern which emerges from studying the aggregate experience.

Analyzing the Sales Problem

Although the art of persuasion may play the dramatic role in making a sale, the primary and really important thing for a salesman to do is on a more mundane, common-sense level. That job is to learn the prospect's viewpoint and adapt to it. In the words of L. Morton Morley, Vice President in Charge of Sales, Brown Industrial Division, Minneapolis-Honeywell Regulator Company:

> "I believe that all the other qualities of a true salesman are of lesser importance. He can have enthusiasm, stamina, intelligence, personality, sincerity, and all the other attributes of a salesman, and still be a failure if he does not have the knack of finding the *points of common interest.*"

And the important points, Mr. Morley adds, are those which are of chief interest to the prospect — not to the salesman. What Mr. Morley is saying is that each sales problem must be analyzed before one can go to work on it successfully, just as in dealing with any other type of problem.

Learning the Customer's Viewpoint. At the risk of deflating the romance of selling right at the start, therefore, let us take Mr. Morley's experience as an illustration:

> Morley's company and another firm were locked in a last-ditch struggle to sell a control system for bleaching processes to one of the largest cotton mills in the South. When Morley was called in to help the district salesman, the prospect mill's purchasing agent — an engineer — was on the verge of signing up with the other firm.
>
> Together with the local salesman and district sales manager, Morley went to the small town where the mill was located. They put up in a local hotel and thrashed the problem over thoroughly. Unless he knew precisely what the problem was, Morley reasoned, he would have very little opportunity of solving it when the psychological moment in the sales interview came. Thus, at the outset, he began getting the facts necessary to orient himself to the customer's point of view.
>
> At the bleaching mill the next day, Morley and his associates entered a large unfurnished room in which about a dozen people were hard at work. They saw the purchasing agent, their "target," sitting at a corner desk bent over his work. He was a huge man, partly bald, with his shirt collar open and sleeves rolled up, and he was perspiring profusely. He beckoned Morley over and indicated chairs. He tiredly asked to be excused for a minute so that he could finish an important bit of work. Obviously he thought he was in for another session of high-pressure salesmanship such as he had been going through with the rival salesmen.
>
> Finally the purchasing agent finished his paper work and opened the conversation by saying: "I've just about made up my mind, but I'm willing to listen to what you have to say."
>
> Now, instead of launching into a glowing and probably disastrous talk about the virtues of his firm's equipment, Morley opened by explaining that he wasn't an engineer but would appreciate it if the purchasing agent would describe the new bleaching operation that was being installed.
>
> The purchasing agent — an engineer, remember — started talking about the process, obviously his pride and joy. Within a few minutes he had become quite enthusiastic and began calling to his secretary for charts and blueprints to illustrate how the new operation would work. The tone of

[1] New York, Prentice-Hall, 1951.

the meeting began mellowing considerably. More important than that, additional facts about the mill's needs in a control system began to appear.

As a result, when the purchasing agent raised the question of servicing and the fact that Morley's electronic control equipment was too delicate for an ordinary workman to fix, Morley, who had been listening carefully, was able to answer him. He could point out several places in which the electronic equipment would actually be easier to repair than a conventional control system.

Although the purchasing agent seemed impressed, Morley kept remembering that he would have to justify his opinion to his superiors. So Morley gave him, not a long song and dance about the technical virtues of the electronic system as such, but the facts that would enable him to support a recommendation to buy it – how it had been tested, tried, and rebought by some of the largest instrument users in the country, how it could save much more than its 30% greater cost over the control systems of Morley's competitors.

Significantly, Morley finally clinched this sale by again keeping the prospect's viewpoint in mind. Knowing that the purchasing agent was not trying to select a batch of instruments but looking for a means of running the plant efficiently, Morley emphasized the reliable, quick service which would be available on a continuing basis. "You've made a deal," the purchasing agent said, and after settlement of the details the contract was signed.

A good salesman will do everything he can to learn the prospect's viewpoint. But remember that he will not, any more than a physician, be able to diagnose the case without seeing the patient too. Opportunities to learn about the sales problem both in advance of the meeting with the prospect and in the actual sales conversation are important. The ability to create and take advantage of such opportunities may mean, as Morley's story illustrates, the difference between a sales attempt that ends "It's a deal" and one ending "I'm sorry, Mr. Salesman, but. . . ."

Preparing for the Sales Conference. Granting the importance of preparation for the sales conference, there is the question of *how* the salesman should go about it. Here is an area in which management can do a great deal to train and improve salesmen and, incidentally, make significant evaluations of a salesman's creative imagination, initiative, and other important qualities.

As might be expected, again there is no easy answer. The extent of preparation needed varies not only with the relative importance of the hoped-for sale and with the situation of the prospect himself but also with the kind of product and industry. A salesman of heavy industrial equipment needs to make a radically different type of preparation, obviously, from that of a salesman of wearing apparel. Nevertheless, concrete illustrations of the ways in which successful salesmen have prepared for representative types of problems ought to be helpful in suggesting the approach needed in betwixt-and-between situations.

In this connection let us consider one of the most interesting of all the 60 cases. The story is told by the 32-year-old head of what is probably the best-known company in the men's wear field – Hickok Manufacturing Company, Inc. President since 1945, Ray Hickok was trained by his father to be a salesman, and he still makes salesmanship his chief interest.

When Ray Hickok learned there was a chance that the president of a chain of stores who was dividing the stores' belt business among Hickok and two other concerns might be lined up as a Hickok exclusive, he found the temptation too strong. He decided to try to make the deal himself. Characteristically, he first talked with his "guides," as he calls them, about the president's situation. He came to the conclusion that this man's big interest was inventory, and sales volume was secondary. Then he went out to make the sale.

"I wasn't content with just listening to what my guides told me," Hickok relates. "The first step I took when I reached the headquarters city of Mr. Jones, as we shall call him, was to take a trip through his stores. I wanted to study his method of display, the amount of space allotted, the method of presentation, what he was doing about training his clerks, and last, but most important, the inventory. In other words, because I knew his chief concern was inventory, I wanted to see with my own eyes just how much duplication there was, how many styles he was carrying that were unnecessary. Then I wanted to check up to see if he had all our best selling numbers in stock."

The next day Hickok kept the appointment he had made in advance with Mr. Jones, and after the "traditional warm up" he got down to business.

"Mr. Jones," he began, "I had a most interesting day yesterday. I spent about ten hours visiting some of your stores here. Looks like you have a lot of money tied up in inventory."

That remark hit home. Hickok's advance conclusion was right; Mr. Jones was the inventory type. But he was a good merchant, too, or he wouldn't have been occupying the office marked "President."

The conversation went on to some of the merchandising problems of the chain. Then Hickok began relating these problems to the specific matter of men's belts. Where only one brown belt was needed at $2.50, he asked, why have two or three? Why not have one good brown belt that the stores could be sure of having in stock at all times?

From his on-the-ground survey Hickok could be specific on a number of styles the stores were carrying that were unnecessary. The president himself began to comment, as Hickok wanted him to, that it was all adding up to excess inventory. "I could almost see him," says Hickok, "multiplying in his head the specific instances I mentioned by the number of stores in his chain."

The conversation continued, covering numerous other points, but all the time Hickok kept the point about the heavy inventory in the president's mind. This approach, hit upon as the result of careful advance thinking, was largely responsible for the president's being won over when the conference ended. (It might be added, as a rueful postscript, that the deal never materialized. Shortly after, Mr. Jones resigned and was succeeded by a new president who had very different ideas.)

Knowing the Market. Preparing for the sales conference may mean walking through the prospect's store, as in the foregoing case, or a tortuous research job. The latter is most likely to be the case in the technological industries, where a good deal of technical proficiency may be needed before the salesman can get even to first base. The management implications of this difference, however, are not that only technicians should be hired as salesmen. This would be fallacious reasoning, for the "art" elements of salesmanship are no less important in the technological industries — particularly as the point of closing the sale approaches — than in others. Personality, manner, enthusiasm, and appearance count whether one is selling tractors or toothbrushes. Rather, the implications are that men should be picked for sales who have native technical curiosity, who are willing to "sweat blood," if necessary, for needed information about the products and their applications. Technical training may be an asset, but its importance is as a means to an end and not as an end in itself — a fact which should not be disregarded.

An illuminating story of sales preparation in a technological industry is provided by Richard H. DeMott, President of SKF Industries, Inc. Incidentally, the sales history of this company, of which this case is one small part, is a good example of the significance of salesmanship to American economic progress. Some 30 years ago, when the incidents described by DeMott took place, the antifriction bearing industry in this country was in its infancy; hardly a machine — or, for that matter, hardly a piece of equipment with a shaft that turned — rolled on ball or roller bearings. Today, modern industry is dependent on these marvels of engineering science and precision. The fact that their use is so widespread is due in no small part to the sales ability and pioneering efforts of people like DeMott in such fields as papermaking, textiles, electric motors, and railroads.

DeMott was district manager in SKF's New York office, and the management of a Brooklyn paper mill wanted his scalp. The SKF people had just installed ball and roller bearings in the mill's Fourdrinier papermaking machine, and in their overconfidence (typical in those days) in the ability of antifriction bearings to cure everything they had failed to account for wire pull, weight of the roll, thrust load, and other factors. The machine soon broke down irreparably, and neither DeMott nor anyone else could solve the problem. This set him to thinking.

"We don't know enough about the paper industry, so how can we suggest workable applications and make sales?" he asked his staff. "Our information about papermaking machinery is pitifully inadequate. We do not know, for example, the operating characteristics of the equipment, nor do we have data on loads, speeds, temperatures, or moisture conditions under which many of the rolls on these machines operate. In fact," he summed up, "we know next to nothing about the industry that we hope to make a major market for antifriction bearings."

To get this information was not easy, DeMott recalls. "It was not just sitting in a public library and boning up. Armed with a 'little black book' (no personal phone numbers) I spent the better part of a year away from home. I met people I had never known existed, doing work I had never known was done, and I recorded information on paper industry equipment such as jack ladders, barkers, chippers, pulp grinders, refiners, stock pumps, and various rolls on Fourdrinier and cylinder-type machines such as breast rolls, table rolls, press rolls, felt rolls, drier cylinder, calender stacks, and many other shaft-turning locations on which ball and roller bearings might be used."

About one year, dozens of hotel rooms, and approximately 50,000 miles of automobile, horse-and-buggy, and plain horseback travel later, DeMott had the answers. It was a lot of work, but it turned out to be worth it many, many times. It was the big first step in subsequently selling to a machinery manufacturer — a company that didn't even want to let DeMott in at first. That company's installation, in turn, was an entering wedge in cracking an entire lucrative industry as a market.

Everybody who has been a salesman or listened to one appreciates the importance in salesmanship of being able to sound convincing. The practical problem, of course, is how to get that way. DeMott's case points up a relevant moral: part of the problem of sounding convincing is familiarity with one's market. Especially in the technological field, the salesman has to know what his product will do in the customer's plant and why. Let the salesman demonstrate to clients that he knows their point of view, and he will not have to worry about being heard up to the point of his clinching arguments.

But suppose, as often happens, that the prospect's point of view is at odds with the salesman's? For instance, when prices are going down, merchants often defer buying the usual merchandise quantities on the understandable basis that it is foolish to buy today if the purchase can be put off until tomorrow when prices will be lower. The manufacturer, on the other hand, is obviously interested in steady orders. In such a case, the salesman's job is not only to be familiar with the facts of the prospect's business but to be able to interpret those facts — at least the ones that concern the sale — in better management terms than the prospect himself.

The salesman has two assets for doing this: (1) he is (or should be) a specialist with expert knowledge of his own; and (2) he is familiar with and can capitalize upon the experience of other firms and individuals in similar situations. To exploit these assets and reorient the prospect's thinking obviously requires the same sort of advance preparation for the sales talk that has been discussed in the foregoing pages.

The sales management of Textron, Inc., faced the very same problem of speculation in merchandise inventories that has just been mentioned. Orders for Textron's Indian Head cloth, for instance, tended to fall when textile prices declined. The challenge which this practice presented to Textron was to show that the merchants were losing business for themselves (as well as for Textron) by holding back on orders in expectation of price drops.

When James E. Robison, Executive Vice President of Textron, approached the president — call him Mr. Smith — of a wholesale house in Philadelphia, he was armed with dramatic figures to show that the prospect was not realizing his full potentials in sales. From these figures Robison went on to outline the objectives and workings of a stock reorder system which would avoid the losses in gross sales margin that occurred when stocks of Indian Head were allowed to go below a certain point. This meant training the clerks to take inventory more regularly and to order on a systematic basis, but Textron was prepared to do that, too.

Smith was "sold."

In the 1948–1949 period, textile prices fell off about 25% as textile production declined about 20%. Against this background the wholesale house, which without the stock reorder system had sold $35,500 worth of Textron's goods in 1948, with it boosted sales in 1949 to $49,500 of Textron's staple line plus $9,000 in secondary quality goods.

This is the kind of experience which is both the objective and the reward of good salesmanship. The decisive factor making it possible, typically enough, was not so much a "smooth" line of talk as an intelligent, informed approach.

Road to Executive Success. The road to success for the sales executive — the salesman nobody meets — is just as long as for the salesman with the sample case, if not longer. There is no royal road — at least none that top sales managers can agree on yet. As an adage, that may sound innocuous. But when we begin to break the sales executive's job down (as best we can) into its main components, and see that one of the components is the ability and interest to plan contacts and associations carefully, tediously, and often over long periods of time, we see that the "pattern of greatness" in selling is not what it is often popularly believed to be as a result of movies, books, and plays.

We may even find that our conception of the ideal sales executive — our mental image of what he should look like, act like, and say — is due for a change. One of the best illustrations of this point is the story told by Harry A. McDonald, a prominent figure in the investment business who in 1949 became the first Republican Chairman of the Securities and Exchange Commission and who, more recently, was appointed Administrator of the Reconstruction Finance Corporation:

"My best inspirations and insights come from people. Not long after I left the Navy I began to hear about Grant of Chevrolet. He had done the miraculous, pushed Chevrolet sales to the point where they had outstripped Ford. His name was magic; his reputation glowed; he was the greatest salesman of them all. To see him and to hear him became one of my ambitions. Grant was to speak at a local dinner, and I looked forward to hearing him then as I have later looked forward to meeting the President.

"My first sight of that man was one of my deepest lessons in salesmanship. Instead of the majestic figure I had expected, I saw a man who would have been lost in a small crowd. What, I wondered, did he have that had enabled him to bring his product into the forefront of the giants? I soon found out. It was not dynamic radiance, although Grant had an intense charm. His speech was not in parables or that of the orator but one of simple declaration. His achievement was not in the play of personalities but in the power of planning and of ideas."

The sales manager whose planned, intense, creative effort bears fruit in the accomplishments of others, not in making the sale himself, has a new sort of thrill. Using research and psychology, and drawing upon the services of experts who may never have sold a dime's worth of merchandise, he may be like the general who master-minds the successful campaign without seeing a single enemy soldier.

Of course, if he has known only the executive side of sales, he is limited much the same as the man who knows only the door-to-door side of sales; that is, he knows only part of the drama of selling. We may wonder if he is not missing something that is important, both to him and to others. As Harry McDonald put it in commenting about his experience:

"In an old-fashioned way I think that the cynicism surrounding mass selling through the new media, what has lately come to be know as 'huckstering,' has come about in large part because its practitioners have lost their contact with *people*."

Creating Confidence and Receptivity

Preparing to make a sale is part of the salesman's job and usually a very important part. But adequate preparation alone never made a sale. Far from it. When a salesman comes face to face with his prospect, the make-or-break part of his job begins in earnest. First, he must win the confidence of the prospect, develop a receptive attitude, pave the way for his clinching arguments. How does he do this?

The stories of a securities salesman, a former car salesman, a movie producer, a former wax salesman, and a former newspaper boy may throw some light on that question.

Making the Customer Want to Buy. Most salesmen do not have the luxury of clients coming to them; they have to seek out the clients, and often they are lucky if they can get in the door. A great many salesmen, furthermore, do not sell products or services which can be easily distinguished from those of competitors. Still, the experience of one of the country's top securities salesmen, who was *not* confronted with these disadvantages or (perhaps better) challenges, is an outstanding example of one of the leading principles of salesmanship:

The career of Gerald M. Loeb, partner in E. F. Hutton & Company, New York, is not a dramatic one. It is a repetitious tale of building brick by brick. It is a story of personal devotion to an austere, back-breaking schedule in Wall Street. Loeb rises so early that by the time he reaches Schrafft's at 31 Broadway, where for 20 years he has breakfasted at precisely 7:30 A.M., he has already read all the morning newspapers from beginning to end. By the time the Stock Exchange opens at 10 A.M., Loeb has spent two hours at his desk digesting the bulletins on late developments flashed him by branch offices and correspondents all over the globe. He maintains a very heavy correspondence with corporation officials, makes many personal calls on business leaders, and keeps almost as well posted on developments in a number of industries as do many insiders.

"I remember one top California executive who told me a great deal about his company," Loeb recalls. "I liked it, and altogether my friends and I came to buy and own about 10% of his outstanding shares, which turned out to be a fine purchase. But suddenly this man shut off his information. At first I could not find out what was wrong, but later he told me that I had scared him. 'You knew so much about my affairs I wondered what your real aim was,' he said. Somehow he feared a sinister motive, such as questioning the quality of his management. Of course, his fears were unfounded, and this was the only time that I have ever encountered such a reaction. Usually after I see the executives of a company, I try to see their competitors, their suppliers, and those whom they sell to in order to get a well-rounded and unbiased view of their situation. This procedure may not sound like salesmanship, but of course it is. People buy more from 'the man who knows' than from any high-pressure sales talk that is given them."

As an ambitious young man from San Francisco in E. F. Hutton's New York statistical department, Loeb soon set himself apart from the statisticians who stayed statisticians. They never got any order-giving clients, according to Loeb, "because their approach was academic. 'What do you think of General Motors?' someone would ask them. 'It's a good company,' they would answer. That was the end of the discussion. I would answer the question with some others. 'Why do you want to know? Do you own General Motors stock? Do you plan buying it? What else do you own? Have you other motor stocks? How much of your capital is invested?' And then they would get a reply that applied to them personally on what they should do and whether I thought General Motors at the price and as things appeared in the market was going up or going down. Such personal attention made another customer every time."

From management's point of view, there are important implications in the moral of this story. Management's challenge is to educate its salesmen to such a belief in the product or service that they can confidently orient their approach and thinking to developing the *customer's* interest in the product — not breaking his resistance with "high-pressure" selling. Put in another way, it is making the prospect want to buy, not "selling" him. As Loeb expressed his own attitude, "I don't sell. People buy from me."

A salesman can be encouraged to grow into this kind of thinking. Do the management "higher-ups" set a good example for him of belief in the company? Is he given opportunities to be "in the know" about product development and problems, sales thinking, management policies, and so on; and is he encouraged to come up with new ideas and criticisms? But questions such as these are only the beginning. There are sterner tests. For instance, how much discretion does the salesman have as to what he sells and how much? And how does management react if, after intelligently studying a prospect's interest in the product or service, he encourages him to buy less than first intended? On the answers to questions such as these depend in no small part the salesman's initiative in attempting to gain the customer's confidence.

Use of Discrimination. Of course, there are all sorts of ways to inspire confidence. Indeed, there is probably no form of selling that does not have a place in some situation or other. The prospect may *want* to be mesmerized, may *want* to see an exhibition of cleverness, may *want* to have the heat turned on. Where one individual (say a businessman) can only be sold a truck by a car salesman talking straight performance facts, another individual (perhaps, but not necessarily, a woman) may have to be sold a car on emotional appeal — design, color, comfort, and reminders about what the Joneses have.

In other words, discrimination must be used — discrimination not only as to *how* but as to *when* and even *whether* to try for the sale. On these points, William A. Blees, Vice President and General Sales Manager of the Crosley Division, Avco Manufacturing Corporation, has some relevant words of advice based on his years as an automobile salesman:

"Selling cars is one of the most competitive occupations. Every town in America has automobile dealers cheek-to-cheek, practically, along Main Street. Every one of these entrepreneurs has a tremendous investment in his dealership. To get it, he must be a man of substance. He probably belongs to the Rotary, Kiwanis, Lions, Elks, or some other fraternal organization; possibly to the American Legion and a local country club. He probably has connections in town politics, is active in community affairs and the church. Consequently, each dealer has as many good friends or contacts as another. The sooner auto salesmen realize that the better. There's no point at all, if you want to remain a successful salesman, in persisting in badgering a brother Elk to buy your Chevrolet if his brother-in-law is the local Ford dealer. You have to watch for different types of opportunities. If you're a Cadillac representative, for example, you must know when the veteran Buick owner is ready to step up out of his range."

Encouraging salesmen to use discrimination in deciding when, how, and whether to approach prospective customers does *not* mean, it needs to be emphasized, that management should take the pressure off salesmen to sell, to produce results. Rather, the meaning is in the kind and method of pressure management uses. Blees has some helpful advice on this point, too:

"One of my earliest associates taught me another good lesson: 'Never grab a lion by the tail.' He was a Chevrolet dealer. He said that there was no point in trying to buck the local Ford dealer, his biggest competitor, in a harmful way. Instead, he concentrated on getting *some* of the sales away from Ford, some from Chrysler, some from Nash, etc. There's plenty of business for everyone, he reasoned.

"Right now, while I'm selling refrigerators, among many other things, I am applying my friend's philosophy. I don't worry about whether Crosley displaces Norge or Westinghouse. They all have good products and I'm proud to be in their company. We want to beat the leader. I try to teach our dealers how to snag *one* or *two* sales from *each* of our competitors. That way, none of them is hurt, and we increase our sales."

By teaching salesmen to "snag" a sale here and another there (in contrast to putting the pressure on them to sell *every* prospect), management helps to instill the kind of attitude in the salesman which makes it easier for the prospect to gain confidence in him. It is a management way of teaching salesmen to "stop, look, and listen" before jumping into their talks. It makes it easier for the salesman to think he can afford to gamble on a "low pressure" approach when his instinct suggests it.

A perfect example of the pay-off to the salesman and his company of the selective approach is given by Mr. John Orr Young, retired cofounder of Young & Rubicam, Advertising, and now of John Orr Young and Associates, Inc., New York:

A number of years ago, Young & Rubicam decided to broaden its clientele beyond the food field, where it was then specialized, and Young put Parke Davis at the top of his carefully selected list of prospective clients. The subsequent story involved many stages and transactions, but the long and short of it was that Parke Davis became a customer.

Explaining how "this conservative manufacturer" was sold, Young says: "I should characterize it as strictly a low-pressure selling job. I was careful in my approach. I did not strain my adjectives, and I did not make the Parke Davis executives feel that I was trying too hard to 'sell' them."

In his book, *Adventures in Advertising*,[2] Young remembers that "Dr. Lescohier, soft-spoken and poker-faced, then vice president and now chief executive of that great company . . . listened courteously but gave no encouraging words or smiles. I thought, however, that occasionally I detected the faintest sort of gleam in his eyes as I talked. I told him that *if* he should ever have occasion to make a change, *if* he were not happy over every advertisement now being produced for his company, *then* I should like him to give Young & Rubicam a trial.

"Had I employed the stage version of hammer-and-tongs agency selling, this prospect probably would have backed away from me," Young thinks. "Had I tried to do a complete and obvious sales job during those first interviews as I was tempted to do, I probably would not have been asked to call again.

"At this point in my selling experience, because I had once failed to sell a good many of my prospects, I had learned the hard way to cut my selling cloth to the pattern of the buyer's personality instead of tearing into every solicitation with a standardized, cut-and-dried, high-powered selling technique. I had started to learn when to turn on the heat and when to use restraint."

Just as this story illustrates something that *can* be taught about salesmanship, it points up one of the critical values that *cannot*. A salesman may be well aware of the nature and importance of both high-pressure and low-pressure approaches. But unless he is astute about human nature, unless he is able to sense when and upon whom to use one type of approach instead of the other, anything else that he knows is next to useless.

To be sure, this "sixth sense" can be developed and made keener by experience. It can be stimulated by incentives and prodding. Beyond these measures, however, management is limited. It will do well to recognize that limitation, making every effort to employ only men with sensitivity to and interest in human nature — and that means more than just typical extroverts, who sometimes are not very perceptive of subtle human values.

Making a Friendly Impression. One very important secret of creating customer confidence and interest might be summed up simply in a single word — friendship. Perhaps, however, this is not so much a different problem as it is a

[2] New York, Harper & Brothers, 1949.

different way of saying some of the same things that have already been said. For example, in 1939, when Richard de Rochemont was producer of *The March of Time,* he "sold" the Vatican, which up till then had been sacrosanct so far as movie cameras were concerned, on the idea of letting him make a documentary film of Vatican City; and he did it by winning friendship at the top level — not through professional arrangers and middlemen, all of whom he by-passed, but "on the basis of legitimate common interest" (astutely presented in his conversations, of course).

There are many ways in which friendship can be demonstrated, and none of them need to seem contrived or artificial. Contrary to what some poor or mediocre salesmen seem to believe, most executives — purchasing agents included! — are pretty nice people. They appreciate the same human gestures as anyone else. The salesman who has a feeling for this fact will not find it difficult to show his friendliness.

Probably one of the strongest illustrations of the value of acts of friendship is the story told by Harold Schafer, President of the Gold Seal Company. This company, now a prosperous sales organization with headquarters in North Dakota, was principally a three-man outfit — and a struggling one at that — back in 1945 when Schafer was trying to sell self-polishing wax to the merchants of Aberdeen, South Dakota.

Stores just weren't buying. Schafer felt on the brink of failure as a salesman when, thinking back over the last few days' work, he decided to take a new approach.

"When I called on a store, if the man who owned the store was washing windows, I started helping him wash windows," Schafer says. "If the storekeeper was unloading a truck load of flour in the back of the store, I helped him unload flour. In one lumber yard I helped unload a couple hundred sacks of cement. In one store I helped wash shelving with soap and water and put on display competitive merchandise. I helped several men sweep their floors on my early morning and late evening calls. A lot of people will say that this is not the right approach, but believe me it works. In every case I stepped right into this work without bothering with the formality of an introduction."

This approach brought tremendous results — sales to 41 of the 44 independent retail stores in Aberdeen. Gold Seal has found that it continues to work. Accordingly, in sales training the company makes it a point not to give its men canned sales talks, not to make them practice before mirrors on their approach, but, rather, concentrates on getting each salesman to develop his own "personal touch."

The moral of Schafer's story applies to sales managers and other executives too.

"Back in 1945 while I was calling on small buyers in retail stores, most of whom owned their own business or were managing it for a close friend or relative," Schafer says, "I found it quite simple and easy to perform a little physical effort to gain the man's friendship. Today in my traveling I am naturally working with buyers and businessmen where it is impossible for me to be of any physical help, but I find that if I give a man a progressive business thought, I arrive at the same friendly association. In other words, it is possible to 'perform something worthy to be remembered' without washing windows or sweeping floors. All business with which I have come in contact in the United States is based on service in one form or the other, and I find a lot of it based on the service of one human being to another."

Finally, the problem of getting the prospect to "stop, look, and listen" can be stated in still another way. Mortimer Berkowitz, formerly Vice President of the Hearst Publishing Company, found it out years ago when he was selling newspapers after school in New York's Union Square. He learned that the boy who simply yells, "Mister, buy a newspaper," does not sell many. But the boy who calls, "Full account of the big fire on 14th Street," or "Society woman jumps out of hotel window," or "President signs new tax bill," does make sales. Why? Because he arouses people's curiosity. He gets them intrigued with what he has to sell. What happens from there on may be a different story, and the problems involved are discussed in the next section.

Making the Sale

Lest the preceding pages with their emphasis on sales-problem analysis, careful planning, and close attention to prospects' viewpoints create any impression that the dramatic and suspenseful elements of salesmanship are not recognized as important by top salesmen, we can promptly point out that this is not the case. Indeed, just the opposite is true. There *is* a romance in selling, and the salsemen who figure in the stories related in the following pages prove it.

Often the romance comes in those climactic moments when the prospect makes up his mind and approaches a decision. It is here at the point of closing the sale, where most salesmen fall down, that the excitement runs strongest — and the top salesmen come into their own.

Here, too, the mysteries of salesmanship deepen. This prospect bought; that one did not. Why? This time the approach worked; that time it did not. Again, why? The reasons are often inexplicable. The answers are buried in complexities of human nature that cannot be precisely understood.

But despite our imperfect ability to understand and master the art of clinching a sale, there are a few principles that sales experience over the years seems to demonstrate.

Capturing Attention. Certainly no one story can illustrate very many essentials of making a sale for more than one industry. However, the story told by David P. Reynolds, Vice President and Sales Manager of the Aluminum Division of Reynolds Metals Company, can serve as a useful basis for a general discussion, interspersed with appropriate observations and comparisons with the experiences of other top salesmen.

About 15 years ago, at a time when Reynolds Metals was attempting to create and expand a market for aluminum foil as a packaging material, its salesmen were running into a lot of trouble trying to convince manufacturers that the conventional lower priced paper labels could be improved upon.

The company had licked the difficult printing situation, Reynolds recalls. A long and expensive research program had succeeded in perfecting a process of printing by rotogravure on foil in variegated colors — a feat which most leading printing authorities had earlier regarded as impossible. "But it was a new and novel idea, and we didn't have the sales to keep those expensive rotogravure presses busy. When you start fooling with rotogravure, it is unprofitable to deal in small quantities. Our new printing process was practical only for mass production.

"I was convinced that we had a superior product and a profitable idea; and I felt certain that if I could only persuade some large producer to take a look at a real display of the finished product, I could sell him in a minute. There was no brief case large enough in which to carry such a display. I decided to try a display coach."

A bus was secured, but the first attempts at improvisation failed. There followed some careful figuring and planning about the kind of display coach that was needed. Reynolds came to the conclusion that he should "shoot the works."

"I wanted to have a display so unique and striking that it would startle any executive, something that would so stimulate his curiosity and awaken his interest that he could not resist stopping to take a look. I had found out from the sales resistance encountered that it was necessary to have something spectacular and to make a daring approach in order to sell foil labels at a price more than twice as much as paper labels."

Here, Reynolds recognizes one of the great principles of putting a sale across — originality of salesmanship. In case after case, it makes the difference not only in capturing the prospect's interest but in *holding* it, just as we shall see in Reynolds' story when we resume it.

Originality in salesmanship can take as many forms as there are sales situations. Samuel F. Rolph, General Manager of the Berrien Springs Division of the Yale & Towne Manufacturing Company, once sold a large order of door knobs to the Robert E. Lee Hotel by having his company make up a sample of a knob with General Lee's face modeled on it. Up to that point the competition for the order had been on a price basis; Yale & Towne seemed out of the running, but Rolph's ingenuity made his product stand out, and he got his order.

In some businesses, of course, there is very little opportunity for product differentiation. The originality of an insurance salesman may have to be in his manner or approach; in the prospect's mind, this often distinguishes the company much more than any clause in the contract. Again, washing machines may be sold — or not — on the basis of the service that the customer is assured of; so may many types of industrial equipment. Another kind of originality was demonstrated by William Bynum, Executive Vice President of the Carrier Corporation, in selling air conditioning equipment for a new building in Texas. The bidding was intensely competitive, and it was not until Bynum introduced a new element — thorough economic analysis — into the architects' thinking about their problem that he got the break that led to the sale.

Just being original, obviously, is not enough. Originality must be calculated. For some more light on that aspect, let us return to David Reynolds' story:

"The inside of that bus was designed like an ultramodern, streamlined supermarket. We installed glass shelves, indirect lighting, and elaborate, ornate display cases within which were artistically arranged actual samples of every product that used Reynolds foil. The major brands of cigarettes were pyramided in accord with the most recent report of actual sales at that time. There were novel arrangements of chocolate bars and kisses, the varied brands of chewing gum, candy bars, dried fruits, foil-labeled root beer and every other thing in the growing roster of commodities that had come to recognize the unique characteristics of foil as a packaging material.

"To top off the panorama within the scintillating coach there was assembled an elaborate array of beer bottles with a reproduction of the brand names of the foremost brewers, printed on sparkling foil labels in varicolors and pasted on actual bottles of beer.

"Previous to this we had succeeded in selling a few foil labels to brewers for their expensive beer, but the volume was unprofitably small. Most beer carried paper labels, much cheaper than foil. The difficult goal that I had set for myself was that of selling foil labels to the 10-cent beer boys. It was there that possibilities of large volume lay.

"The dream display coach was completed. Its glamour surprised and thrilled even me. It represented the expenditure of a lot of money, and it was up to me to justify the investment by demonstrating that it could be made an effective selling auxiliary."

Notice how Reynolds is planning here to appeal to the prospect's *senses.* It is an important point, and top salesmen typically make the most of it whenever they can. Norvin H. Rieser, President of the Rieser Company, Inc., capitalized on visual appeal in breaking down the resistance of druggists in 1915 to carrying Venida hair nets. In the window of one of the few New York druggists to whom he had sold, he displayed a backdrop, painted by the best artist he knew, showing a charming lady in negligee sitting at her dressing table and putting on a Venida hair net. Traffic was stopped by that display, and a long succession of sales to all 187 stores of the Liggett chain was started. But from the prospect's (Liggett's) point of view, the eye-opener was not so much the painting as the crowd and traffic jam – and people going in to buy.

Dramatic devices are no substitute for sound selling, but sometimes they help. R. L. Hockley, Vice President of the Davison Chemical Corporation, recalls an associate who began tossing $20 bills, one by one, in the general direction of the door. When the prospect, an automobile dealer to whom they had not been able to sell undercoating, asked what the idea was, Hockley's friend answered: "That's what you're losing every time a car goes out of here without an undercoating job." The sale was made. Here again an appeal to the senses was partly responsible.

Perceptual senses are not the only ones that count. In a situation where a luscious painting or a demonstration with $20 bills is inappropriate, the salesman can appeal to his prospect's sense of humor, or his patriotism, or his sportsmanship. David F. Austin, Vice President – Sales, United States Steel Corporation, once won his company a good account by helping the prospect straighten out a mix-up with an important customer. When the prospect lets the salesman do a good turn for him, it is difficult not to reciprocate. Buying on this basis may not be "logical," but it is human nature.

It should not be necessary to emphasize that appeals (sometimes "techniques" is a better word) of this sort, even when they work, are only a part – and often a very small part – of the process leading to a sale. Their importance is nonetheless great because they usually have to do with the decisive period when the prospect makes up his mind. Basic to everything, it must always be remembered, is whether the product *as the salesman presents it* is in the buyer's self-interest.

Helping the Prospect Make a Decision. Now let us go back to Reynolds Metals' "dream display coach." Since Reynolds had gambled time and money on it, the pressure was on him to make the investment pay off:

"I called our local division manager in a midwestern city and asked him to designate the toughest customer in his territory. He smiled and said, 'All right, you asked for it – and here it is.' He named a large brewery. 'Why, our men can't even get in the front door!'

"This corporation owned an extensive chain of breweries throughout the country. Their leading brand of beer sold for ten cents.

"I put in a telephone call for the president of the firm. I couldn't get him on the phone. He wouldn't even talk to me. O.K., I thought, I'll have to make a different approach.

"I drove [the new display coach] to the premises where the local brewery was located, right up to the front entrance, and parked, almost blocking it. I waited nervously and impatiently.

"It seemed to me that an eternity had passed, although it was only an hour or two, when a gentleman came through the door and started down the drive. But the bright, gleaming coach caught his eye. His curiosity got the better of him. He could not resist the impulse to turn around and walk back."

The point illustrated here is that a salesman has to get up to the decision-makers with his story. All his careful advance preparation will go for naught unless he can reach the men who do the buying.

But this is often a problem. With Reynolds it was a case of being turned down for an interview by the top man. Often it is more subtle than that. Often the salesman is blocked on his way up the ladder by men under the decision-maker; and when this happens, there are human relations difficulties to contend with. It is a good rule of selling not to climb recklessly over people's heads. Like all rules, however, there are times when the situation may justify breaking it. (Here again, there is no way to "teach" a salesman what to do. It is a problem of judgment.)

William K. Beard, Jr., President of Associated Business Publications, says that his most memorable sales experience involved a time when he was selling advertising in a trade publication and the advertising manager of an important account which had just canceled its contract told him that if he were "smart," he wouldn't go up to the sales vice president in an effort to renew the business. Beard figured that the stakes justified the risk, and so he "went upstairs" with his story. In this case it happened to work; often, despite the best of planning, it does not. Generally, however, the salesman will find, as Beard did, "that the man way up the ladder is a pretty human sort. That's one reason why he got there." Indeed, he is often more approachable, once the salesman *has* met him, than his subordinates.

Can the Prospect Sell Himself? David Reynolds reached the top men, too, but by a more unique means. What happened when he did is even more interesting:

The first curious visitor to the display coach which Reynolds had parked at the front of the brewery turned out to be the purchasing agent.

"He inspected the coach. The diversified exhibit of beer bottles with their gleaming, sparkling foil labels arrested his attention and held his interest. He was tight-lipped, but there were indications that an impression had been made. The purchasing agent left the coach and returned to the office. He came back shortly, bringing with him another gentleman. This turned out to be the sales manager. His eyes swept the interior of the coach, but it was the beer bottles with the bright foil labels that fascinated him.

"The sales manager was as noncommunicative as the purchasing agent had been. There was no verbal indication that my sales talk was making any impression. I realized that I was confronted with a crucial test in my effort to break down sales resistance, to get across a new idea.

"Then the sales manager returned to the office There was still no indication that I was getting anywhere. I was dejected and trying to devise another line of sales strategy when the sales manager returned. He had brought the president of the company with him. I was both excited and elated.

"In our sales talks we made it a practice to stress the fact that aluminum-foil beer labels are impervious to water. The advantage of that could be demonstrated by the fact that this prevented them from coming off when the bottles were placed in cold water or were iced to keep the beer cold. In talking to the president I purposely avoided our chief selling point, eye appeal. I felt that the display would make that point self-evident. As the president of the brewing corporation walked through the bus, I could see that he was startled by our dazzling, modernistic display on wheels. I enthusiastically gave him my spiel about aluminum-foil labels being waterproof and that they would not come off in cold water or when iced as paper labels always do. He hardly waited until I had covered the idea when he interrupted to say: 'Boy, your greatest selling point is eye appeal. Why those labels are beautiful. They impart the impression of a product with high quality and class.' "

Here Reynolds is recognizing that basic principle of making a sale: if possible, let the prospect convince himself. Usually, of course, the salesman will have to lead him a great deal more than Reynolds is doing in this case. There are many ways of doing this. Some of the best ways would be classified as indirect. They involve suggestion, restatements of customer viewpoints, anecdotes, and so on.

One of the best of them is asking questions. Frank Bettger, regarded by Dale Carnegie as the best teacher of sales training in America today, learned this years ago from a top salesman of an earlier generation, J. Elliott Hall. Bettger was electrified by Hall's demonstration of meeting objections by asking questions. According to Hall, if the prospect said he couldn't make up his mind, the salesman should ask questions to help him pinpoint the trouble spots. If the prospect said he wanted to go home and "think it over," the salesman should ask questions to help him find out just what it *was* he wanted to think over. The idea, in other words, was to help the prospect recognize what he wanted and then to help him decide how to get it — not to persuade or influence him in the usual sense.

But no approach works all the time. Sometimes the only solution is the exact opposite of indirection and restraint. Graham Patterson, the publishing head of the *Farm Journal* and *Pathfinder*, once managed to get General Wood of Sears, Roebuck interested in farm-journal advertising, after the ordinary means had failed, by openly challenging him to do better than Montgomery Ward if he *didn't* advertise in farm journals. (Patterson did not go away with the order he wanted that time, but his tactics brought him a lot closer to doing so.)

The rest of the Reynolds story, to which we can turn now, illustrates a final technique that is often useful at the close of a sale:

It was Thursday when Reynolds attracted the attention of the brewery executives, and the president asked him to bring the display coach back on Saturday. "He explained that the thought he had in mind was to telegraph the manager of one of his breweries, whose advice he valued, and direct him to come to the home office. He wanted him to see the display and register his reaction.

"Of course it was not necessary for him to insist or to ask me twice. It was with great anxiety that I waited for Saturday; in fact I could hardly wait. I reviewed every detail of what had taken place, trying to decide what had been the most significant thing in that sales discussion. I decided that it was silence, keeping quiet after the president pointed out to me that the major selling point of foil labels was eye appeal. From there on I kept my mouth shut and let him talk, after agreeing that he had put his finger on the quality in foil labels that excelled.

"This was the first time I had observed that being a good listener is helpful in making a sale. So long as the prospect indicates an inclination to talk, it is wise for the salesman to listen. An occasional discreet question that keeps the customer talking sometimes is the most effective method of leading to a sale.

"The crucial day arrived. I piloted the display coach back to the office of the brewing company and waited anxiously. The important prospects finally arrived. The out-of-town brewery manager was impressed with the gleaming labels on the beer bottles. But he was skeptical about the wisdom of paying twice as much for them as for paper labels. Again I bit my tongue and kept silent. The president of the company made my sales talk for me. He soon had his associate enthusiastic about the idea, convincing him that the foil label would be a profitable sales stimulant. He argued that the foil label would mark the beer as a distinctive beverage and that it would have a good psychological effect on the customer as he sipped it.

"The president of the company sold himself as he persuaded his subordinates that the decision to adopt foil labels was a good investment. The result was that the corporation gave me an order for 100,000,000 beer labels. It was the largest single order that [we] had ever sold and the largest purchase of foil labels that had ever been made."

Conclusion

Salesmanship seems to be a great defier of logic. The outcome of any given sales conference is affected by intangibles and luck. Prospects may add up to averages or percentages, but each one is an unpredictable human being when you are dealing with him individually. Furthermore, whether the man who failed to make a sale did the best anyone could, or whether the man who succeeded could have done better, are questions which can seldom definitely be answered by either the salesman or his sales manager.

The fact remains that positive, purposeful effort will produce more sales than simply calling on people or hit-or-miss plugging. As Edward C. Bursk pointed out in his pioneering analysis of low-pressure selling five years ago, making the prospect feel he is reaching the buying decision himself may dull his resistance and thus unleash his natural buying urge, but to get him to feel that way and still lead him to your particular product takes even more skill than high-pressure selling. "More is required of salesmen than a series of soft and subtle stratagems to replace their old exaggerated claims and emotional appeals; they must utilize something strong and purposeful, like the customer-problem approach." [3]

In any event, it is clearly important for a salesman to make the most of as much experi-

[3] "Low-Pressure Selling," HARVARD BUSINESS REVIEW, Vol. XXV, No. 2 (Winter 1947), p. 239.

ence — his own *and* others — as he can. He never does the *best* that could be done, but by constantly searching, examining, and evaluating sales experience he can sometimes come close to it. Horace B. Van Dorn, Vice President of the Joseph Dixon Crucible Company, Pencil Sales Division, expressed the top salesman's attitude this way:

> "Selling is one of the subtle arts, which throws mind against mind, tongue against tongue, firmness against firmness. Salesmen are in conference all day long, and as Bacon has said, 'Conference maketh a ready man.' The ebb and flow of conference is a joy to me. It always is to a salesman. He has much to accomplish with spoken words. As I reflected upon a life of selling contacts, the experiences that leap out are those made memorable by something said, something said to me or something I replied. Such experiences are educative, disciplinary, and wholesome."

To the many points which can be perceived from the experiences quoted in these pages — the value of little things, the role played by fate or circumstance, the fact that people are not "sold" but that they "buy," the value of perseverance and creative imagination, and all the rest — we must add, therefore, one more: the priceless value to the salesman of actual selling experience.

That is why I think it is so significant that *all* of the 60 stories in *How I Made the Sale That Did the Most for Me* can be classified under one or more of what Richard N. W. Harris, President of the Toni Company, says were "hammered home" to him as "ten of the vital points of successful selling." Despite their abbreviated form these points cover the fundamentals we have been discussing:

(1) You can't go off "half-cocked."
(2) Your product must be good.
(3) You must do an educational selling job.
(4) You must have an aggressive sales policy.
(5) Don't start "too big."
(6) Think of your market in terms of individuals, not cold statistics.
(7) Your idea must be right.
(8) Your product must fill a need, economic or otherwise.
(9) You must have confidence in your product.
(10) You must keep ahead of your competition.

Certainly, the experience of successful salesmen *does* point up a number of valuable object lessons — and top management *does* have reason for increased effort in developing salesmen. Successful salesmen are not just born that way; nor, at the other extreme, can successful salesmen be turned out by the application of a scientific formula. Somewhere in between these two misconceptions is the truth that careful selection and training can make good salesmen better salesmen.

Robert N. McMurry

8 The Mystique of Super-Salesmanship

In contrast to the advances of modern industry in such areas as automation, electronics, chemistry, and physics, selling as an art and science has made little or no progress since the early days of the Industrial Revolution. Today, as then, "representatives" attempt by various occult devices to persuade others to buy and use their wares. In terms of the methods he employs, the salesman of today is essentially no better qualified, in my judgment, than the "drummer" of yesteryear.

Merchandising methods have improved with the advent of self-service and vending machines, and advertising has taken advantage of motivation research. Consumer sales have been made much easier because of the widespread availability of consumer credit. But salesmanship — as an art applied at the face-to-face level — is just as primitive today as it was 100 years ago. It works, but no one seems to understand quite how and why.

It is probable that, in general, no phase of American business is less efficient and less well controlled costwise than is distribution. In many instances, no one knows precisely what sales should cost. The only measure is what they *do* cost, which may be quite inaccurate. Whatever the total expenses of distribution, the sums spent on the salesmen usually constitute a major component — a component made larger by the fact that a very high proportion of those engaged in selling cannot sell.

Now, we all know that selling is qualitatively different from all other aspects of business and industry. It does not lend itself to the empirical, quantitative research methodologies of the more exact sciences. Instead, it tends to have a "mystique" of its own which is peculiarly baffling. For example, debates rage perennially on this topic: *Are salesmen born or made?* Even the most successful practitioners of the art rarely know precisely how they accomplish their magic. There is, therefore, great uncertainty as to how one proceeds to penetrate such a mystery.

Still, I believe that if American sales efficiency is to be maximized and the appalling waste of money and manpower which exists today is to be minimized, a constructive analysis must be made of what selling really is and how its effectiveness can be enhanced. Answers to the following questions must be obtained:

- How variable is the selling job? Is it made up of about the same main elements everywhere, as many people seem to assume?
- What is the role of the salesman in consummating the sale? To what extent does he "seduce" the prospect into buying, and to what extent does he use pressure to make the sale?
- Putting aside what in our more idealistic moments we might *wish* to be true, what really distinguishes the truly good salesman from the "hack"? To what extent is he a "wooer" and an "actor"? Is the possession of these qualities an unmixed blessing?
- What kinds of training are valuable? Is it reasonable to expect the intelligent salesman to develop unaided his own presentation or "pitch"?
- What are the implications of the nature of salesmanship for building and maintaining a hard-hitting, productive sales force? What is an effective philosophy of supervision and leadership?

I shall discuss these and other questions in this article. In general my emphasis is on consumer-goods selling, although much of what I have to say applies to industrial selling as well. Those who tend to assume that industrial buying lacks the personal, emotional element of consumer-goods buying would do well, I think, to turn to the first conclusion of a new marketing study: "In his buying habits, the industrial buyer is more human than industrial marketers have realized. [He] . . . not only has the same biological needs that you and I have, but he also has the same psychological drives, urges, desires, ambitions." [1]

The Selling Spectrum

Is selling characterized by the same needs and problems everywhere? This question has already been ably discussed for HBR readers by George N. Kahn and Abraham Shuchman who made a major distinction between two kinds of selling — creative and maintenance.[2] I agree with them completely. However, the people we have to deal with — the salesmen, existing or potential — are not so black-and-white; they are not just of two kinds, but range over a spectrum from one extreme to the other. Thus, thinking particularly of creative skill, I find it useful to array salesmen in terms of positions requiring increasing amounts of that ingredient, from the very simple to the highly complex — as for example:

• *Positions where the "salesman's" job is predominantly to deliver the product, e.g., milk, bread, fuel oil* — His selling responsibilities are secondary. Obviously good service and a pleasant manner will enhance customer acceptance and hence lead to more sales. However, few originate many sales.

• *Positions where the salesman is predominantly an inside order-taker, e.g., the haberdashery salesman standing behind the counter* — Most of his customers have already made up their minds to buy. All he does is serve them. He may use suggestive selling and upgrade the merchandise they buy, but his opportunities to do more than that are few.

• *Positions where the salesman is also predominantly an order-taker but works in the field, as the packing house, soap, or spice salesman does* — In his contacts with chain store personnel, he may even actually be discouraged from applying the hard sell. As with the delivery salesman, good service and a pleasant personality may enhance his personal acceptance, but he too does little creative selling.

• *Positions where the salesman is not expected or permitted to take an order but is called on only to build good will or to educate the actual or potential user* — Examples here are the distiller's "missionary man" or the medical "detailer" representing an ethical pharmaceutical house.

• *Positions where the major emphasis is placed on technical knowledge, e.g., the engineering salesman who is primarily a consultant to the "client" companies.*

• *Positions which demand the creative sale of tangible products like vacuum cleaners, refrigerators, siding, and encyclopedias* — Here the salesman often has a double task: first he must make the prospect dissatisfied with his or her present appliance or situation, then begin to sell his product.

• *Positions requiring the creative sale of intangibles, such as insurance, advertising services, or education* — This type of sale is ordinarily more difficult than selling tangibles, of course, because the product is less readily demonstrated and dramatized. (Intangibles are often more difficult for the prospect to comprehend.)

Degrees of Difficulty

The men in the first classifications are salesmen by courtesy only. While they are not without value in bringing in additional business, few in any sense *create* business. They perform useful services but someone else, usually a supervisor or someone from the home office, must make the initial sale. In the case of name brands like Swift, Colgate, or Seagram's, of course, the demand which advertising and product acceptance have created is such that the merchant *must* stock the product.

The creative or "specialty" salesmen at the other end of the spectrum actually move merchandise which cannot be sold in equal volume without them. They have an infinitely more difficult selling task. For example, the prospect may never have heard of the product and at the outset may have no desire whatever to purchase it. He may even be prejudiced against it. And if he wants it, he may want competing products still more, or not be able to afford it. Such sales

[1] Hector Lazo, "Emotional Aspects of Industrial Buying," in *Dynamic Marketing for a Changing World*, edited by Robert S. Hancock (Chicago, American Marketing Association, 1960), p. 260.

[2] See Chapter 4, "Specialize Your Salesman!"

situations require creative salesmanship of the highest order.

Enormous Demands

Businessmen and business writers often assume, it seems to me, that specialty selling is hard because it calls for initiative, imagination, and qualities of that order. It may indeed be demanding in these respects, but I do not believe that this is why there are so few good specialty salesmen. Here are the characteristics that really make the job difficult:

(1) Specialty selling ordinarily demands almost constant door-to-door or office-to-office ("cold turkey") canvassing.

(2) Field sales positions have the disadvantage of being lonely. The representative must work by himself without the supportive presence of an associate or a supervisor.

(3) Specialty selling is fatiguing. The hours are often long and irregular; many positions necessitate extensive travel and frequently require tiring demonstrations.

(4) The salesman is always in an inferior status position vis-à-vis his prospect. He must be willing to accept rudeness and rebuffs as a matter of course.

(5) In many instances the salesman sees himself as the perpetual intruder, forcing himself on people and into homes where he is not only unwelcome, but often actively resented.

(6) In creative specialty selling the frequency of rejection is higher and more important than in other kinds of selling. For example, a salesman of accident and health insurance is expected to make at least 36 prospect contacts by cold canvass each week. If he can sell 4 of these, he is regarded as performing very well. Thus he must steel himself to an average of 32 rejections 50 weeks in the year.

No one without a well-defined capacity to take punishment (often with a real need for constant self-punishment) can tolerate such activity. If, as often happens, the salesman is working on straight commission without a draw or guarantee, the torture is even worse. This is one reason why much selling is deprecated, and the work attracts so many neurotics.

Since a need for security, certainty, and a predictable future characterizes the majority of the working population, the demands of salesmanship generally, and of specialty selling particularly, are intolerable to many. (Actually, dependence, insecurity, and free-floating anxiety are *endemic* in America.) My guess is that not more than one person in a thousand is so constituted that he will be successful and find challenge and security in direct sales. Few people have the ability to accept rejection with equanimity. The turndown is not only an affront to their self-esteem, but a frightening experience. It is no wonder that many salesmen are reluctant to ask for an order; if they do not ask, they are never rejected.

The high rejection rate accounts for the fantastic rates of turnover in many direct-selling organizations. A turnover rate of 400% per year seems to be acceptable much of the time — and in experience the rate may run as high as 750% per year. Most firms have a hard core of 10%–20% who are veterans, while the remainder come and go with lightninglike rapidity.

Now, success as an inside or route salesman does not necessarily qualify a person to engage in creative selling — or vice versa. Each type of sales work requires its own, unique configuration of traits, attributes, and qualities in its practitioner. Hence, if a productive sales force is to be established, the first and fundamental step to take is *to ascertain the category of sales to be undertaken and decide precisely what qualities the incumbents will need.*

Role of the Salesman

To understand the role of a top-notch salesman, we must first review what happens within the buyer while a sale is being consummated. Here I shall focus on products sold on a door-to-door basis. This kind of selling more dramatically mirrors the universal problem than does any other type.

Dynamics of the Sale

To begin, everyone has an almost infinite number of needs and desires. All of them, conscious or unconscious, are dynamic and strive constantly for expression. It is never necessary to *create* needs and desires as the sales texts say; they are there all of the time. Accordingly, the problem is not to *arouse* needs in order to initiate buying action; it is to determine which among existing needs are the most powerful; which lend themselves best to strengthening through the satisfaction of related needs; which will necessitate the purchase of the salesman's product for their gratification; and how readily their gratification can be rationalized.

Of course, as writers often remind us, many consumer purchases are essentially nonrationally determined. A need or needs exist of which the buyer may be conscious, but these are usually reinforced by secondary needs of which he is only marginally conscious or totally unconscious. The sight of the article, a description of it, and especially a presentation of what it will do for the buyer causes him to invest it with attributes and properties, real or fancied, which give it unusual value to him. The merchandise may be said at this point to have "seduced" him. This is the point at which he begins to discover that he likes it and wants it. The procedure is analogous in many respects to the act of falling in love — and is equally irrational.

The role of the salesman in consummating ("closing") the sale may be summarized thus:

¶ He is the "procurer" who uses the merchandise to seduce the prospect so that the latter falls in love with it and wants to buy it.

¶ He provides logical justifications to his prospect for performing what would often impress others as an irrational act, e.g., the purchase of an article which the buyer appears neither to need nor to be able to afford.

¶ It is he who, when necessary, applies the pressure to effect a "close."

Seducing the Prospect

The act of seduction consists of presenting the merits of the merchandise vividly and in glowing terms and by painting a very alluring picture of the pleasures or services it offers. Often the prospect and the sales representative engage in joint fantasies of a highly voluptuous character. "Think, Mrs. Smith," says salesman Steve, "how luxurious it will be to bathe in the pure, soft water that your new water softener will give you." More than one salesman has so learned to pitch his voice that he creates an almost hypnotic effect on his listeners. Many persons are by nature highly suggestible. A dramatic presentation made with rising and falling inflections in the evening to a fatigued group can heighten the listeners' mutual suggestibility to the point where they will buy without being altogether conscious of what they are doing. The astute salesman then does not ask for the order; he simply tells the prospect, "Sign here." The more vivid and intimately personalized the picture, the more effective the sales presentation.

Providing Rationalization

Now let us turn to the second function: providing the customer with plausible rationalizations for buying. Once having induced the prospect to fall in love with the merchandise or service, there is no question but that he will want it. On the other hand, the satisfaction of this need may arouse guilt in him, and inevitably there are competing needs and desires — shall he buy an encyclopedia or a new TV set when the house needs a new roof? He needs support, preferably authoritative and logically buttressed. If he can generate these rationalizations himself, fine — but he may need the salesman to do it for him.

Closing the Sale

The third function — closing the sale — is important because in all too many instances the customer wants the merchandise and has convinced himself that he should buy, but is still unable to reach a final decision to do so. (Indecisiveness, as a by-product of dependence and insecurity, is also endemic to America.) It is at this point that the salesman may be called on to apply pressure for a close. Pressure takes many forms:

- At its simplest, it is sheer animal dominance: the salesman is merely a stronger character than his prospect. He states authoritatively, "Sign here! The down payment will be $10. I'll take it in cash or by check."

- A variant of the foregoing ploy is where the salesman stays and stays until the customer signs to get rid of him.

- A more subtle type of pressure exploits the prospect's inherent anxiety. Its theme, with variations, is, "If you don't buy now, you'll always regret it."

- An even more subtle device is to base the sale on the prospect's objection. This is a form of dialectical entrapment. The prospect is led to commit himself to buying if the salesman can overcome his major objection.

- The salesman "takes the prospect's measure" by interrogating him at length about his needs, his preferences, the use to which he will put the product, what he likes and dislikes about what he presently has or is using, and so on. He then proceeds to adapt his presentation so that the prospect cannot rationalize a refusal to purchase.

- Of all techniques, the use of the demonstration, particularly one in which the buyer participates, is one of the most effective. For example, in the sale of an automobile, nothing is more likely to arouse a desire for immediate, contractual ownership than the thrill of sitting behind the wheel of a chrome-laden behemoth and being the master of 200–300 horsepower.

Inside the Personality

So much for the functions and techniques that come into play in making a sale. They are important, especially insofar as they help to show what kind of person a good salesman must be, but in and of themselves they do not make a good salesman. This is a point worth emphasizing. Sometimes writers and speakers convey the impression that the successful salesman is a bundle of the right techniques and concepts. I do not believe that experience confirms this. Techniques certainly can help, but selling is a human task that can only be explained satisfactorily in human terms. We must look a good deal further — into the mysteries of personality and psychology — if we want real answers to sales managers' problems.

The Wooing Instinct

What is the "mystique" of super-salesmanship? What enables some persons, with or without technical competence, to sell, while others cannot seem to? Where is the source of "creative" salesmanship? Why is it said by many that salesmen are "born, not made"?

My answers to these questions are not popular ones, and they will not endear me to some audiences. But I feel they are much more realistic than the glib, glad-handing treatments that so often have characterized "trait and work habit" discussions; they get us much closer to *people*, as contrasted with abstractions or ideal types. We all need a stiff corrective, I am afraid.

It is my conviction that the possessor of an *effective* sales personality is *a habitual "wooer," an individual who has a compulsive need to win and hold the affection of others.* He is not born with this need; it is the product of his early environment. But it develops so early in life that for all practical purposes it might as well be inborn.

To the degree that a salesman possesses this trait, he is characterized by the conviction that he is really unloved and unwanted. His reaction is to attempt to use every means at his disposal to "buy" the acceptance and affection of all of those with whom he comes into contact, using personal charm, flattery, gifts, and similar inducements. Partly as a result, he has great empathy toward others; he is sensitive to every nuance of their reactions to everything he says and does. He has, so to speak, a built-in radar which is invaluable in sales contacts. He senses the usefulness to himself of *compatibility.*

His wooing, however, is not based on a sincere desire for love because, in my opinion, he is convinced at heart that no one will ever love him. Therefore, his wooing is primarily exploitative; he seeks to win the affection of others the better to use them for his own selfish purposes. In consequence, his relationships tend to be transient, superficial, and evanescent. There is always an element of ambivalence, of repressed latent hostility in all his relationships.

The typical "sales personality" is not consciously aware of his predilection for wooing people. He does it entirely out of habit, rarely by design — but constantly, so that he is said "always to be selling." The fact that his wooing is intuitive explains why he so often has difficulty in explaining how he accomplishes results. He finds it easy to describe the steps to the sale (arouse interest, induce conviction, answer objections, make the close, and so on), but almost never does he indicate how he accomplishes these effects as he passes from step to step and finally makes the close. This is why many books on salesmanship are so fatuous. Wooing in a sales context is as difficult to teach as wooing in a boudoir. And if the student is not a wooer by nature, to try to make him one is comparable to trying to make a Don Juan out of a John Calvin.

Differing Styles

While "born salesmen" are essentially similar in certain psychological respects, they do not necessarily take identical approaches. The qualities which will make an individual highly acceptable to one prospect may have a diametrically opposed effect on another. Just as each customer is unique in his appearance, manner, mode of expression, and personality make-up, so does he have a correspondingly unique potential to tolerate or to find distasteful any given qualities in others.

Thus, no single salesperson can possibly be equally attractive to everyone, no matter how earnestly he tries. For this same reason, no one, no matter how competent, can sell all types of customers. Moreover, the types of buyers one man can sell often cannot be sold by another — and vice versa. This is why a change of field representatives almost invariably brings with it a loss of accounts (although there may, of course, be gains in other accounts and additions of new customers). Let me illustrate:

The two champion vacuum cleaner salesmen in a Midwest city were as unlike as day and night. One, an ex-railway brakeman, was big, beefy, and loud. He closed by browbeating his prospects. Some probably bought to get rid of him. The other was a thin, pallid, anemic-appearing youth who, at the appropriate moment, would fall on his knees and break into tears and literally beg the prospects to buy, explaining that if he did not close *this* sale, he would lose his job and he, his wife, and his five children would be dispossessed. He sold as many machines as his colleague, but it is probable that the women he sold would have been impervious to the approach of the other man, and vice versa.

Other Qualities Needed

Along with the wooing instinct, several less glamorous, more pedestrian qualifications are important:

1. *A high level of energy* — The person who is not a self-starter, with a high continuing level of drive, rarely is consistently productive. Many of the best salesmen are hypomanics whose energy and optimism are inexhaustible.
2. *Abounding self-confidence* — This often is a neurotic compensation for or denial of strong buried feelings of inadequacy or inferiority. Nevertheless, it enables the salesman to accept rejection without too much inner anguish.
3. *A chronic hunger for money* — Many salesmen are highly narcissistic; they love to show off. This often requires money. The man with a low level of aspiration or standard of living rarely has sufficient incentive to exert and extend himself.
4. *A well-established habit of industry* — This means that the individual is uncomfortable when not constructively occupied. Since he must work without close supervision, he must be totally self-disciplining.
5. *A state of mind which regards each objection, resistance, or obstacle as a challenge* — The salesman is one who can never hear the word "no"; it does not exist for him. He must also be competitive by nature. Many successful salesmen hate their prospects; they have been rejected by too many whom they regard as their intellectual and cultural inferiors. Closing the sale thus constitutes a "victory" over a buyer.

All or Nothing

If a man is not a natural wooer and has not demonstrated that he has the foregoing five qualities, he is a poor risk. No training program or system of supervision can inculcate them in him. He either has them or he does not, *at the time of hiring.* He can be given information and taught skills, but his character and personality are subject to little change. At the same time, if he *does* have the foregoing attributes, he may superficially be quite unimpressive. He may be ill-favored in appearance, use poor English, lack education and culture, and even be somewhat deficient in intelligence. Nevertheless he will still get the orders. For example:

The leading salesman for a number of years in a national vacuum cleaner marketing organization looked very much like an ape. He was short, he had a low forehead, he had practically no neck (his head was hunched between his shoulders), he always looked as though he needed a shave, and his hands hung nearly to his knees. In the summer, he wore no underwear so that the hair on his chest came through the loose mesh of his polo shirt. He was a Greek immigrant who spoke poor English in a guttural voice. In short, at first glance he appeared to be the type of man from whom housewives would run screaming if he appeared at the front door.

In fact, however, he consistently sold more vacuum cleaners than any of his 5,000 colleagues, most of whom were better looking and better educated than he, simply because he had a substantial measure of the attributes I have discussed (including that of being a natural "wooer"). He knew how to win and to hold personal acceptance.

Effective Training

How much training is needed, and of what type? Where the salesman's primary function is delivery or order-taking, formal training need not be very complicated. It is principally in the creative sale of tangibles and intangibles where training makes its greatest contribution. As a *minimum*, and keeping in mind that indoctrination can be successful only if the right men have been chosen to take it, formal sales training for creative sales work must cover:

1. *Orientation* — It is important to acquaint the new representative with his employer, his opportunities, and the special features of his work. More specifically, it is vital to sell him on his company, his job, and his product. This training must ordinarily be conducted inside the firm by staff personnel.
2. *The product or service and, if necessary, its demonstration* — In most instances, information concerning competing products or services should

also be given by staff personnel. Ordinarily, unless the representative is thoroughly grounded in this latter area, he will be at a serious disadvantage.

3. *The procedures to follow in booking orders, making necessary reports, and so on* — This obviously should also be done inside the firm.

4. *Time management* — Since the salesman spends only a fraction of his time before prospects, it is imperative that he be shown how to utilize his time with the utmost efficiency. While the principles of this may be presented in a formal course, time management can actually be taught only in the field and then only by constant drill and close supervision.

5. *Sales techniques* — These are, as indicated, of great variety, and the question of what should be presented depends largely on the product and the market. At a minimum, the training program should include:

- How to prospect for prospects.
- How to make the pre-presentation survey.
- How to get in to see the prospect.
- How to "take the prospect's measure," i.e., ascertain his needs, both latent and overt.
- How to make a selling presentation (and, if necessary, a demonstration).
- How to anticipate, cope with, and answer objections and handle resistances.
- How to begin to ask for the order — i.e., how to take the prospect's "temperature" and what to do when he says "no."
- How to make the close.
- How to maintain continuing good relations after the order is signed.

It is in this last area of salesmanship skills that many sales organizations fail to make the most of their personnel resources. Supervision is too busy or too indolent to spend the requisite amount of time in the field with the men; yet the only really good place to practice is right in front of the prospect. The mistake is to assume that because it is to the salesman's self-interest to develop himself (particularly where he is working on commission), he will do so voluntarily. In actuality, he must be *forced* all too often to improve himself.

The Do-It-Yourself Fallacy

As I look around at the ways most companies train sales personnel, I am struck by a variety of mistakes. A significantly large number of these can be traced to an erroneous assumption that underlies almost countless plans, policies, and decisions. This is the belief that the more intelligent the salesman is, the greater will be his facility at adapting himself to the demands of his work and working out a presentation which will have maximum effectiveness.

The truth is that the salesman needs a well-defined structure, a prepared "pitch" to follow in making his presentations. In spite of years of practice, even the best specialty salesmen experience great difficulty in originating a presentation or coping unaided with a new or unusual objection or resistance. They often have very retentive memories and have acquired a substantial storehouse of answers and ploys which they can use as the occasion may demand, but practically none of this material is ever original. They are, therefore, best compared to actors who must be fed their lines. Without the support of a predetermined sales "pitch," they are like the actor who, when called on to speak extemporaneously, is often at an utter loss. Sometimes when their presentations are interrupted or they are thrown off stride, they find it necessary to make an entirely fresh start.

Few salesmen have much imagination, and almost none have any perspective on the broad marketing picture. The ideal candidate is one who will accept a presentation which has been worked out for him and modify it only enough so that it "sounds like him" and not obviously "canned." In short, conditions here are similar to those which many observers have found in manufacturing. There we have learned that the "brains" must be taken out of the shop; real thinking is not for the operators.

Skills as an Actor

In a well-planned presentation, the prospect's objections come to serve as cues to the salesman's "routine." If he has been properly trained, he will have been exposed to every conceivable objection so that none will take him by surprise and disrupt his presentation. He will know the correct answer to each resistance. Hence, just as the actor may engage in a sparkling and scintillant dialogue on the stage, none of which is original, so the company representative is enabled to give brilliant answers to the questions and objections his prospect may raise. He can thus be the complete master of the situation without having originated any of his brilliant lines himself.

Not only does this type of training enhance the salesman's self-confidence, but it greatly improves his productivity. This is due, in part, to the fact that he is not thrown off stride by objections he cannot answer, and in larger part to the fact that, having been drilled in what to say, he is less likely to flounder or to give the wrong response and thus endanger the sale. Further, once having learned his lines, he can relax and use the same material again and again. It can be made sufficiently flexible to meet nearly every contingency and requires little or no intelligence to employ.

The fact that the salesman does not originate his presentation does not mean that he cannot learn to speak his lines with elegance, feeling, and apparent total sincerity. Many salesmen are born actors. Many are narcissistic and are exhibitionists at heart. They are never happier than when in front of a prospect making a "pitch." They love to be the center of attention and find that an audience inspires them to surprising heights of artistry. A number have learned, for example, even how to manipulate their eyelids in such a manner that a tear can be excreted on demand:

> One appliance salesman uses a three-step referral plan. Each purchaser gives the names of 10 friends, 6 of whom will allegedly buy. For each of these 6 purchases he is to receive a "commission" of $15, and another $15 for each of the 36 who buy as a result of the 60 recommendations made by the 6. Finally, he is to be paid $15 for each of the purchases by the 216 who buy as a result of being nominated by the 36.
>
> The salesman shows the prospect how much he is about to receive. Using a so-called "eggchart," he explains how he will get $90 from his nominations, $540 on the purchases of the 36, and $3,240 on the purchases of the 216. At the bottom of the eggchart is a picture of a "treasure chest," overflowing with golden doubloons. The salesman then points to the treasure chest and a tear trickles down his cheek. He says to the prospect: "I am crying because I am so happy for you. For a down payment of only $50, you may receive as much as $3,870. This will much more than pay for your new appliance." (The appliance is a $450 item sold on this plan for $777.)

As may be seen, this type of presentation requires little intellectual ability (or ethics) but a high degree of acting skill. Indeed, my own studies indicate that there is little or even a negative correlation between level of intelligence as measured by tests and sales success. Obviously, if a salesman's intelligence is in the very low range (e.g., IQ below 80), he will have difficulty benefiting from the training given him.

However, it is equally true that too high a level of intelligence (e.g., IQ of 120) is equally disadvantageous. This is not because the salesman cannot learn; it is because he is unlikely to remain on the job. Either he quickly seeks to move up into management or starts to look for a position with more challenge or with equal earnings but not as much work and with fewer rejections.

The Compensation Question

All selling positions, with the exception of missionary and some detailing activities, lend themselves in varying degrees to incentive compensation. In spite of this, a surprising number of representatives are either paid on straight salary or receive bonuses or profit sharing, neither of which have much incentive value. While sales positions on straight salary tend to be the easiest to fill, because of the security they offer, it is also to be remembered that too great a desire for security is inconsistent with the temperament needed for creative selling. Straight salary may be appropriate for delivery men and order-takers, but it tends to be fatal in creative activities.

I know of one firm that studied the productivity of 1,500 heavy-equipment salesmen. Its survey indicated that while those on straight salary produced an average sales volume of $135,000 per year, those on an incentive averaged $262,000 per year. Studies of door-to-door or specialty salesmen also indicate that straight salary compensation is frequently impractical in that kind of selling.

Quality of Supervision

The final and in many respects the most important element in a productive sales force is leadership. It has been said that "no sales organization is better than its first-line supervision." What kind of supervision, specifically, is needed?

Firm Hand Needed

Several considerations are involved. Among others is the fact that a number of men may be chronic "problems." Included in this group are many *prima donnas* with their frequent total disregard for reality. Particularly troublesome to supervise are the high-pressure, specialty types — the "bombers," the "dynamiters," and the "wheeler dealers." They tend to be confidence men first and salesmen second. Since they are, first of all, completely selfish, they are incapable of loyalty to anyone — employer, associates, supervisors, or prospects. They are, almost without exception, "lone wolves" of the first order.

Again, the primary motivation of many "star" salesmen is, in my observation, an amalgam of greed and hostility. The latter is directed principally toward their supervision and toward the public to whom they sell. Their attitudes toward authority are extremely ambivalent. On the one hand, they resent being told what to do; on the other hand, they are basically dependent and have a constant need for help and guidance which, nevertheless, they feel impelled to deny as unmanly. In consequence, they are chronically demanding and dissatisfied. Nothing that can be done for them will please them or awaken their loyalty.

Most important, since these traits are basically symptomatic of their immaturity or neurosis, they are resistant to reason, logic, admonitions, and threats. They cannot be changed. The very immaturity which provides them with their charm and affability (their principal asset in selling) also ironically takes its toll in their business relationships and private lives. Few are happy and relaxed. Some destroy themselves by means of gambling, women, or the bottle.

In consequence, a firm hand is required to manage them. Under no circumstances should an attempt be made to win their good will by what are essentially appeasement tactics; these are invariably interpreted by them as evidences of weakness and lead to new and unreasonable demands on supervision.

Although the high producers may growl and grouse under firm direction which structures their activities in detail and maintains strict discipline, they invariably feel more secure and comfortable under it. This type of firm supervision is equally appropriate with the more docile, submissive, and conformist personnel — the delivery men and order-takers. The latter, too, do not resent discipline if it is fairly and evenhandedly administered.

To structure the salesman's activities and provide close supervision does not necessarily imply autocratic or bureaucratic leadership. It merely means that in conferences with a salesman the supervisor gives him:

1. A clear statement of his duties, responsibilities, and the scope of his authority.
2. Materials with which to work, make reports, and keep necessary records.
3. A statement of what management expects of him so that his production goals for a given period are specifically defined. He should have a chance to express disagreement with these expectations if he wants to.

Staffing & Structuring

It is no news to good marketing men to point out that selling and management are two widely differing activities. Competence in one does not guarantee ability in the other. The real problem is what to do about it. Management can choose between two major alternatives:

¶ *Complementary staffing* — This approach is based on the recognition that *all* of the requisite traits for competence in sales supervision are practically never found in one person. Accordingly, each sales management position is staffed with *two* executives.

The first is the traditional, "hell-for-leather," "go out and get the business" type of sales manager. He is the dynamo, the man who constantly maintains the drive and pressure for sales; he is the inspirational leader. But he is not to be expected to be concerned with detail, with report making, and with maintaining a constant follow-up on his men.

The detail of the work is for a second man. He handles the minutiae of the job, prepares the reports, and follows up on the individual salesmen. He is the record keeper.

Many sales organizations have acquired this type of double or complementary staffing on a trial-and-error basis. Its sole drawback is the occasional tendency for the roles of the two men to become reversed; that is, the second man is promoted into the top or dominant position with the first man reporting to him. When this occurs, nothing but trouble ensues.

¶ *Rigid structuring* — This approach is especially practical at the first levels of supervision where complementary staffing is not feasible. Its rationale is that most salesmen need continuing help and close supervision in planning their activities and in utilizing their time and efforts most effectively. It also assumes that, left to their own devices, most will do only the minimum which they believe their supervision will accept. Hence, the initiative for much of their activity and its direction must come from without, notably, from their manager. It is he, therefore, who principally determines what his men will accomplish.

Since the first-line supervisor must, perforce, be primarily a salesman — especially in the many companies where he has production as well as supervisory responsibilities — he cannot usually be expected to possess most of the qualifications required of a manager. There are, of course, exceptions to this rule, but they are few in number. In consequence, every phase and aspect of his job must be defined and structured in detail.

Conclusion

There is only one final answer to the problem of inefficient, ineffective sales activity. It is to be found in strong, imaginative, aggressive — even ruthless — leadership at the top of the sales organization. Just as nearly every growth company today reflects the initiative and drive of one man, the daring entrepreneur,[3] so nearly every dynamic and productive sales organization mirrors the drive of one man, its sales manager. It is he who sets the group's objectives; it is he who structures the activities of everyone below him; and it is he who often relentlessly applies continued pressure for superior performance. Within the established structure of policies and politics, he provides opportunities for challenge. He is liberal in his recognition for missions well accomplished, but he demands results — and gets them.

If a subordinate shows initiative and imagination in his work or performs beyond the call of duty, he is rewarded. But the effective sales manager has no unrealistic expectations concerning the role of the great mass of long-service, career sales representatives who compose his organization and provide its backbone. They are the privates in his sales army; they do what they are told. He runs a taut, well-disciplined operation. It is not a democratic one in the conventional sense, but everyone knows what his duties are and what is expected of him.

The greatest contribution of such a manager is not only that he gives the group direction and order, but that, because of his personal strength of character, he imbues the entire organization with a sense of security and certainty. He thereby creates an excellent esprit de corps.

To be sure, he runs a one-man show; he will develop no replacement for himself (he cannot, because he cannot tolerate anyone equal to him in strength). And when he leaves, his successor will have to come in from the outside. But while he is on the job, he and his men will *produce.* His company will have sales representatives who feel that they have a unique and often highly personal contribution to make. In many cases, their presentations will be colorful and dramatic. Often they will bring romance and excitement into lives which are otherwise drab, arid, and sterile.

Typical of such a force's enthusiasm is the close used with great success by one specialty salesman of silverware. With his samples, he carries two tall candlesticks. As he approaches his close, he places his gleaming silver place setting on black velvet display pads on the dining-room table, lights his candles, and turns out the lights. In the romantic atmosphere which he has thus created, he makes his final pitch. He tells the prospect housewife:

> "Madame, there are three apocalyptic moments in every woman's life: when the man she loves tells her he loves her and wants to marry her; when she holds her first-born in her arms; and finally when she looks down on her first sterling silver table service. Sign here, madame. Please use this pencil and press hard; there are four carbons."

[3] See Theodore Levitt, "Marketing Myopia," HBR July–August 1960, p. 56.

Ray C. Brewster

9 More Psychology in Selling

How can we improve our salesmanship? This is indeed a timely question with our economy so heavily weighted on the production side. If we are to find some means of equalizing production's vast advances, we need a more dynamic approach to the unprecedented marketing problem which lies ahead.

Present Inadequacies

That there is much room for improvement can be shown by a brief review of the various factors bearing on sales performance:

1. *Recruiting* — We are not keeping up on our recruiting facilities. According to Walter Ayers, sales director of the Ford Motor Company, while there was one salesman for every 14 workers in other lines in 1940, four years after World War II there was only one salesman for 28 workers. And this does not represent just a postwar lag; nor is it the result of a proportionate gain in per-salesman efficiency. The significant point is that in the face of our growing marketing problem, selling is subject to a long-run trend of decreasing recognition.

If the reputation of selling as a profession continues to deteriorate, the pool of high-caliber recruits will dwindle further. Mothers do not want their sons to be "drummers." Recent admissions of students indicate a waning interest in selling, while engineering, medicine, and other fields are becoming more popular. Accordingly, salesmanship is not billed as a feature course in many schools.

Sales and advertising clubs, in collaboration with individual manufacturers, are doing some special and inspired work to counteract this trend, but apparently they do not have the continuing strength to accomplish the task by themselves. It will take a well-organized national program to restore selling to its "rightful estate."

2. *Training* — In all the manufacturing companies I have observed, the general level of sales training is woefully inadequate. Many manufacturers program their training of new men for one week or less. Few companies have developed a scientific curriculum making use of recent advances in our knowledge of psychology and human behavior. Many lack trained staffs for teaching. Usually, as much as 75% of the training time is applied to imparting information on company products, policies, routines, etc. — which is a prime prerequisite for the salesman in the field but not the same thing as proficiency in selling techniques. And only a minority of companies have developed plans for continuing training beyond occasional sales meetings.

Some companies depend entirely on letting older salesmen train the new ones. The danger is that these "teachers" may not be really well trained themselves — or, even if they are, may not be able to impart their wisdom and experience. For what good there is in this kind of field training, I have found it advisable to put a new salesman out in three territories with at least three older salesmen over a period of three to six weeks; this lessens the possibility of having the salesman frozen in a wrong pattern and at the same time tests his aptitude for the work. If he passes muster up to this point, then he gets the needed several weeks of intensive training in the basics of salesmanship in the home office.

The tendency to overlook the importance of this basic grounding is understandable. Knowledge of the product, for instance, is something tangible and obviously useful — as well as easily taught. In contrast, salesmanship, whatever else it may be, is also a psychological phenomenon which must engage the conscious and subconscious mind; and as such it has long been subject, if not to charlatanry, to very superficial treatment. I know of one college specializing in business administration and marketing where they teach the same rules of selling as were taught there 30 years ago, and another leading college that just recently rejected the idea of including psychology in its selling courses.

The significant point is that the colleges are not to blame for such a state of affairs. They merely reflect what most manufacturers want and have put into their own training courses. Here, again, sales and advertising clubs have worked for improvement, but against heavy odds.

3. *Administration* — Part of the problem lies in administration. In many companies there are two or three people authorized to hire salesmen. They hold widely divergent views in hiring; they evaluate differently. The candidates are trained by a different group, who again have highly personalized ideas on selling. The salesmen are then supervised by one group in the field and still another from the home office. Everybody gets into the act with a different philosophy on salesmen, selling, and management. The result is confusion and frustration among salesmen. They soon lose face and faith, grow unresponsive and mechanical.

Let me illustrate what can happen. When I started as sales manager for a toilet goods company, years ago, my first recommended assignment was to fire a certain salesman in the Texas territory. Upon investigation, the man proved to be really a good salesman who had developed an inferiority complex because of conflicting instructions and requirements from his immediate superiors. No less than three executives in the office and one in the field were telling him what to do. As a result, his attitude had so deteriorated that nothing could be done for him in that company. Yet he later became a top salesman in a competing company.

Such a situation may be extreme, but it is far from uncommon to have a lesser but still critical degree of management neglect of salesmen and misunderstanding of the nature of their jobs. The result — in my own observation of several thousand salesmen over a wide variety of companies — is that most salesmen fail to grow more skillful with experience as do men in other professions; neither do they grow in functional understanding of what they are doing — right or wrong. In fact, only about 20 out of every 100 salesmen keep their production curve going up throughout their careers. The rest slough off to varying degrees after "learning" and "consolidation" periods which last six to eight years — and that represents a real economic loss to their companies.

4. *Understanding* — The lack of understanding about salesmanship is, it seems to me, the one great weakness underlying all the others. I do not refer to the kind of thinking that produced the old stories about the traveling salesman and the farmer's daughter — or of their modern sublimation (truly great as a play but just as erroneous and damaging), *The Death of a Salesman*. Rather, I refer to the fact that even salesmen and sales managers, conscious of the dignity and economic importance of their work, still fail, only too often, to realize the true scope of salesmanship.

A typical group of salesmen will ask for more information about their products; will show interest in the mechanical features of selling like routing, introductions, appointments, use of business cards; will respond to exhortations about personality improvement; and so on. But they appear insensitive to the psychological factors — except the gimmicks and the quackeries like "always look at the bridge of your prospect's nose, because then he thinks you are looking into his eyes but you avoid the danger of his dominating you," which they enjoy only to laugh at. Their attitude is that if they find the right prospects, get themselves well liked, and know enough about their products to present the merits of their wares, then that's the best they can do and they either make the sale or they don't.

Of course all salesmen of any success at all instinctively approach their prospects, organize their data, and exhibit their personalities in such a way as to exert persuasion (high-pressure *or* low-pressure). The point is that until they accept selling as in fact the psychological phenomenon of persuasion, they cannot consciously do more and better what they already do instinctively, and thus cannot realize their full potential.

If any reader has any question at all about this point, just let him dictate a memorandum describing his understanding of selling; and then compare it with similar statements from his sales manager and his five top salesmen; there will be little or nothing in common in his group or, for that matter, with any other sales group.

Role of Psychology

Accordingly, it seems to me that if we are to expect salesmen to become as effective as they *ought* to be, we need to revitalize our whole concept of salesmanship. Specifically, I think we need to broaden and reorient the concept to include the most up-to-date psychological knowledge that is available.

Associating salesmanship with the functions of the mind is certainly not new. Rather, it seems to have been vaguely recognized in top-level discussions for some time. The fact remains that it has been studiously avoided in formal, organized efforts to improve salesmen and salesmanship. This may be so for the same reasons that "impulse selling" was a suspicious and whispered expression in retailing 20 years ago, and "open display" was taboo in 99% of the department stores; we kept away from them because they sounded complicated — and too different.

Our persistence in clinging to a narrow concept of salesmanship is indeed strange in view of the fact that the aim of selling is to persuade, to lead people's minds. Certainly, this objective calls for a fairly sound psychological training on what moves minds and how to do it.

Perhaps the greatest selling fault in a sales presentation is the poor "opener," resulting from the unconscious habit of thinking and feeling in terms of "self." It is as difficult as it is important to think in terms of the prospect or customer. When a salesman's mind is unconsciously host to the "self attitude," he will have trouble in trying to talk convincingly from the other side of the counter or desk. Particularly in the opening of a sales presentation, right at the point when resistance is strongest and needs most to be lulled, the salesman's attitude is crucial.

Similarly, the second most troublesome thing that corrodes salesmanship is the "close" of the presentation. Persuasion may have led the customer to *want* to buy, but he needs an urge for action; his natural inertia must be overcome. And this cannot be achieved unless the salesman acts in terms of the customer's mind, has the feeling of mental leadership. Otherwise, as is all too often the case, the salesman becomes timid, has the subconscious fear of unsuccessfully trying to make the prospect do something that he does not want to do. No one can conceal fear; it shows in the voice, mannerisms, posture, fluency. And fear paralyzes the dynamic "umph" necessary for a close. In my judgment this is the most responsible factor in the high cost of making a sale.

The same thing applies to the sales presentation as a whole. Preplanning is valuable not only because it represents a conscious effort to arrange the selling facts so as to persuade the prospect, but also because it preconditions the salesman and gives him psychological leadership and natural forthrightness. I have seen many incidents where this factor was the measure of success — as for example:

A big hospital had resisted all attempts to sell it a leading brand of ether. The "big guns" of the company tried to make the sale, and one after another admitted defeat. Finally, a new young salesman was allowed to try. He made his presentation confidently — admitting that he wasn't a scientist or an M.D., but arguing that a company like his which sold 89% of all the hospitals at a premium price *must* have a superior product — and urged that the buyer, who had to be satisfied the hospital got the best product for anesthesia regardless of cost, visit the plant and examine at first hand the technical reasons for his company's success.

Subsequently, the sale was made. Note this neophyte's demonstration of confidence in his own company *and* in the hospital's high standards. In other words, the determinant was better psychology, not a more imposing array of technical facts.

Now, let me try to show more specifically some of the possible ways that psychology enters into the success or failure of a sales presentation — in other words, why it is so important and deserves so much more attention than it is getting in most companies. (The fact that my applications may appear less than precise to trained psychologists is only another indication of the need for further research into the whole subject.)

Conscious and Subconscious

The most significant point is the distinction between the conscious mind and the subconscious. We might compare the two parts of the mind with a watch. The face is like the conscious mind, while the works represent the subconscious; the conscious mind tells the time, the subconscious supplies the wherewithal.

The conscious mind can think, but it does not get very far without drawing on the subconscious, where a large part — some psychologists say all — of our previous impressions and experiences are recorded. If the conscious mind were not backed up by this storehouse of thoughts and ideas, it would be inoperable. Yet, though we cannot use the conscious mind without the subconscious, we can use the subconscious without the conscious — as when one puts his foot on the brake of his car at a sudden sign of approaching danger.

The conscious mind with its power to think tends to act as a guard. For example, when somebody wants to change our mind or make us buy something, our conscious mind instantly and automatically goes on the defensive and occasionally adopts an attitude of negative aggression. In contrast, the subconscious is a more pliable and an agreeable sales target. Provided it has no previous prejudices or deep-seated behavior patterns to the contrary, it tends to accept what seems interesting, without protest.

In selling, the salesman's problem is to relax the guard of the conscious mind and get his sales ideas into the subconscious. Resistance cannot completely stop him from implanting his ideas there, but it can defer, distort, or weaken them before they enter. For example:

Suppose a salesman says: "Here is a razor which is better than all other razors." The prospect's subconscious mind might immediately like to have one. But his conscious mind would probably challenge that presumptuous statement and regard all further statements of the salesman suspiciously. He would consciously think: "I have two good razors now. I don't need any more. I question the salesman's veracity."

But suppose the salesman says: "Would you be interested in a new kind of razor if it would cut your shaving time in half and if it would give you a closer and smoother shave?" The prospect's conscious reaction would be different. "Yes," he would think. "If there is such a razor, I would like one. Prove it."

In other words, removing the prospect's resistance at the outset means that the salesman does not have to fight the negative, defensive conscious mind and instead can appeal that much more effectively to the subconscious acquiescence or desire to be kind to the salesman and to buy.

As a matter of fact, the salesman can even turn the defensive guard into a positive ally; he needs to do this particularly when making a sale to industrial buyers. For the thinking mind is able to call upon the subconscious and direct it to select and assemble the pertinent material necessary to support a buying decision.

Establishing Rapport

The ability to establish contact with other people's subconscious is called "rapport." This is what the wise salesman seeks to achieve from the very beginning of his sales call — for instance, by starting off with a statement or question on which he is reasonably certain of mental agreement. Of course, having thus established rapport, the salesman must be careful not to lose it later; if he goes on to take undue advantage of it by using unsound logic or dishonest tactics, the alert conscious mind of the prospect will quickly act to close the channel to the subconscious. But if the salesman remains true to the sincerity and engaging spirit of his opening, then he can go on to win cooperation and maintain agreement throughout his presentation. To illustrate:

A manufacturer developed a floor merchandising cabinet which very intelligently displayed its belt products. Much expensive research was done to establish the efficacy of the cabinets. Tests proved dramatic increases of sales — up to 79%. But since the cabinets cost retailers $300, there was considerable sales resistance.

The salesmen were briefed on the merits of the cabinet, its cost, and the impressive findings of the research. In other words, management gave them "all the facts." Yet at the end of five months, 92 salesmen had sold less than 25 units.

Then the salesmen were briefed again, but this time they were trained on the psychological approach to the problem. In contrast to the previous approach, which was to explain how and why the cabinets would sell *x*% more of the product (thus immediately bringing the retailer's guard up and leading him to think, "If it is that good, why should I invest in a display to sell your merchandise? — give it to me, and we will both sell more"), the psychological approach suggested opening with something like this:

"Mr. Jones, probably the thing you are most interested in is what you can do to make each square foot of occupied space in your department earn more profit. And probably your second most important problem is how to increase "impulse sales" on the most profitable items. I mention this because I believe I may have something which can help solve these problems."

Obviously, such an opening was calculated to gain instant agreement. And when the salesmen went out again, results were quite different. These same salesmen — all 92 of them — in the next four months increased sales of the cabinet units by more than 250%!

The speechmaker who starts with a funny story is also trying unconsciously to get agreement. And when we say, "How is your golf?" or "What a wonderful day!" we are doing much the same thing. Rapport is vital to many types of human relationships. In some of them it is often a matter of "doing what comes naturally," as the song goes; in others — selling, for instance — it takes skill and planning, at least to gain maximum effectiveness.

Suggestion

While the subconscious can never forget the facts and ideas that it holds, the conscious does not always have the power of instantaneously recalling them. Suggestion is often the best activator. The power of suggestion is well known. We use it in our daily lives. When we try to recall a forgotten name, we invariably resort to suggestion — association. Psychiatrists use it. Speakers use it.

Jacob apparently understood the power of suggestion when he put spotted and striped rods over a watering trough where pregnant cattle would see them. When they drank, if you remember the Bible story, they became spotted and striped themselves. Or, to cite a more scientific instance, it was recently reported in medical journals that out of 700 pregnant women 99% went through childbirth without any pain; this involved no drugs, no hypnotism — just suggestion, carefully implanted to secure muscular cooperation and subconscious control of fear.

The value of suggestion in selling should be obvious. Not only is it useful in establishing rapport; when the proper foundation for agreement has been laid, suggestion will help to keep rapport active. This is partly true because suggestions are easily accepted by others as their own ideas. The salesman can fortify this impression. To revert to my case about the display cabinets, when the salesman selling them got along in his presentation, he would occasionally refer to the opener. "Mr. Jones, we agreed that you were interested in making more profit per square foot," he might say. Suggestions, to be effective, must be laid on a proper foundation. They must be relevant, sound, and easily acceptable as the customer's own thinking.

Of course, Franklin D. Roosevelt was a past master at this kind of selling. In every speech he delivered to persuade people he used but one simple formula. For example, if he was addressing a labor group, he would say in effect:

> "My friends, you are interested in greater job security. You want better old age benefits, vacations with pay, and, above all, a fair living wage. We are in agreement on these objectives, I am sure.
>
> "I mention these things because I believe in them and I think I may have a plan which may make all of them immediately possible.
>
> "Here is the first thing I will do. . . . Here is the second. . . . Here is how I will get this for you. . . .
>
> "Since we all want more security, now and in old age . . . and since I have a plan which I have shown will work, your best bet is . . . vote for me."

Customer's Viewpoint

Creative ideas in salesmanship, advertising, and plays are dreamed up to sell, please, or move people, to influence their minds. So it would seem then that one of our chief problems in selling is to be realistic in appraising the customer, in trying to understand his mind. Integrity in a presentation depends on honest concern for the customer's point of view; this may be obvious in the case of industrial buyers, but it is just as true when dealing with consumers. If a presentation is not demonstrably tailored to the real needs or wants of the prospect, it will lack this integrity, and the prospect's conscious mind will reject it.

It is this integrity, faithfully representing the customer's interests, that imparts the ever necessary dignity to a customer's decision to buy. Man instinctively clings to certain dignities which endow his life with little personal glories. He is proud of the dignity of his birth, no matter how humble. He loves the dignity of personal superiority and glories in the dignity of leadership. And, above all, nothing is more precious than the dignity of making his own decisions — particularly decisions to buy. Unless the prospect instinctively feels that his contemplated decision to buy is sound, voluntary, and in line with his own best interests, it will not "pass" in his conscious mind — even if the need or want is fairly substantial.

A somewhat different but completely parallel approach to this problem of customer "know how" is described by Edward C. Bursk in his analytical and very practical paper published six years ago in the HARVARD BUSINESS REVIEW under the title of "Low-Pressure Selling." He observes that selling "is too closely related to the bewildering variousness of human nature — and this, again, is one reason why low-pressure selling, with its flexibility and adaptability, is both more effective and more fun." [1] Low-pressure selling insists upon a deeper, clearer understanding of the human mind and the all-important requirement to let the customer make his own decision in dignity — without force. The importance of this factor can be illustrated by what happens when it is neglected, as for example:

[1] Winter 1947, pp. 241–242.

A salesman was using a high-pressure approach to sell a dramatic big-scale Father's Day promotion to a department store last May. The presentation progressed very soundly until the salesman suggested sales gains for the store which were unrealistic. Then his unreasonable request for additional floor space revealed him as having a "self attitude." His recklessness with promised benefits and his selfish demands robbed his presentation of integrity. Result: a really interested buyer, sensing a proposal lacking in integrity, could not accept values that logically justified a decision to buy. There could be no dignity in his decision.

Psychological Check Points

To check the psychological soundness of a sales approach in terms of its power to create and maintain rapport, here are three rules:

1. *Tune in on the buyer's wave length* — Did you ever try to tune in on a small station with one of those early model bedside radios? Half the time two or three other stations would come through all scrambled up, so you usually turned to a more powerful station. Selling is like that. If the salesman does not tune in on the buyer's wave length, he gets nothing but confusion. Either he fails to make the sale, or it takes longer than it should.

To illustrate, I recently heard a salesman presenting a floor merchandising cabinet to a chain drug store which had the Rexall agency franchise. The first thing the salesman did was to develop fear in the mind of the druggist. He showed that the merchandising cabinet would accelerate sales on the advertised line at the expense of Rexall. In other words, the salesman forgot the buyer's point of view in his determination to sell what he was interested in. Everything he so convincingly said in his presentation put the retailer on the defensive and increased resistance. He wasn't tuned in — even though he otherwise had a fine presentation.

Afterwards the salesman changed his presentation to meet the psychological needs of the situation and said something like this: "Bill, there is a lot of business around here that you are not getting and could. I know, because I have the purchase records of your competitors. You would be interested in picking up this extra business so long as it was plus and wouldn't interfere with the regular sale of Rexall, wouldn't you? Especially if you could get one of these efficient floor merchandisers free — and on top of that, the extra 4% profit on this 'special deal'?" This presentation was tuned in with what the Rexall man thought and felt. It disarmed him, got agreement, and made a sale.

Note particularly that it is not possible ever to tune in on the buyer's wave length by dialing "I," "me," or "my." Those stations are not on a buyer's set. But "you" and "your" are.

2. *Head right; see things as the buyer does* — Sometimes a buyer and seller are like people starting back to back and walking in opposite directions. The more they talk, the further apart they get. This happens when the salesman does not arrange to head for the same objective as his prospect.

For example, a salesman was having a great deal of trouble interesting a very successful doctor in his pollen allergens. Then the doctor happened to mention that his son suffered from hay fever and had to live in a different section of the country to keep his allergy under control. Acting on this knowledge, the salesman started at once to talk about the doctor's son and the reasons why the particular pollen allergen he was selling might prove more beneficial than the ones the son had tried in vain. He ended up making a sale despite his false start, which indicated an improper "tuning in."

Note that this does not mean talking about what you think the buyer *ought* to be interested in, but about what you know (or have good reason to think) he *is* interested in. You can always win arguments with customers — arguments, not sales. The moment you talk in terms of the customer's interest, however, you avoid arguments and win sales.

3. *Avoid "interference" by staying tuned in* — Recently, I heard an important publisher address a large audience. He started off by discussing the fascinating work of war correspondents and their experiences in Korea. He talked very knowingly about the possible outcome of the war. Like the rest of the audience I was spellbound — until finally the editor got around to his own business problem (which turned out to be the reason for his address). When he started talking circulation, editorial content, and so on, the audience immediately settled back to deliberate on how hard the seats were and how stuffy the room was.

Although our speaker was brilliant and dynamic, he did not stay tuned in and promptly lost his audience as a result. The salesman who makes this mistake with his prospect pays the same penalty.

Natural Selling Formula

I believe that there is a natural formula for a successful sales presentation. It is based on the psychological principles we have been discussing.

The four steps in this formula are outlined in Exhibit i. In the following pages I shall discuss certain points about them that I feel are particularly significant and show in a little more detail how and why they work.

Show Openers

There is certainly nothing new in the thought that a sales presentation should describe the

EXHIBIT I. THE NATURAL FORMULA FOR PERSUASIVE PRESENTATION

Step	Generic term	Explanation
Step I	Show openers. Establish mental accord.	Make openers something customers surely want. Relax conscious defense mechanism. Keep openers logical — possible — provable. Be able to relate them to your product, naturally, in presentation. Build integrity in presentation.
Step II	Declare your hand. Tie in product.	Tie in openers to your proposition. Establish "I want what you propose — prove it" attitude. Fortify psychological position by leaving decisions to prospect.
Step III	Prove openers.	Prove only each point in openers — no variation. Summarize when points are proved — with brevity — tersely. Relate proved points to original agreement. Keep prospect's mind on track. Blend steps III and IV into one close.
Step IV	Showdown. Pay me — Close!	Refer to original accord. Refer to proof. Suggest affirmative action. Repeat customer need. Give choice and alternative for affirmative action.

benefits of the product to the buyer. Yet in probably 85% of all presentations the real customer benefits are obscured, subordinated, and often presented at the wrong time. As a result, the prospect gains time to develop additional and considered resistance.

The average salesman thinks too much about his order and the expected resistance. He becomes fearful and is forced to operate a mental offensive with defensive tactics. For example, a short while ago an experienced $10,000-a-year automobile salesman came into my office to sell me a certain car. His actual opening was this:

"I understand that you came in recently to buy one of our cars — and that nobody followed up on your inquiry. This certainly shouldn't have happened. However, I am here to tell you all about our beautiful new '53 models. This is the one [here he showed me the catalogue] I think you would like best . . ." and so on, with all the price details and other facts about the motor, clutch, and differential.

There was nothing engaging in these openers — not even a first-class apology. So no matter what he said from there on out, my resistance was bound to grow in effectiveness. He spoke of no specific thing that I wanted; certainly there was no effort to develop "accord" at the outset; and he "headed wrong," introducing elements that were not important.

He had no understanding of the psychological steps which he should have taken. Yet later on in the discussion I discovered that he had spent hours in memorizing population figures, income groups, and so on by counties and towns. He was a student of all the mechanical facts. But nobody had ever shown him really how to sell. To him, selling was just good talking and personality. He knew there had to be a close, but had no idea how to work up to it. Yet isn't all this really pretty typical of what salesmen are doing all around us?

That salesman could have turned his organization's slip-up into an excellent selling opener by saying something like this:

"Mr. Brewster, you were good enough to visit our showroom recently and indicate an interest in our cars. To my astonishment, I have just found that there wasn't an immediate follow-through. We certainly could never afford to miss the opportunity of doing business with you. From your standpoint, there may not be any special reason why you should buy a car from us, but I can assure you that we have a very strong reason for wanting you for one of our customers. It would be very important to us to have you drive one of our '53 models.

"Furthermore, Mr. Brewster, I believe you mentioned that Mrs. Brewster has had some trouble with her arm and that driving and parking a heavy car with a long wheel base have become quite a problem for her. [Of course he might not have found out about this, but he could have made a personal tie-in some other way.]

"I mention this because since my company pioneered power steering, I think we may have a dependable solution to Mrs. Brewster's problem without forcing her to a smaller car. She could literally turn the wheel for parking with the pressure from one finger." And so forth.

In other words, that salesman, with a good healthy apology could have converted a regrettable incident into a real advantage in the form of an opener. Adding a touch of believable flattery, repeating his prospect's name a few times, and making some personal reference, he could have had a perfect opener, gaining complete accord and even conscious cooperation on my part.

People naturally resist persuasion unless it is in the direction of something they want. This is why proper openers are all-important. If every presentation had them, sales results would multiply even if the content of the rest of the presentation were not improved proportionately.

Declare Your Hand

But no matter how good his openers, a salesman still has a big job to do in most cases. The prospect is still skeptical. "What has all this, interesting as it is, to do with me?" he thinks. "What are you leading up to?"

Accordingly, the psychology of selling requires the salesman to take a second step in order to delay suspicion in the prospect's mind and to consolidate the "mental accord" established by the openers. He must offer the prospect the dignity of choice. While the conscious mind may be willing to buy, it does not want anybody making decisions for it. Accordingly, the salesman needs to say something like "I mention this because I think I may have a solution to that problem" or "I think I may have a product which will do these things." Several important things are thus accomplished: (a) the salesman anticipates what the prospect is likely to be thinking; and (b) he avoids making a challenging positive statement like "I will prove that I have what you want."

Step II may be regarded as one of psychological politeness. It gives graciously, yields to the other fellow's mind the privileges of selection and decision. It helps to consolidate rapport and widen the salesman's entree into the subconscious of the prospect.

Normally, Step II should be cut in innocuously and fast, as a tail end of Step I.

Prove Openers

The first two steps should convince the prospect that the salesman is talking about what he approves of and that proof will be offered to establish specifically what was originally agreed upon. The salesman can now go on to the third step. In doing so, it is good practice for him to refer occasionally to his openers. This refreshes the prospect's confidence, and it also keeps the presentation on the track. Furthermore, since the conscious mind quickly considers the idea in the openers its own, repetition often puts the prospect in the state of mind where he wants the proof to be satisfactory. He wants to buy if he can do so without pressure.

The power of a salesman to impress his proof lastingly in the prospect's mind, following good openers, can be shown by an everyday example:

A few years ago a clothing salesman sold a prospect on the virtues of a vicuna coat. However, the prospect had three topcoats already and couldn't afford the price of an additional expensive vicuna, so he didn't buy. But three years later he did need a topcoat. He was still so completely sold on vicuna that he went out of his way to return to the particular store where the salesman worked. This time he did buy — with practically no further effort on the salesman's part. Nothing would change his conviction about the virtues of vicuna.

In Step III the salesman proves just the material in the openers, with no variations or deviations. This keeps things from getting complicated, emphasizes the common objectives, and also saves time.

The Close

Again, some reference to the openers used is indicated when the proofs have been established. This sort of repetition crystallizes the whole presentation and makes it more acceptable. The salesman can wind things up with a confident suggestion for positive action. For example:

"We pretty well agreed, Doctor, that it would be a good thing for the practice of medicine if there was a product which would give a faster and more sustained hemoglobin gain — especially without the usual nausea to the patient. The clinical testing I have shown you pretty well establishes that the product does give a faster, more sustained hemoglobin gain — without nausea. I think that perhaps you may properly wonder if this product will perform for your patients as well as it did in the 5,000 tests for those scientists. Try it on your next ten food-iron deficiency cases; check your results carefully against these scientists' findings. I'll leave this literature marked for further reference — the product is available for your prescription at your pharmacy — it costs no more than ordinary products. Would you like these samples to get you started, Doctor?" And so on.

Knowing that he builds agreement and cooperation as he proceeds, the salesman has good reason for the confidence that he needs to close his presentation successfully and clinch the sale. He feels the rapport that he builds in the prospect's mind. When he gets to the all-important close, there is no subconscious reason for hesitancy or fear to get that name on the dotted line. He can "let go." Normally he can devote to the close as much as 40% or 50% of the presentation time.

Then the instant a sale is completed, the conversation should be diverted to plans for merchandising, displaying, and other services which salesmen can and should render and which will hasten the satisfaction from the purchase. In other words, the salesman should assume a continuing responsibility. Real salesmanship only begins with the order. What happens after that is what determines the effectiveness of the salesman both in terms of volume and selling cost.

Example from Radio

A splendid example of the psychological pattern of a short hard-hitting sales presentation is given verbatim in the following transcription of a Roy Rogers radio commercial for Quaker Oats:

Step I: "Would you like to do the very same things that Roy Rogers did when he was your age?" (The children in the audience, having just heard thrilling exploits of their hero, want to do what he does and be like him.)

Step II: "Do you know what you would likely eat for breakfast tomorrow? A good hearty delicious bowl of Quaker Oats." (This statement ties the product in naturally. It consolidates the agreement made in Step 1. It sets up the pattern of the presentation to follow.)

Step III: "Yes sirree! Here's the facts straight from Roy Rogers himself. He says 'Partners, I was raised on Quaker Oats — the giant of cereals.' " (Roy's voice was dubbed in here, and what he says is proof believable to kids.)

Step IV: "So, fellows, every time you eat Quaker Oats you are getting the cereal that Roy Rogers was raised on, the cereal that helps grow the stars of the future — stars in games, sports, and other activities. You get more growth, more endurance, from oatmeal than from any other whole grain cereal. So, if you want to be able to do the things that Roy Rogers does, eat Quaker Oats for breakfast every day." (This close represents 40% of the presentation. It is strong and logical, and refers back to the openers in asking for logical action.)

Once a sound formula like this is thoroughly understood and practiced, it can henceforth be employed unconsciously and automatically — much in the same manner that we compose sentences in ordinary conversation, not thinking whether the subject or the predicate is in the right place but getting them there just the same. But an unsound formula never seems to form an exact habit pattern.

Conclusion

The most sober thought that we can hold for the future is that for the first time in history the stability of our economy will be based primarily on our ability to sell. Probably what we need to sell is enough goods to provide a 30% better standard of living than at present. We must therefore find a perfection and efficiency in distribution that can only come out of a deeper and clearer knowledge of what moves people to buy — easier, faster, and more.

In this discussion I have dealt entirely with present salesmanship and one direction from which a better, more secure economy might come. I do not suggest that this discussion covers the entire subject of selling. Neither do I want to imply the slightest criticism of the remarkable job which has been done in distribution. Rather, my aim has been to stimulate serious thought on a subject which is vitally important to the future of business.

Without more basic research on people and their ways of thinking, we cannot cope with the problems that lie ahead in retailing, wholesaling, advertising, displays, transportation, and salesmanship. In the meantime, however, thoughtful sales managers could make very good use of what we already know about the psychological aspects of selling.

The Role of the Sales Force Manager

Raymond O. Loen

10 Sales Managers Must Manage

¶ The department head of a major corporation recently told me: "The division head to whom I report can talk for hours about modern concepts of managing, and it sounds like chapter and verse from a dissertation about how to be a modern executive. But almost as soon as he gets back to his operating responsibilities, he seems like a different man. In my area of responsibility, for example, he gets unduly engrossed in the very problems he says he expects me and my people to handle."

¶ A staff marketing manager had just completed discussing the modern concepts of managing to which he said he subscribes when the phone rang. It was a customer with a complaint which line sales should have handled. Yet the marketing manager assumed undue responsibility for the matter, apparently without realizing that he was violating one of his avowed precepts of managing.

¶ A field sales manager with whom I met several times proudly proclaimed the progress he was making in developing his salesmen. Yet my meetings with this sales manager were interrupted repeatedly by his salesmen, most of them asking for solutions to fairly routine sales problems. It was apparent that the salesmen brought such problems to him only because they had learned that he wanted them to do so. I do not recall a single instance where the sales manager asked any of the salesmen to suggest a solution.

Managing vs. Doing

Anyone who attempts to examine the difference between the theory and the practice of managing can find hundreds of similar examples throughout his business environment. Why is this so? Companies *try* to instill the management point of view in their executives by:

- Hiring graduates from the top-rated business schools.
- Putting managers through their own management development programs.
- Sending their managers to management courses and seminars.
- Encouraging their managers to read and study modern methods of managing.

The inherent assumption in such actions is that if managers are exposed to many and varied approaches to effective managing, they will be able to translate what they see and hear for application to their particular jobs.

The fact is that *most practicing managers have relatively little time to study managing.*

And when they do study the subject in any depth, most find it is complicated and elusive. Either the subject is treated with far more semantic sophistication than they can realistically apply, or it has a ring of academic gobbledygook. The result: most managers find, perhaps subconsciously, that they are managing by *doing*. They are excelling in the very skills that earned most of them their jobs as managers, i.e., solving *non*managing, technical problems!

Almost any manager today can talk the language of managing in terms such as planning, directing, and controlling. But the test of being an effective manager is really to understand managing well enough to practice it in day-to-day responsibilities.

Analyzing the Job

Today's sales manager often exemplifies this problem of managing by doing. Let us look briefly at the sales manager's job and training in order to better appreciate the problem. The effectiveness of the marketing effort in many companies is dependent on the sales manager and his ability to get results through his sales personnel. The difference between a capable sales manager and a not-so-capable sales manager can make a significant difference in sales, profits, and whether or not the cost of a marketing program pays off. In such instances, sales managers are responsible for hiring, training, motivating, and directing the sales personnel, who in turn persuade customers to buy. This latter job of persuading customers is a challenging one and is the ultimate payoff for the salesman and the company. Usually it is also a job that the sales manager learned to do well before becoming a manager. As a result, most sales managers sell — what they like to do and do well — when they should manage. Indeed many think they are managing when they are in fact selling — often duplicating the efforts of their salesmen — or performing some other nonmanaging activity.

Every sales manager has certain nonmanaging activities which he alone must perform. But how much is he contributing to the marketing effort when he spends his time unnecessarily on nonmanaging activities instead of on managing which would enable him to multiply his efforts many times through his people?

Most companies today spend a great deal of money to train their sales personnel. Yet many of these same companies appear to expect their sales managers to learn their jobs by osmosis. Or if they provide organized training for their sales managers, it is restricted largely to company procedures such as hiring, forecasting, and budgeting, or to increasing functional knowledge of marketing, personnel, accounting, engineering, production, or the like. A sales manager must certainly understand the necessary procedures which he is expected to follow as well as the additional functional knowledge which will generally help him technically or provide him with a broader perspective. But the training which is usually neglected is a *clear concept of what constitutes managing,* so that the sales manager can best apply the procedures or utilize the increased functional knowledge in order to multiply and maximize his efforts through the individuals in his department.

What Are the Elements?

Even though managers understand many aspects of managing, they have trouble distinguishing the elements of managing from those of nonmanaging activities in their actual day-to-day activities. Our experience indicates that most sales managers have difficulty deciding which activities are managing, and which are nonmanaging or "doing." For example, which of the following activities would *you* say are managing, as distinguished from nonmanaging (i.e., doing), activities:

1. Calling on an account with one of your salesmen to show a customer that company management is interested in the account.
2. Making a sales presentation to a prospective customer in order to show one of your salesmen how to do it.
3. Making an independent call on an officer of a large account in order to cement customer relationships and promote business.
4. Explaining how to solve a work problem which one of your people has just brought to you.
5. Filling out a form to recommend a salary increase for a member of your department.
6. Explaining to one of your people why he is receiving a salary increase.
7. Interviewing a prospective salesman referred to you by an employment agency.
8. Giving a telephone report of progress to your superior.
9. Asking one of your salesmen what he thinks about a selling idea you have.

10. Planning and deciding on a dollar sales objective by account.

11. Deciding what the cost budget request shall be for your sales office.

12. Reviewing monthly sales reports to determine progress toward specific sales objectives.

13. Deciding whether to meet a competitive price based on considerations beyond what the salesman has access to.

14. Deciding whether to recommend adding a position.

15. Drafting an improved sales office layout.

16. Asking your salesmen to establish tentative six-month objectives for the number of personal sales calls to be made on target accounts.

17. Giving a talk about your company's progress and plans to a local service club.

18. Transferring an account from Salesman A to Salesman B because Salesman A did not devote the necessary effort to develop the account.

19. Phoning a plant manager to request help in solving a customer delivery problem for one of your salesmen.

20. Planning the extent to which your salesmen should use staff services during the next year to accomplish over-all sales objectives.

Concept of Managing

Before looking at suggested answers and explanations to the listing, let us consider a proposed simplified concept of managing for sales managers.

Managing can be defined as planning, directing, and controlling the activities of other people in the same organization in order to achieve or exceed desired objectives. It does have other meanings, but the managing we are concerned with here is the managing one is expected to do when he wants to get results through others.

It is easy to confuse selling with managing because one who sells is expected to get sales results through customers and prospects. Selling is not managing, however. The essential difference is that a person in a managerial position has authority and responsibility to get a job done through others in the same organization — and these others are expected to recognize his authority and responsibility to help accomplish the over-all objectives of the enterprise.

Helpful Classifications

How does an objective differ from a forecast, or a budget, or a program? How does a policy differ from a procedure? These and other elements of managing can be distinguished and classified under the headings of planning, directing, and controlling:

Planning	*Directing*	*Controlling*
Developing . . .	Supervising	Measuring
forecasts	Delegating	Evaluating
objectives	Motivating	Correcting
organization	Coordinating	
policies	Counseling	
procedures	Staffing	
programs	Training	
schedules		
standards		
budgets		

In addition, communicating, deciding, and improving are applicable to each of the elements of managing. A manager must communicate and decide in accomplishing the other elements of managing, and he should certainly strive to improve in all elements of his managing. Definitions for each of these elements of managing along with examples tailored to the sales manager are listed in EXHIBIT I.

Suggested Answers

Now let us look at suggested answers (with explanations) to the managing versus doing activities listed earlier:

1. *Doing.* This may be a highly necessary activity, but it is selling, not managing. The direct purpose of the call is not to get results through others.

2. *Managing.* This is training.

3. *Doing.* This is selling. The direct purpose is *not* to get results through others.

4. *Managing.* This is supervising, assuming the manager does not have his people come to him (so he can feel sufficiently needed or productive) for routine solutions to recurring problems which they are capable of handling. It would be counseling if a more formal, planned personal discussion were needed.

5. *Doing.* The actual filling out of the form is clerical. Instructing your secretary how to fill it out would be a managing activity in that it would be delegating.

6. *Managing.* This is motivating.

7. *Doing.* This may be an essential activity, but the manager is actually performing a personnel function in the same way that he is selling when calls on accounts. When he does interviewing, he is not currently getting results through others. Deciding to hire someone after all the recruiting and selecting has been done,

however, would be considered a managing activity.

8. *Managing.* This is communicating for the purpose of control, provided the manager is doing so to receive possible guidance and direction. Otherwise it may be plain communicating, which anyone does whether he is a manager or not.

9. *Managing.* This is communicating, probably in order to develop a selling program, and it could be a form of motivating if the manager's main purpose is to have the salesman participate in developing the idea in order to get later acceptance.

10. *Doing.* The manager is developing objectives — which is a managing activity — but he is not delegating; he is developing objectives by account which his salesmen should be best qualified to do since they work closely with the accounts. Were he to review the sales objectives of one of his salesmen, he would be managing, in that he would undoubtedly be planning part of an over-all sales objective to be accomplished by the salesmen as a group.

11. *Managing.* This is planning — developing a budget. Putting the budget in its proper form would be clerical.

12. *Managing.* This is measuring and evaluating.

13. *Managing.* This is probably coordinating — making sure that any price deviations are consistent with an over-all plan. This would be a doing activity, however, if procedures and controls could be set up in such a way that certain pricing decisions could be delegated.

14. *Managing.* This is developing the organization structure.

15. *Doing.* This is a methods engineering function. Deciding to get an improved office layout would be a managing activity.

16. *Managing.* This is developing objectives as well as standards of performance.

17. *Doing.* This is performing a public relations function.

18. *Managing.* This is correcting — taking corrective control action. This could also be considered the disciplining part of supervising.

19. *Doing.* This may be necessary, but it is the inside part of a salesman's job. The direct purpose of the phone call is *not* to get results through, but rather for, your salesman.

20. *Managing.* This is developing a program of marketing strategy to achieve group results.

We can see that the difference between doing and managing can be subtle in many instances. Indeed two sales managers can appear to be performing identical activities; yet we would say one is managing and the other is not — depending on whether one's *intent* is to get results through others.

Awareness of Managing

I have pointed out that every sales manager has certain nonmanaging activities which he alone must perform. In fact, *some of the sales manager's nonmanaging activities may be more important than his managing activities* in accomplishing the objectives of the enterprise. For example, this may be true where the sales manager is asked to establish and maintain working relationships with decision-making executives in large volume accounts; it may also be true where the sales manager is asked to participate in local community affairs because significant business is placed locally.

However, in most companies, managing responsibility is generally greater or more important than doing responsibility. Accordingly, *it is important for the sales manager to have an awareness that he is not managing when he personally does selling, public relations, or the like.* Only with this kind of awareness is he apt to strive to do as much managing as he should in his current job; only with this awareness is he apt to be able to develop himself as much as he should for the broader responsibilities where managing activities assume even greater importance to his company.

Teaching Managing

If sales managers are to manage as well as they should, top management will need to provide the climate and instigate or approve certain actions. Three examples of such actions follow.

1. *Developing and disseminating a company-wide managing philosophy.* This involves considering and communicating the facts that the company recognizes managing as a separate and distinct activity, and that managers should develop managing skills.

It is also highly desirable to relate the managing philosophy to corporate purposes or long-range objectives in terms of the products to be made, services to be rendered, markets to be served, obligations to all concerned, and profits and growth to be sought. For example:

In a few companies, the presidents have actually conducted a managing program for those re-

EXHIBIT I. DEFINITIONS OF THE ELEMENTS OF MANAGING WITH EXAMPLES TAILORED TO THE SALES MANAGER

PLANNING—
DETERMINING WHAT NEEDS TO BE DONE BY WHOM AND BY WHEN IN ORDER TO FULFILL ONE'S ASSIGNED RESPONSIBILITY

FORECAST
A projection about what will happen by a certain time. Example: The amount of dollar sales which will be realized for the year.

OBJECTIVE
A goal, target, or quota to be achieved or exceeded by a certain time. Example: The amount of dollar sales which a person will strive to achieve or exceed for the year. An objective is often higher than a forecast.

ORGANIZATION
Design of the number and kinds of positions, along with corresponding duties and responsibilities, required to attain or exceed objectives. Example: The number of sales, clerical, and managing positions required to obtain annual sales of $3 million in a certain geographical area.

POLICY
A formal or informal practice which serves as a general guide for decision making and individual actions. Example: Policy of Product Performance, in which the company guarantees customers that its products will perform or function as advertised.

PROCEDURE
A detailed method for carrying out a policy. Example: A claim and complaint procedure for effecting a product performance policy.

PROGRAM
Strategy to be followed or major actions to be taken to achieve or exceed objectives. Example: Obtain trial orders of New Product A in five major accounts.

SCHEDULE
A plan showing when individual and/or group activities or accomplishments will be started and/or completed. Example: A salesman's daily call plan for a week. (Often a program and schedule are combined.)

STANDARD
Criteria for determining the degree to which the individual or group performance has been met. Example: At least 10% of a salesman's total business is to be new business.

BUDGET
Planned expenditures required to achieve or exceed objectives. Example: The dollar savings required to support the necessary staff for achieving or exceeding an annual dollar sales objective.

DIRECTING—
EXERCISING LEADERSHIP AND HUMAN RELATIONS SKILLS IN IMPLEMENTING AND CARRYING OUT APPROVED PLANS THROUGH OTHERS IN ORDER TO ATTAIN OR EXCEED OBJECTIVES

SUPERVISING
Giving day-to-day instruction, guidance, and coaching to subordinates in implementing and carrying out approved plans. Example: Explaining to a salesman his part in carrying out the marketing plan.

DELEGATING
Assigning work, responsibility, and authority so that everyone can use his abilities to the utmost. Example: Asking subordinates to offer a suggested solution whenever they have a problem.

MOTIVATING
Inspiring and encouraging subordinates by giving or offering tangible and/or intangible reward for achieving or exceeding objectives. Example: Commending a salesman in a sales meeting for exceeding his target business objective.

COORDINATING
Seeing that activities are carried out in relation to their importance and with a minimum of conflict. Example: Holding sales meetings when it is impractical to make customer calls.

COUNSELING
Holding a planned discussion with a subordinate about how he might do better work, solve a personal problem, or realize his ambitions. Example: Holding a planned private discussion with a salesman to help him realize the need for planning better how to utilize his time.

STAFFING
Seeing that qualified people are recruited and selected for each planned position. Example: Hiring a salesman for a new territory.

TRAINING
Explaining and/or showing in planned individual and group meetings how to perform one's duties and responsibilities. Example: Accompanying a salesman on calls and helping him evaluate his effectiveness after each call.

CONTROLLING—
MEASURING PROGRESS TOWARD OBJECTIVES, EVALUATING WHAT NEEDS TO BE DONE, AND THEN TAKING CORRECTIVE ACTION TO ACHIEVE OR EXCEED OBJECTIVES

MEASURING
Determining through formal and informal oral and visual reports the degree to which progress toward objectives is being made. Example: Reviewing of monthly sales performance reports to determine progress toward group and individual objectives.

EVALUATING
Determining which are significant deviations from planned performance as well as the importance of various factors which affect results. Example: Calling on accounts with salesmen to determine whether sales problems are customer centered, salesman centered, or policy centered.

CORRECTING
Determining and taking control action designed to correct an unfavorable trend or to take advantage of an unusually favorable trend. Example: Planning and holding training meetings with salesmen to improve their abilities in making customer surveys which are intended to help increase sales in target accounts.

COMMUNICATING — Keeping subordinates, associates, superiors, and others informed about plans and activities through discussions, reports, letters, memos, and the like. Example: Explaining a new procedure in a meeting with subordinates.

DECIDING — Making a judgment about a course of action to be taken. Example: Determining whether to request a salary increase for a subordinate.

IMPROVING — Developing more effective and/or economical procedures, policies, organization, products, equipment, and/or facilities. Example: Adjusting account assignments so that existing sales force can handle significant additional business with no increase in staff.

porting to them who, in turn, have conducted the same program for those reporting to them — and so on down through first-line supervision. The purpose is to ensure common understanding about both corporate objectives and a corporate managing philosophy.

2. *Developing and implementing a program or programs designed to help sales managers having similar responsibilities to translate "textbook" managing into reality.* This includes learning how to distinguish managing from doing in their particular job. For instance:

One large company has its sales managers attend several programs which it conducts. First, sales managers, along with other functional managers in the company, participate in a program designed to define and gain understanding of managing as a separate and distinct activity. Next, sales managers, along with other functional managers in the company, attend another program covering company marketing functions such as selling, customer service, advertising and sales promotion, and market research. Then, to exchange ideas and solutions to mutual managing problems, sales managers attend still another program designed specifically for sales managers with similar responsibilities.

Where this company uses several of its own programs to develop its sales managers, other companies with less complicated products and organization can accomplish similar results with only one program. Specifically:

Another large company uses a one-week program developed specifically to teach managing to its sales managers. The program is divided into nine sections: introduction, planning, organizing, directing through communication, directing through human relations, directing through leadership, directing through personnel development, measuring results, and cases in professional management. The program has planned follow-up. It is also being extended to cover both staff personnel who work with sales managers and potential sales managers.

3. *Ensuring that the sales manager's work conditions will allow him to manage.* Even the best training or management development program in the world does not guarantee that a man will practice what he has learned. Most management seminars and courses leave the manager with an implied, "Go ye therefore and sin no more." But the manager finds that it is a long road from the conference room to the job. As a result there are hundreds of thousands of dollars largely wasted in training and development programs every year. To ensure putting the managing theory into practice — to ensure real learning which many say can occur only on the job — there are three main considerations:

- The sales manager, like any other manager, is going to do what his boss tells him to do or expects of him — provided he wants to stay on the payroll. If, however, top management has not been exposed to, or is not in general sympathy with, the managing concepts promulgated in a sales manager's program, the sales manager will be seriously limited in trying to apply what he learned. Indeed, the program may do more harm than good since the sales manager may become frustrated — perhaps to the point of leaving the company. This upholds the need for a company managing philosophy, but it also supports the need for the sales manager's top management to participate in developing and conducting a sales manager's program. Leaving the job entirely to corporate staff or to an outside consultant is not going to produce the desired results.

- The sales manager's job content should be scrutinized to provide him with the responsibility and authority he needs to be able to manage. There are still hundreds of companies which hold their sales managers much more responsible for handling personal sales than for getting sales results through their salesmen. Then there is this kind of situation:

  An industrial products company relieved most of its sales managers from responsibility for personal sales. But it reserved many managing decisions for the general management level or for headquarters staff. The result was that the sales managers complained that they were largely funnels for information going up or coming down — such as routine pricing decisions or nominal salary increases for their people.

- The management control reports which the sales manager receives and submits to top management should be designed to prod him into doing a balanced job of managing. Frequently the sales manager is asked to get along with control information developed primarily for accounting purposes. Not enough companies have analyzed the specific needs of the sales manager and designed their reports to help him *manage*.

- Often the sales manager is told that one of his prime managing responsibilities is to help increase corporate profits, but he has neither a profit contribution objective nor the scorecard to tell him how he is doing. His control reports are often limited to sales performance and sales expense budget compliance, which are translated into profit figures only at division or headquarters levels where accounting statements are customarily prepared. Under these conditions, the sales manager is tempted to accept unprofitable business because when his total sales are reviewed, the large unprofitable order contributes to making him look better than the small profitable order.

¶ To encourage their sales managers to manage with corporate objectives in mind, a number of companies give their sales managers responsibility for achieving a profit contribution, gross profit, or marginal income objective as related to those factors under control by the sales manager.

Probably most top managements would agree that it is desirable to teach sales managers how to manage and that these actions make sense. Why, then, haven't more companies done so?

Bars to Progress

There are a number of reasons why companies have not taught their sales managers to manage as well as they should. What are the more prevalent bars to progress?

(1) There has been an overreliance on internal and external management development programs designed for managers in general. Sales managers have often been expected to learn managing cafeteria-style, taking some knowledge from here and some from there. Putting this knowledge into a meaningful framework for a particular job has been left largely up to the individual sales manager. As the director of personnel in a major corporation recently put it to me: "Sales managers learn blue-sky theory about managing in a typical management program, but by themselves they don't make the transition from the program to the job."

(2) Companies think that it is impractical to get sales managers together for any length of time — else the wheels of business will stop turning. They think that it is difficult enough to get the sales managers together for vital administrative matters such as the introduction of new products, policies, or procedures.

I am sympathetic with this viewpoint, but it seems to me that the problem is more one of determining how important the sales manager's *managing* is to the success of the marketing effort. A company can find the method (not necessarily a conventional one), the time, and the money for anything it believes is really important.

(3) Some companies fear that if you emphasize a sales manager's role as a manager, he will get grandiose ideas of his job and will no longer want to "roll up his sleeves and get his hands dirty" — he will no longer feel compelled to continue to know the business. The fear is that the sales manager will become insulated from what is going on — that his men will be able to pull the wool over his eyes, that he will have to consult his people whenever top management wants specific information. This is what one executive meant when he told me: "Our company isn't large enough for us to afford sales managers who just manage."

Such an argument is reasonable, perhaps, when the main responsibility of the sales manager is not to get results through others. But, as I have contended throughout this article, if the sales manager's main contribution to a marketing program's success is to get results through his salesmen, then he should have a clear concept of managing as applied to his job. This means clarifying how he is to exercise judgment in keeping informed about details of customers, the market, problems and activities of his men, and so forth in relation to his responsibility to manage and to perform nonmanaging activities.

In general, it is a misconception that a manager who manages doesn't "get his hands dirty." But there are time limitations. Shall the sales manager keep informed about details of customers at the expense of developing the individuals in his department or of planning field implementation of marketing strategy? Shall he manage by exception? If so, how? And what is an approximate dollar value of a sales manager's time as he performs various managing and nonmanaging activities?

A program which has been carefully developed to provide discussion of, and the basis for sound answers to, these kinds of questions is certainly going to give the sales manager a better *modus operandi* than when he has to develop the answers primarily by himself.

(4) There are companies which rely largely on procedures and controls to see that a sales manager does his job. They teach him the procedures for hiring, training, forecasting, reporting, and so on, and see that he follows them — teach him to be a mechanic, not an engineer. This is fine for companies which can develop enough procedures and foolproof controls and which can find sales managers who do not mind being automatons with relatively little responsibility for independent judgment and creative

solutions to management problems. The only problem is that it is very difficult to attract and hold high caliber people who are qualified for and want responsibility.

(5) Many members of top management have not yet learned to distinguish between managing and doing. Although management theorists and those who stay abreast of management thinking have had this awareness for a long while, it usually takes years for sound management theory to be translated into practice in the majority of companies across the country. This is a problem particularly in sales management, where many top executives have worked their way up through top field sales performances; their own past skills may have been largely in doing.

It seems to me that the over-all impediment to getting sales managers to understand managing has been primarily one of recognition of what managing is.

Conclusion

Not too many years ago, the most prevalent practice in training salesmen was to give the new salesman a demonstrator, a price list, an order pad, and a kick in the pants to get out there and make those calls. In some ways, it seems to me, today's training for sales managers is about where sales training was then. Many a sales manager is put in the job and told to manage. If he gets training or development, as he does in many companies, much of it misses the target.

My thesis has been that if the sales manager's most important responsibility is to manage, then basic to his training and development should be an understanding of what managing is. But to get this understanding, I submit, requires a simplified concept of managing and a program specifically designed around the day-to-day duties and responsibilities of sales managers in similar jobs in the same company — otherwise they do not really learn to distinguish managing from nonmanaging or doing.

The courses of action I propose are applicable to both large and small companies. The results of these actions can have a significant effect on a company's profit and loss statement where the sales manager's role in the marketing effort is an important one.

Robert T. Davis

11 Sales Management in the Field

◖ The Life Insurance Agency Management Association recently kept track of the careers of 100 insurance salesmen who were assigned at random to competent and less-than-competent local managers. These salesmen were given a battery of tests when hired and graded A or B. After several years, an examination of the personnel records revealed that salesmen who worked for competent managers had a much greater chance of success than their unfortunate brethren with incompetent superiors.

Specifically, 48% of the A salesmen succeeded under good supervision; only 27% under poor supervision. Correspondingly, B salesmen with good supervision had nearly five times as much chance for success as their counterparts with poor supervision. Moreover, a B salesman with a strong manager had the same chance as an A salesman with a poor manager.

◖ The same research association analyzed salesman-turnover figures for a single life insurance company and sent questionnaires to over 650 salesmen — both "survivors" and "terminators." The study concluded that dissatisfaction with local supervision was the single most important reason for salesman termination.

◖ New salesmen in a large typewriter company were assigned to a local branch for 8 to 12 months of "feet-wetting" experience in the field. During this period, and with a minimum of training, these men "cold-canvassed" special territories. If they survived this baptism under fire, they were sent to the firm's central school for 5 weeks of training before being assigned a regular sales territory.

The sales vice president was not surprised when the turnover statistics showed a termination peak between the third and sixth months of employment. He was, however, extremely upset to find a second peak equally as high during the three months immediately after the training course. Investigation showed that the salesmen received their best supervision at the training school and missed it sorely when given permanent field assignments.

Obviously, marketing executives have failed to give adequate attention to their field sales managers. Package and product design, product testing, marketing research — all have been subject to careful scrutiny — and rightly so. Now executives need to take as close a look at their strategically situated field sales forces.

Poor performance not only is costly; it also tends to be self-perpetuating. And the problem is more widespread than most businessmen realize. For example, in an intensive study of 54 companies in 26 industries, I talked with and observed the performance of over 150 sales executives and field sales managers.[1] In the majority of these cases the men involved expressed some important dissatisfaction with present or-

[1] For a complete report of the findings of this study see my book, *Performance and Development of Field Sales Managers* (Boston, Division of Research, Harvard Business School, 1957).

ganization or policies. The evidence strongly indicates that too many sales executives have underestimated the importance of local managers or taken their performance for granted.

Their Importance

A strong field sales management group is important because of two common characteristics of the typical sales operation:

- The separation of the home office from the field organization.
- The intangible aspects of the selling job.

Let us examine these two characteristics in terms of the local management function.

Serving as Liaison

Since most branch offices are at a distance from headquarters, there is a constant need for a liaison officer. The salesmen need a contact with the company; the home-office executives need a pipeline to the field. Moreover, the marketing vice president is freed for important overall planning and policy matters if he is relieved of local details. The field manager can be his alter ego, his "eyes, ears, and arms in the field." He insures compliance with the home-office policies, makes many operating decisions, initiates or carries out local selling strategies, represents his company in the community, relays communications to and from the home office, and supervises the field personnel.

The alternative to local management is central control, with either a minimum of direct contact between the field and home personnel or an executive group that spends most of its time on the road. Some companies go to this extreme, but a majority do not. Among the 54 companies studied, branch and regional managers in 21 have little authority and are considered primarily supervisors and salesmen. By contrast, managers in another 10 have complete operational authority and, in addition, help formulate local and national sales policies. Managers in the remaining 23 companies have considerable operational leeway, including planning local sales programs, developing and supervising branch personnel, setting quotas and budgets, and establishing local control devices.

But, regardless of company practices, field sales managers can be valuable adjuncts to the sales executive using them. He cannot be in all places at the same time, but he can be represented everywhere by competent local managers.

Personal Support

We can further appreciate the importance of field sales managers by looking at them from the selling end of the organization. Salesmen are far more dependent on local managers than is generally realized. The competent manager not only contributes to the emotional requirements of his men, but he develops their skills and work habits and helps to condition their customers for subsequent calls.

Consider, for example, salesmen's attitudes. Most salesmen operate alone, at a considerable distance from their colleagues, and in an environment of constant competition. They are faced many times each day with the problem of trying to induce buying action. Buying is based on rational *or* nonrational factors, which greatly complicates the task of persuasion.

Because there are no simple rules, selling can be extremely frustrating. At the end of a day, the salesman may have to measure his accomplishments in such nebulous terms as, "I seem to have made some progress with these accounts," rather than in the more satisfying terms of orders received. Nor can the salesman plan his future tactics mechanically. At the crucial point of face-to-face contact with the buyer, he is beyond the help of predetermined formulas.

Most executives agree that because of these job peculiarities salesmen do have pronounced peaks of emotional ups and downs. They welcome local supervision, not only as the tangible link with the company, but also as the sounding board for their thoughts and ideas. Without this contact, their attitudes may be negative. As one businessman sees the problem:

> "I think that loneliness is perhaps the salesman's greatest handicap. Many people work alongside their boss, and if he is a right boss, they get a lot of help as well as companionship from him. A salesman does not have this hourly contact with his boss. Nor does he have hourly contact with associates whom he can talk to and use as sounding boards for his ideas. In fact, he is likely to spend a large part of his day with prospects who — at first, at least — have their defenses up against him." [2]

Role of Coaching

The local manager does more than help to establish positive attitudes among his salesmen.

[2] William B. Given, Jr., "Broadening the Horizon," *Dun's Review & Modern Industry*, September 1953, p. 42.

He is an important contributor to the salesman's knowledge of selling techniques, product characteristics, and proper work habits.

Ordinarily, the salesman's ability depends a great deal on the efforts of his field supervisor. To be sure, some companies run formal training courses and expose their salesmen to lectures, seminars, demonstrations, role-playing sessions, case discussions, film presentations, and so forth; but even in these instances local managers have a great deal to do with the eventual success or failure of the formal training. Not only must these managers give their tacit support to the approved sales techniques; they must also follow up the initial training with on-the-job coaching. It takes time to develop skills, to change work habits and attitudes, to learn product adaptations and improvements, to practice new presentation procedures.

In a petroleum company, for example, several salesmen complained that the techniques they learned at the training center had to be dropped in the field because, as their spokesman said, "Our manager has his own approach to selling." This insistence by some managers on a personal approach to selling has caused a number of sales executives to state that one of the essential requirements for promotion in their companies is "selling orthodoxy."

Local managers also contribute to the salesman's development of good work habits — to his routing and record-keeping procedures, call preparations, and working hours. In addition, they have the very important responsibility of providing the proper field services. Salesmen need competent backing-up at the local office. Samples and displays must be prepared for use, sales records maintained for ready reference, and the necessary secretarial help provided.

Preselling Influence

Equally important, the local manager can personally influence sales. For instance, he can help create favorable buying attitudes among customers by his good-will calls on them, by the image he creates of his company through his personal activities, by his use of advertising and other promotional materials, and by his manipulation of the terms of sale.

In this sense, a number of the managers I interviewed talked about management selling as distinguished from order-taking selling. Order taking, they pointed out, is the traditional job of salesmen, while management selling is the responsibility of field and home-office executives. The manager does not take orders during a call; he only intends to create a favorable climate in the buying firm — a climate which is sometimes the result of reciprocity appeals, sometimes the result of purely social contacts. Regardless, management selling can open the door for the line salesmen.

Managers can also influence sales through their ability to determine sales programs. For example, the terms of sale may be an important factor in buying action. In some companies, branch managers have authority to set trade-in allowances on the purchase of new equipment. In others, local prices are determined by the field manager, and, in still others, managers have the right to accept or reject the customer as a credit risk.

Whether we look at the manager's direct or indirect impact on salesmen, there is no doubt as to his influence.

Management Development

Not only does the competent field manager strengthen the selling skills of his men, but also he helps identify and bring along for advancement those unusual men with management potential. This aspect of manpower development is customarily called "vertical" training as opposed to "horizontal" or in-grade training. There are at least four reasons why vertical training is primarily the responsibility of local managers:

(1) In large organizations, potential managers can be easily overlooked if selection depends entirely on the far-removed and sometimes sporadic efforts of headquarters personnel. The local manager is in an ideal position to watch for promising candidates.

(2) Management potential is hard to measure, and reasonable judgments require considerable periods of personal contact. A field manager has (or should have) this contact more often than home-office personnel.

(3) One of the best techniques for identifying potential managers is exposure to management situations during their working periods. The local manager is again best able to give his candidates one or two juniors to train, a sales meeting to conduct, new sales applicants to interview, or a sales program to prepare.

(4) The attitudes, knowledge, and work habits of the potential manager are shaped to a large extent by his field supervisor. As a result, whether he chooses to or not, the supervisor is constantly affecting the potential manager's ability to succeed.

It can be seen, therefore, that the responsibility of the field sales manager may be an awesome one. Even if top management's policy is to reduce his authority to a minimum, with the burden for as many decisions as possible on headquarters, there are a number of responsibilities that he has by virtue of his strategic position in the sales department. He cannot escape them, even if he wants to, and management cannot help letting him have them, even if it wants to. The only questions are how much responsibility he has *relative* to other field sales managers (for, as we have seen, some have more than others), and how well he carries out his responsibilities.

Their Performance

How well do field sales managers contribute to sales operations? Do they use their time wisely? My study throws some light here.

Evaluation of Activities

Any general description of management activities is to a certain extent deceptive because it implies the existence of some management prototype, and of course there is none. But, as a basis for a general evaluation of performance, it is useful to note that field sales managers are active in five broad areas:

- Developing salesmen.
- Supervising salesmen.
- Personal selling.
- Operating an office.
- Planning and public relations.

The extent to which managers *are* active in each of these areas varies widely from company to company, and there is a good deal of controversy in management as to how active they *should* be in the different areas. Here are some important differences to keep in mind:

(1) The development of salesmen has two major aspects — (a) recruiting and selecting, (b) training and coaching.

There seem to be few hard and fast rules about the role of local managers in the selection process. In some companies managers have wide latitude; in others they have none. Yet there are some basic patterns. To some extent selection is a more pressing problem for large-city managers than for their small-city counterparts. Most large-city managers play some part in the selection process, even if it amounts to no more than making final hiring recommendations. Since manpower is more plentiful in the larger cities, most of these managers recruit regularly at local schools and other sources. Often their candidates are assigned to small-town branches whose managers have no other reliable source of manpower.

The training of salesmen, on the other hand, is generally a local management activity regardless of city size.

(2) Supervising the salesmen, the second major management activity, includes (a) control and (b) motivation — two aspects of management almost impossible to avoid.

Managers can hardly operate without controlling to some extent. Tasks must be assigned, even if the assignment involves no more than the delineation of a general sales territory. Likewise, most managers gather performance facts and evaluate their men almost automatically. The outsider may question the facts collected and the criteria used for judging performance, but he would be hard pressed to find any field manager who had no opinions at all about his men.

Nor can the manager very well avoid motivating salesmen. By his everyday actions and words, he influences sales-force attitude and morale. In effect, managers motivate — or fail to motivate — by almost everything they do.

(3) The activity most heatedly debated by executives and field managers alike is that of personal selling. We must differentiate two kinds of personal selling: joint visits by the manager with his men and independent selling in a personal territory. Joint visits are generally considered sound management tactics. Not only are they a useful training technique, but they enable the manager to keep in close contact with his men and the markets. The assumption of a personal territory, on the other hand, is viewed with misgivings by many executives.

(4) Practice varies widely among the companies as to the amount of time local managers spend on office duties — customer service, record keeping and paper work, pricing and trade-ins, credit and collections, inventory control, advertising and promotions, and various housekeeping chores.

To some extent, the time involved is a function of the layer of management. First-line supervisors seldom are as concerned with office problems as are branch, regional, and divisional managers. The importance of office duties also varies with branch size. Managers in the larger centers usually have assistants who supervise many details of office administration. Small-town managers, on the other hand, generally handle details themselves.

(5) Finally, field sales managers spend their time on a variety of miscellaneous tasks attendant on their being the local authority. They not only provide over-all direction for their people, but they are the customers' point of final contact with the firm and top management's representative in local matters beyond the authority of the sales force.

In effect, they are the local trouble shooters. Whether the trouble concerns an irate customer, an upset salesman, a ruffled home-office dignitary, or a sudden slump in sales, the manager is usually expected to solve the problem. Timewise, emergencies take a large share of his available hours.

Strengths & Weaknesses

In appraising the performance of local sales managers in the job just described we should, to be perfectly fair and accurate, use a different yardstick in each company. We should take into account the preferences of personal management; for example, in one company the manager may like to concentrate on the office details and that may be important to his boss at headquarters, but in another company just the opposite may be true. The problems of a branch may be unusual, as in the case of the new office in an undeveloped territory, where it is most important to select and train new salesmen.

Marketing strategy may also pose different requirements. For instance, the local managers of a packaged goods manufacturer may be expected to spend much of their time selling directly to grocers and wholesalers because the regular salesmen are primarily missionary men. Also, it is not completely fair to judge the several layers of field management in a large company upon the same basis, because the importance of technical, human relations, and analytical skills usually varies with the different levels of management.

While taking such differences into account, I believe that my study of the activities of the 150 field managers still points up a number of management strengths and weaknesses that cut across the board. In general, the study shows that field sales managers are most skillful at personal selling, trouble shooting, running an office, maintaining satisfactory customer relations, and insuring acceptable communications with headquarters. On the other hand, they are weak when it comes to developing and supervising salesmen and devising local sales strategy. In EXHIBIT I this conclusion is stated in terms of the different skills that field managers need.

EXHIBIT I. STRENGTHS AND WEAKNESSES OF FIELD SALES MANAGERS

Skills in which managers are strongest	*Skills in which managers are weakest*
Technical (the mechanics of the job)	Analysis
Human relations	Planning
with customers	Human relations
with superiors	with subordinates

In other words, the study shows that local managers are, in effect, supersalesmen instead of administrators. As one executive said, "They are doers instead of delegators; seat-of-the-pants operators instead of planners." We might imagine a very simple scale of functions on which selling appears at the left, managing at the right. Neither function is necessarily confined to its extremity; it spreads into a few gradations between "pure" selling and "pure" managing. Some salesmen, for instance, supervise junior salesmen, control a suboffice, or perhaps direct one or two office subordinates. In like manner, some managers have selling responsibilities, as in the case of the packaged goods manufacturer cited above. But keeping this in mind, the field management function should still be decidedly different from the selling function and appear well to the right of it on our imaginary scale.

Inherent Danger

That this is a problem of some magnitude is shown by examining executives' statements about the performance of their local managers:

Among the 54 companies mentioned earlier, 24 executives said there were no performance problems, but the other 30 executives itemized 60 complaints about their field managers:

Area of complaint	*Number of complaints*
Developing and supervising personnel	27
Analysis and planning	15
Operations	4
Development of management replacements	10
Home-office relations	4

Is this situation all bad? Measuring the effect of "watered down" local management is nebulous. It was apparent that few of the companies were in financial or sales difficulties; a poor supervisor can maintain his branch quota even though he does it through personal selling. But what happens when he leaves without having developed replacements, or when market conditions change abruptly, so that greater selling depth is needed in his organization? The greatest danger to a management group which concentrates on personal selling is the loss in manpower development — a loss that may take years to materialize.

Shortcomings Explained

Although the field sales managers studied do seem to have major weaknesses, they are generally considered to be successful men. They seem secure in their positions, and many have received promotions. How can this fact be reconciled with their weaknesses as managers?

In many instances, their inadequacies are balanced by compensating strengths. As a consequence, any piece-by-piece analysis of performance is less meaningful than an over-all appraisal. But in many other cases their shortcomings are apparently not offset and the man's standing in his organization still does not seem to be affected adversely.

Four influences seem to be most important in shaping management performance and explaining this paradox. Let us examine them briefly.

Personal Experience

Managers tend to perform in terms of their own backgrounds and experiences. Skills developed in the past are relied on in the present — a wholly natural phenomenon. The influence of past experience becomes significant when we realize that most field managers receive little or no management training; hence, they must rely on their premanagement background. In other words, a number of managers perform as supersalesmen because selling is their only proven business skill; they have no alternative.

Industry & Product

In many cases management performance reflects industry and product characteristics. Insurance and securities salesmen frequently maintain their customer contacts after promotion to management because these contacts are too personal to be automatically assigned to other salesmen. On the other hand, managers in companies selling door-to-door devote a great deal of their energies to recruiting and training new salesmen, a necessity in an industry having such high salesman turnover.

Local Situation

Some managers attribute certain aspects of their daily performance to particular branch conditions. One such sales manager I interviewed, who had had an incompetent predecessor, spent most of his time hiring and training new salesmen, a problem of minor significance to another manager who had followed a strong predecessor. And in some new branches, as I saw in one company selling an appliance door-to-door and in another selling office equipment direct to industrial users, the neophyte manager may personally have to make many large initial sales to cover branch overhead.

Again, there are frequent observable differences between managers in large cities and managers in small towns. Most small-town managers, whose operations are usually limited, supervise their salesmen and office personnel directly and engage in more personal selling than their large-city counterparts. Under these conditions, it is only natural for them to become more doers than delegators, the opposite being true for the city manager.

The manager's selling is also frequently an economic necessity. The sales vice president for one company said that he could afford to maintain most of his smaller branches (about 90% of his total of 240) only by assigning the biggest accounts to the managers. The managers are paid a salary and small commission. The alternative is to pay a full 15% commission on these sales to the salesmen and also support a nonselling manager. This is an alternative the executive considers financially impossible.

Superior's Expectations

The most significant influence on management behavior is the superior's expectations. Although managers are responsive in their performance to the requirements of the market and the peculiarities of their branch situations, they are even more alert to the requirements of their sales superiors. Since sales superiors are generally the ultimate judges of job performance, this alertness is essential to job success.

What performance requirements do sales executives have? A great many, to be sure. In some companies managers are expected to develop and supervise their salesmen, to prepare men for advancement, and to represent the sales executive in the field. In other companies performance requirements are less comprehensive.

Frequently, the key requirement is simply to break the sales quota, regardless of how. Very often, too, the sales executive at headquarters has a few performance checkmarks; if the manager meets these satisfactorily, he is free to operate on his own in other respects. These checkmarks are sometimes rational, sometimes not. Unfortunately, for every executive who wants his managers to train their salesmen, there seem to be several who expect only a clean desk, the ability to drink as well as the vice president, the ability "to see things as I see them," or the willingness to talk all day about manpower development.

Incomplete or unquestionable performance criteria are not the only evidence indicating unsatisfactory executive attitudes about field sales managers. There are other signs, such as:

¶ *Executive statements that salesmen succeed or fail through their own efforts.* If a salesman who wants to succeed is given enough information about products and selling techniques, so argue the proponents of this view, he will become an outstanding performer. In the words of the sales vice president of one large office equipment company, "Sales success is the result of confidence. Confidence comes from product knowledge." Or, as this philosophy is sometimes further expressed, the skill of selling can be reduced to four or five or six steps, the mastery of which means sales success.

The assumption behind this belief is that the impact of field sales managers on salesmen is of no importance or can be taken for granted. Such an assumption does not, in my opinion, check at all with the facts.

¶ *An organization which minimizes the role of field sales managers.* In one national company 60 salesmen report to a single regional manager, a span of control that makes impossible any real contact between the manager and his men.

A general condemnation of these practices is, of course, unwarranted. A well-educated, highly specialized sales force — for instance, an experienced group of turbine salesmen — will obviously need less supervision than a group of door-to-door salesmen selling low-price utensils. But it is fair to say that in a good number of companies, at least, a scanty field management group is primarily the result of inadequate executive understanding about the functions of local managers.

¶ *Inadequate policies for the selection and the training of field sales managers.* Despite stated misgivings, many sales executives promote men to management primarily on the basis of selling ability. There are a number of reasons for this practice. In the first place, many executives have not spelled out the requirements for management and thus rely on the one obvious attribute, salesmanship. Such a measure is simple and easy to defend. Moreover, the fiction has developed in many organizations that the reward for sales success is advancement. Salesmen have grown up in this environment, and any attempt to change the system would damage morale. Finally, a number of executives insist that their local managers pay their own way by selling. Not surprisingly, therefore, they feel that managers must be outstanding salesmen.

Conclusion

The jobs of selling and management are not the same and do not call for the same skills. Competence as a salesman is no guarantee of management potential.

We can appreciate the distinction between salesmen and managers by contrasting their important working relationships. A salesman has key relationships with *customers*, superiors, and colleagues; a manager has key relationships with *subordinates*, superiors, and colleagues. To the salesman, customer relationships are most important; to the manager, subordinate relationships. There is no evidence to indicate that relationships with customers and with subordinates require the same skills. If they did, all outstanding salesmen would make outstanding managers, which we know to be false.

A strong salesman is frequently aggressive, the dominant force in the sales contact. He may practice what Edward C. Bursk refers to as "low-pressure selling,"[3] but in his efforts to induce buying action he cannot be passive, except perhaps in a sellers' market. But these traits (admittedly generalized) that make him good at selling handicap him in administration. He would tend to *drive* rather than to *lead* his men. He would tend to say to them, "This is the way I did it. You do it that way too."

As one executive told me during the course of my study, the sales field is a relatively poor source of its own management replacements. He felt that the kind of man who has potential management traits is not attracted to selling, and that the man who gravitates to the sales field does not have management characteristics. Selling by itself is seldom adequate preparation for management. If an executive argues otherwise, it would seem reasonable to assume that one of two things is true in his company:

- Selling requires some management activities, such as directing juniors.

[3] Edward C. Bursk, "Thinking Ahead: Drift to No-Pressure Selling," HBR September–October 1956, p. 25.

- There is no actual field management, the transition to management occurring at a higher echelon in the organization.

When the jobs of selling and managing are not properly differentiated, there tends to be a self-perpetuating cycle of management. Not only are managers expected to behave as salesmen, but their replacements are selected on the basis of selling ability and receive little or no management training. Thus, the pattern of inadequate field management tends to perpetuate itself. Today's managers become tomorrow's top sales executives and continue the cycle under which they developed. In fact, they know of no other pattern to follow.

Furthermore, any attempt to break the cycle will cause immediate morale problems. Salesmen have grown up under a system that measures sales success by promotion to management. A man who does not receive a promotion, then, is thought to be not fully successful.

If promotions are suddenly made on the basis of other criteria, such as the ability to train subordinates or the ability to analyze and plan, then something must be done to save face for the star salesmen with no management potential. In one company, the problem was so severe that the sales executive started a special program to educate salesmen about the attractions of a permanent selling career. This was one of the problems which induced the General Electric Company in its new compensation plan to distinguish managers from individual contributors and to provide that individuals in each group could earn commensurate salaries.

Steps to Improvement

The first step in any attempt to improve the performance of field sales managers must be to raise the expectations of their performance. The quality of management will not change drastically so long as sales executives continue to select, train, and evaluate their field managers on inadequate bases. Most of the weaknesses outlined in this article reflect either similar weaknesses in the sales executive group or a failure of the executive group to appreciate the functions of local management.

Because job success means primarily "obtaining the approbation of the boss," we must not assume that success and competence are synonymous terms. The competent manager meets certain standards based on an impartial analysis of his job requirements. Such performance may or may not be approved by the superior, depending on that superior's personal standards and expectations. Some men are successful but not fully competent; others may be competent but not successful.

That distinction has real meaning whenever the superior has incomplete standards of performance. For one thing, management training programs, to be effective, must start with the top layers of management and work downward into the organization. Only in this way will more adequate performance requirements be established by superiors. Unfortunately, most of the management training programs covered in my study cut into the *middle* ranks of management as a starting point.

Moreover, personnel devices based on the assumption that competence means success should be viewed skeptically. It is significant that most of the observed job descriptions, man specifications, standards of performance, and rating forms fail to distinguish between success and competence; the managers described or rated are evaluated without reference to their different superiors. To illustrate:

> The sales personnel director of a large rubber company told me with pride that his company's newly developed rating form was not only a significant technique for measuring performance, but was used conscientiously in the field. The form included nine rating factors, among which were loyalty and dependability.
>
> The New England regional manager for the firm, who was well regarded by his sales vice president, in a separate interview agreed that he used the form — but in a most unexpected manner. He said, "This new form really helps to distinguish the good men from the poor. And here's what really counts — loyalty and dependability!" As far as he was concerned, therefore, the other seven factors had no significance.

A rating form without reference to the separate performance requirements of the sales superiors has limited significance.

Finally, the fact that acceptable performance depends on the superior's expectations points up the real need for making national sales executives aware of the problem. Unless they know what is happening and are given evidence about the performance of their field managers, it is unlikely they will make any changes. Ultimately, the improvement of field sales management performance rests on a top management that *wants* to improve performance.

J. S. Schiff and Michael Schiff

12 New Sales Management Tool: ROAM

Foreword

Revenues and costs . . . in marketing, these elements of course are critical. But the authors of this article insist that too often another major factor is ignored when a company is considering, say, expanding in a territory or introducing a product. They have dubbed this factor ROAM, an acronym for "return on assets managed" (a term they feel is more meaningful than the familiar "return on investment").

The significance of capital budgeting to a company, involving as it does long-term commitments and relatively large sums, has brought about the development of sophisticated procedures to evaluate proposals for expenditures.

Proposals that affect product marketing in which no additional investment in plant or equipment is required may be of equal significance to the company's future. But they usually do not receive the same attention or depth of analysis.

Decisions on expansion or contraction of a market, addition or elimination of a channel of distribution, changing the product line, and increasing or decreasing the field sales force are resolved by applying a procedure commonly referred to as *incremental revenue and cost analysis.* Management compares the expected change in sales revenue with the expected impact on cost; if incremental revenues exceed incremental costs, the proposal is considered a viable one.

Further, management may go on to contrast the proposal under scrutiny with others, and, still more sophisticatedly, to weigh projections of incremental revenue and cost for subjective probability values (though note that the elements assessed still are limited to revenues and costs).

What is missing from many calculations in marketing revenue-cost analyses is consideration of the fact that the company will be committing working capital to the venture. Accounts receivable and inventories are investments that must be included in determining a course of action. Moreover, we contend that these investments take on the character of assets as "fixed" as a piece of machinery, however liquid they may appear on the balance sheet.

In this article we elaborate on these contentions and present an example of how a marketer should make allowance for more than revenues and costs in calculating his projected "return on assets managed." (We prefer this phrase, rather than the well-established "return on investment," because it differentiates the active role of management from that of the investor seeking a return on funds risked.) Then we describe a training program which a large business organization has operated to acquaint field marketing managers with ROAM.

Atlanta or Cleveland?

Consider competing proposals for expanding markets submitted by two hypothetical district managers of a company, one in Atlanta and the other in Cleveland, as shown in *Exhibit I*.

In a comparison of incremental sales revenues with incremental costs, the profit contributions shown are identical. If management deems the levels of district profit contribution to be adequate—perhaps by reference to current performance—it may accept both proposals.

Exhibit I. Alternative proposals for expanding district markets

	Atlanta	Cleveland
Expected increases in:		
Sales	$100,000	$100,000
Cost of goods sold	55,000	55,000
Gross margin	45,000	45,000
Marketing costs	15,000	15,000
Profit contribution	$ 30,000	$ 30,000

Industrial practice ends the analysis at this point. Rarely, if ever, does the marketer consider any incremental accounts receivable and inventories necessary to service the projected increase in sales. Perhaps the fact that they are labeled *current assets* in the conventional balance sheet and are classified as "near cash" or elements of working capital deters the company from further probing. It must be remembered, however, that the balance sheet is prepared to serve the needs of the banker, creditors, investors, and so on—external users, not operating managers.

Cash is shown in first position under the heading *current assets* in the balance sheet because it is available to liquidate liabilities; yet, from an operational point of view (beyond the need of meeting day-to-day obligations), cash is a sterile asset in that it produces no revenue. Listed after cash are the two typically largest elements of current assets, accounts receivable and inventories. They are classified as current because of their expected conversion into cash either within a year or within the company's operating cycle.

Treating them thus meets the banker's or creditor's requirements, since they concern the company's liquidity. As a result, the sequence used in listing current assets is generally based on the "order of liquidity."

But it is impossible to imagine that incremental sales increases, as proposed by the Atlanta and Cleveland district managers, could be accomplished without any impact whatsoever on accounts receivable and inventories. The additional volume will inevitably produce additional accounts receivable, and there is no doubt that additional inventories will be carried to serve the new customers.

Of course, gains in sales volume do not necessarily yield proportionate increases in accounts receivable and inventories. What happens to these assets is also affected by the planned product mix, the level of inventory service to be offered, the expected credit terms, and paying patterns of the new customers. Accordingly, changes in the required investment in receivables and inventory must be determined independently.

More realistic picture

Now let us reconsider the Atlanta-Cleveland situation, this time including a realistic expectation of the incremental accounts receivable and inventories. The modified proposals are shown in *Exhibit II*.

A more realistic picture now emerges, for it is revealed that Cleveland customers will require more extended credit terms than those in Atlanta. The turnover in Atlanta is about 8 times (line 1 divided by line 6), or an average of 45 days outstanding, while the Cleveland district turnover is 4 times, or about 90 days on the average. Additionally, the inventory requirements vary. The slower turnover in Atlanta, 1.7 times (line 2 divided by line 7), requires an average inventory of $33,000 to service, while less than one third of this amount is needed in Cleveland.

(The proposal should now be projected over the expected period that the market will continue to be served, and evaluated on a present-value basis, using the company's cost of capital as a basic measure. It is omitted in this article for the sake of simplicity.)

Now that the proposals summarize all the pertinent data and reflect the comparable returns on assets managed, it is clear that expansion in Cleveland is more desirable. Of course, both alternatives may still be acceptable under certain conditions, but management is now able to make a more intelligent choice.

Exhibit II. Modified proposals for expanding district markets

	Atlanta	Cleveland
Expected increases in:		
1. Sales	$100,000	$100,000
2. Cost of goods sold	55,000	55,000
3. Gross margin	45,000	45,000
4. Marketing costs	15,000	15,000
5. Profit contribution	30,000	30,000
6. Accounts receivable	12,000	25,000
7. Inventories	33,000	10,000
8. Total investment	45,000	35,000
9. Profit on sales (line 5÷line 1)	30%	30%
10. Turnover of investment (line 1÷line 8)	2.2 times	2.9 times
11. Return on assets managed (line 9×line 10)	66%	87%

Not-so-liquid assets

The desirability of applying refined return-on-assets criteria to decisions of this type is not based exclusively on its superiority over the approach that ignores the reality of working capital commitments. Nor do we espouse the procedure simply because it makes decisions more congruent with total corporate objectives. We support it on the grounds that commitments of working capital are generally far more fixed than commitments of so-called fixed assets.

Expenditures for plant and equipment are recouped periodically from revenues yielded by sales of products and services. The depreciation methods authorized under our tax laws permit a relatively early and rapid recoupment of capital investment. To illustrate:

□ A company buys a machine for $100,000 and is permitted a depreciation of $20,000 the first year. At the end of that year the company has $20,000 in cash, or its equivalent, flowing to it from sales of the products or services produced by the machine, *and* a machine one year old, which may well be functioning as economically or even better than it did at acquisition. The second year returns an additional sum, and so on.

Contrast the incremental investment in inventories and accounts receivable. Using our earlier situation (*Exhibit II*), if the marketer elected to accept the Cleveland proposal, he would invest $35,000 in current assets. Once these current assets have been invested, they are not available for any alternative use as long as the company elects to stay in this market at the higher level of activity. At the end of year one, the full $35,000 is invested and cannot be used for any other purpose. The working capital invested in Cleveland has taken on the character of a fixed asset.

From an operational viewpoint, fixed assets in the traditional sense are more like current assets, and those generally classified as current assets tend to resemble fixed assets. This is not a mere play on words. It means that (a) because commitments of working capital are indeed long term, they deserve as much study and analysis as do decisions involving capital expenditures; and (b) failure to consider the effects of marketing decisions on working capital could well lead to decisions that decrease the return on assets.

A thorough understanding of this concept is critical for every manager who makes decisions affecting either directly or indirectly the level of inventories or the range of accounts receivable committed.

Indoctrinating managers

Recognizing that the ROAM concept is valid in many marketing situations is one thing. Convincing middle management of it may be another.

Some time ago Sylvania Electric Products, Inc.

became aware of the long-term commitments of working capital stemming from decisions by its field marketing management. Accordingly, Sylvania designed a training program consisting of lecture-discussion periods and case studies for these managers. In the sessions Sylvania attempted to show clearly the relationships among day-to-day decision making, marginal contribution, and the investment base of inventory and accounts receivable. The program leaders tried to make field marketing managers aware that they were responsible not only for producing a planned profit contribution, but also for maximizing the return on assets they control.

The marketing executives' quick grasp and ready acceptance of these essentially financial concepts were extremely gratifying. On the basis of this experience, Sylvania made the school a regular function and added a decision-making technique using computerized simulation. At this writing, some two years later, about 150 Sylvania managers, and a few from other organizations, have participated in the exercise.

Called Sylvania Marketing Management Simulation, it is described in the remainder of this article.[1]

Timers, Lockits, Noburns

Participants in the simulation exercise are assigned the task of managing a division that markets the following items: Timers (timing devices used by industry as a component and by consumers in the home); Lockits (a new product, used mainly in industry, that prevents burglary or tampering with equipment); and Noburns (a fire alarm system which is bought primarily for the home).

The three products are marketed directly to original equipment manufacturers as well as to other industrial and commercial organizations. The consumer market is reached by retail outlets. The terms of delivery are f.o.b. area distribution centers from which shipments are made.

The division is organized into three geographical areas: West, South, and North. A high degree of decentralization exists in the company, and each area is completely independent of the others. The management of an area is charged with the responsibility for decision making in its area and the resulting profit contribution and return on assets managed. While it is possible to interchange inventory and personnel between areas, decisions made in one area normally do not affect conditions in another.

Total industry sales are affected by a general economic factor which is related to the gross national product and influences all product sales equally in all markets.

Some seasonal variation affects the three products. In each area, however, the seasonal fluctuation for any product is the same for both the consumer and the industrial markets.

The three areas are growing at different rates as a result of local economic conditions. Within each area, however, this growth factor affects equally all products and both the consumer and the industrial markets. Some differences in demand for Timers, Lockits, and Noburns prevail also in their respective markets.

Putting it on paper

Six reports summarizing current conditions in the business are provided for each month.

The statement of operations, an example of which is shown in *Exhibit III*, is an income statement which also contains information relative to ROAM. It should be noted that this report incorporates only those elements of income and expense that are influenced by decisions of the area managers; the investment includes only the accounts receivable generated by area sales and the inventory levels as determined by the managers.

There are no arbitrary allocations of expenses or assets, and therefore no reasons for quibbling about them. Nor is there the possibility of producing artificial results by arranging to overuse services that are not effectively charged or to avoid services for which a manager feels he is being overcharged. Avoiding arbitrary allocations leads to a logically developed responsibility reporting system. The report therefore reveals profit contribution by product and by market resulting only from managerial decisions.

Another report, a summary report, sets forth selected financial and marketing information by product, market, and totals for each area. A sample, using the same team, month, and area, is shown in *Exhibit IV*. Note that this report calls for budget values related to performance. Typically, the participants prepare marketing plans and compare performance to plan. In the exhibit the budget values have been omitted.

The four remaining reports cover (1) divisional operations, in the form of *Exhibit IV*; (2) sales

1. The bulk of the material that follows is drawn from our manual, *Instructions for Participants—Marketing Management Simulation* (New York, Sylvania Electric Products, Inc., 1966).

Exhibit III. Sample statement of operations

TEAM	2	COMPANY	TEAM 2
PERIOD	5	MONTH	MAY
		AREA	NORTH

	TOTAL		TIMERS		LOCKITS		NOBURNS	
	CONSUMER	INDUSTRIAL	CONSUMER	INDUSTRIAL	CONSUMER	INDUSTRIAL	CONSUMER	INDUSTRIAL
LIST VALUE	$ 949,734	$ 723,333	$ 534,684	$ 443,263	$ 111,800	$ 192,470	$ 303,250	$ 87,600
DISCOUNT	427,381	361,667	240,608	221,632	50,310	96,235	136,463	43,800
SALES	$ 522,353	$ 361,666	$ 294,076	$ 221,631	$ 61,490	$ 96,235	$ 166,787	$ 43,800
COST OF GOODS SOLD	390,067	292,488	227,916	188,946	39,577	68,134	122,574	35,408
GROSS MARGIN	$ 132,286	$ 69,178	$ 66,160	$ 32,685	$ 21,913	$ 28,101	$ 44,213	$ 8,392
PERCENT OF SALES	25%	19%	22%	15%	36%	29%	27%	19%
TOTAL GROSS MARGIN BY PRODUCT			$ 98,845		$ 50,014		$ 52,605	
PRODUCT ADVERTISING			9,000		6,000		7,000	
WAREHOUSE EXPENSE			9,387		2,509		4,076	
TOTAL PRODUCT EXPENSE			$ 18,387		$ 8,509		$ 11,076	
PRODUCT CONTRIBUTION			$ 80,458		$ 41,505		$ 41,529	
PERCENT OF SALES			16%		26%		20%	
CUSTOMER COSTS								
PROMOTION	$ 12,000	$ 5,000						
PERSONNEL EXPENSE	37,200	19,300						
TECHNICAL SERVICES	8,000	15,000						
BONUS EXPENSE	3,754	1,494						
TOTAL CUSTOMER COSTS	$ 60,954	$ 40,794						
CUSTOMER CONTRIBUTION	$ 71,332	$ 28,384						
PERCENT OF SALES	14%	8%						

BONUS % SET	5%
BONUS YEAR TO DATE	$ 34,406

RECAP

TOTAL SALES	$ 884,019
COST OF GOODS SOLD	682,555
GROSS MARGIN	$ 201,464
PRODUCT EXPENSE	37,972
CUSTOMER EXPENSE	101,748
ADMINISTRATION	38,000
TOTAL EXPENSE	$ 177,720
AREA CONTRIBUTION	$ 23,744
PERCENT OF SALES	2%

ACCOUNTS RECEIVABLE - CONSUMER	1,060,267
ACCOUNTS RECEIVABLE - INDUSTRIAL	361,666
TOTAL ACCOUNTS RECEIVABLE	1,421,933
TOTAL INVENTORY VALUE	$ 798,619
TOTAL ASSETS MANAGED	$ 2,220,552

Exhibit IV. Sample summary report
[Dollar figures in thousands]

		TEAM	2	COMPANY	TEAM 2
		PERIOD	5	MONTH	MAY
				AREA	NORTH

		TIMERS	LOCKITS	NOBURNS	CONSUMER	INDUSTRIAL	TOTAL
LIST VALUE	MONTH	$ 978	$ 304	$ 391	$ 950	$ 723	$ 1,673
	THREE MONTH	2,876	924	1,321	2,930	2,191	5,121
	YR TO DATE	4,732	1,525	2,440	5,021	3,676	8,697
	BUDGET						
SALES	MONTH	$ 516	$ 158	$ 211	$ 522	$ 362	$ 884
	THREE MONTH	1,517	479	711	1,611	1,096	2,707
	YR TO DATE	2,496	790	1,314	2,761	1,838	4,599
	BUDGET						
MARKET SHARE	MONTH	26.4%	20.1%	18.9%	23.8%	21.7%	22.9%
	THREE MONTH	25.8	20.3	18.7	23.3	21.4	22.5
	YR TO DATE	25.5	20.1	18.8	23.0	21.2	22.2
	BUDGET						
GROSS MARGIN	MONTH	$ 99	$ 50	$ 53	$ 132	$ 69	$ 201
	THREE MONTH	328	160	184	437	234	671
	YR TO DATE	547	264	337	752	395	1,147
	BUDGET						
CONTRIBUTION	MONTH	$ 80	$ 42	$ 42	$ 71	$ 28	$ 24
	THREE MONTH	272	135	151	259	119	150
	YR TO DATE	453	223	285	447	206	275
	BUDGET						
CONTRIBUTION/SALES	MONTH	15.5%	26.6%	19.9%	13.6%	7.7%	2.7%
	THREE MONTH	17.9	28.2	21.2	16.1	10.9	5.5
	YR TO DATE	18.1	28.2	21.7	16.2	11.2	6.0
	BUDGET						
SALES/ASSETS MANAGED	MONTH	13.20	15.16	12.41	5.90	12.00	4.77
	THREE MONTH	12.93	15.32	11.70	5.89	12.01	4.71
	YR TO DATE	12.47	15.16	13.36	5.90	12.01	4.73
	BUDGET						
RETURN ON ASSETS MANAGED	MONTH	204.6%	403.3%	247.0%	80.2%	92.4%	12.9%
	THREE MONTH	231.4	432.0	248.0	94.8	130.9	25.9
	YR TO DATE	225.7	427.5	289.9	95.6	134.5	28.4
	BUDGET						

force numbers, salaries, and expenses by area; (3) unit sales details by area; and (4) inventory matters by area.

'Year' of decision

With the aid of the computer, the field marketing managers can undergo a full year of decision-making experience in 12 hours.

The decisions the area managers can make are interrelated and quite extensive. In any one-month period they can:

□ Hire, fire, train, and transfer salesmen.

□ Revise salaries, the bonus rate, or travel and entertainment expenses.

□ Order products from the plant for normal delivery or to be expedited.

□ Transship from one area to another.

□ Modify the three-month forecast of goods to be ordered from the plant.

□ Alter prices, trade discounts, or credit terms.

□ Change expenditures for advertising, promotion, or technical services.

□ Shift the sales force's emphasis on the three products.

Since the objective of the exercise is to place the managers in a realistic setting and demonstrate the impact of their decisions on financial results as well as shares of markets, authority is rather broadly extended. Though all these decisions may not normally fall within the purview of the manager, he may well influence them, albeit indirectly, in a very practical manner.

Credit terms can serve to illustrate this point. Typically, extension of credit is not a marketing or sales management decision, but *persuading* the credit manager is a normal activity. Hence, in the simulation the end result is assumed, and the participants are given full decision-making authority for establishing credit terms.

The decisions made affect the business in "real-life" fashion. For example, unit costs increase if orders for goods from the plant vary greatly from the forecast or if expediting is necessary. Increased expenditures in advertising, promotion, and sales personnel boost sales for a time, but then become decreasingly effective. Extending credit produces more sales volume but also increases accounts receivable, which in turn affects ROAM.

Each manager is provided with a series of charts that enable him to plot the key data and thereby discern more readily the combined effect of his decisions on such critical factors as sales, shipments, market share, profit contribution, and ROAM.

Exercise in action

The optimum number for the exercise is 35, organized into 5 groups of 7 managers each. Two men are assigned to co-manage each area, and one man is appointed general manager of the division. Each group works as a team throughout the exercise.

The program runs for three days, beginning with an orientation session after dinner on the day the trainees arrive. Here the program leaders describe the purpose of the exercise, establish the groups, distribute manuals spelling out the details of the simulation, and explain the schedule. Afterwards the participants read their manuals and then meet to discuss them in group sessions.

The following morning is devoted entirely to a review of the manual and a question-and-answer period. By the end of the morning, the groups are ready to submit their first sets of decisions and tentative annual marketing plans for their areas.

During the midafternoon a lecture-discussion on the planning and financial management concepts presented in earlier programs serves to refresh the managers' minds and point up the nature and purposes of the exercises. Then the groups are given their first set of reports reflecting the results of their decisions. That night the participants make the second set of decisions and submit a formal marketing plan for the year.

The second day is devoted to decisions and report analysis until a full year of operation is completed. That evening each group meets to prepare a critique of the year's activities and to develop a plan for the following year.

The third and final day is divided into two periods. Each manager delivers an oral report. His presentation must be more than mere rationalizing or "Monday morning quarterbacking," because the audience is thoroughly conversant with his situation. Since the simulation is noninteractive—that is, the decisions of one group do not influence the others' operations—it could be likened to a discussion by golf pros who have just completed independent play over the same course.

The last period of the program consists of a general discussion of application. It centers on the question: How can we apply all that we have learned during these three days to our specific tasks?

New era at Sylvania

Measuring the tangible effects of an educational exercise of this kind is at best extremely difficult. Sylvania nevertheless seems very satisfied with it. Recently, in an address to marketing executives, Alfred C. Viebranz, executive vice president of Sylvania, made these comments on Sylvania Marketing Management Simulation:

"Basically, we have redirected the thinking of our entire sales organization. Our sales managers now think and act like businessmen. They know how their decisions affect the overall objectives of the company. Yet they still go out and get orders—indeed profitable orders—but beyond that they understand how to get the maximum mileage from the assets they control. Thus they are making a positive contribution to the company's ROI.

"This program has also had a direct effect on our salesmen. The knowledge gained by our managers from these programs has filtered down. Our salesmen who call primarily on the principals or senior executives of business organizations now come as business consultants rather than mere stock takers or order writers. They have also educated many of our customers to think about their businesses in terms of the key measure—return on investment.

"This program has made it possible to promote from within more readily. It has prepared and continues to develop our people for greater responsibility. Additionally, we have attracted many bright people from the graduate schools of business. This three-phase program is an extension of the kind and level of education these young people have been exposed to on their campuses."[2]

Summary

As a rule, marketing proposals are evaluated by a restricted consideration of two factors: revenue to be generated by the proposals, and the incremental costs to be incurred. Rarely does the marketer direct attention to the manner in which the proposals may affect his investment in inventory and accounts receivable.

Furthermore, these current assets are far more fixed than those assets typically referred to as "fixed." Hence, marketing proposals should be carefully studied in terms of their impact on current assets as well as on revenues and costs.

A simulation exercise, as devised by one organization to educate marketing executives in this approach, has proved to be an extremely effective teaching tool. This is a step in the direction of making field marketing managers realize that their decisions should be evaluated not merely in terms of sales volume, market share, and profits, but also on the basis of a critical criterion, return on assets managed.

2. Remarks delivered at the Sixth Annual Strategy Conference of the Sales Executives Club of New York, October 11, 1966.

Andrall E. Pearson

13 Sales Power Through Planned Careers

Many large companies today are launching major efforts to improve their methods of attracting and developing outstanding salesmen and sales managers. To a remarkable extent, however, the results are disappointing.

As good men are lost and the less capable men remain — and rise — in the sales organization, executives become concerned about their company's lack of sales power and of progress in this obviously vital area. Too often they then resort to another set of expedients: the crash hiring program and the ruthless housecleaning. The latter shakes morale and continuity; the former brings in a new crop of candidates who often fare no better than the old.

How badly they do fare is illustrated by the experience of one major consumer goods company where, of the 1,380 college men hired since 1962, 1,102 have already left. By any standard, an 80% turnover in three and a half years is dangerously high, especially when it includes some of the most promising men. While this company's turnover experience is extreme, there are many that lose half or more of each year's incoming recruits over a three-year period. Considering the increasing difficulty of attracting high-caliber men into sales work in the first place, this high turnover among newer men is especially frustrating.

Sales Force Outlook

The lack of good men in the sales force — and available to the sales effort — is felt with increasing severity as the importance and complexity of the selling job grow. It has, of course, always been important. There was a time when the sales force was "the apple of every president's eye," and thus received the attention and guidance of top management so essential to aggressive and innovative sales management. The decline in interest in it today may be traced to, among other things, the growing popularity of the "marketing concept." Executives have come to think in terms of strategic planning, product line innovation, and acquisition strategy. These new words and the concepts they denote are important to modern business, but top management is also finding out that they are no substitute for an effective sales force. The need for a different kind of salesman and more effective sales management in the years ahead is suggested by these two examples:

¶ A food manufacturer finds his products maturing and becoming increasingly "price sensitive"

— that is, the consumer buys **the best "deal" offered** that particular week, rather than being persuaded by the flow of media advertising for the products involved. Thus the manufacturer must get the support of the grocery chain in featuring and displaying his products in order to build volume. This means the manufacturer has to have a sales force capable of persuading increasingly sophisticated grocery chain buyers of the profitability of supporting his promotion. In order to accomplish this, the salesmen must be able to deal with break-even analyses, "out think" the computer with regard to inventory implications, and show why the promotion doesn't merely borrow from next week's sales. Obviously, this job is a far cry from the old days of "loading the trade" and hoping everything will work out all right.

◖ A manufacturer of commercial office machines finds the technology of his products changing so rapidly that men in the field three or four years do not know as much about the product line as do new sales trainees coming off the line. And the pace promises to quicken. In the old days, a few weeks at the plant usually provided enough background for new men to go out and sell for 30 years.

Overhaul Needed

Thus the sales organizations of many companies today — in both industrial and consumer industries — are caught in a pincer, between (a) an urgent need for an upgraded, expanded sales force, and (b) inadequate, ineffective techniques for the development of this manpower.

These are the generalized findings of a study of sales manpower development in 30 large companies which McKinsey & Company undertook recently. Of the companies investigated, those in consumer fields all have sales forces of more than 350 men, while the industrial companies have sales forces of 75 men or more. Significantly, these companies are the sales leaders in their respective industries, and in most instances they also are regarded as having very effective programs for developing sales power.

The major finding of this study is that a few advanced companies are, in fact, overhauling their sales manpower development processes. A new pattern, cutting through the old haphazard ways, is taking shape. Although the changes are relatively recent, they are already showing positive results. The turnover rate is declining, especially among the high-potential performers. The caliber of the men who are **recruited** and stay is improving in terms of education, training, and job performance. The age profile of the sales organization is improving as younger men are attracted and retained. The depth of competence in the organization is growing as more qualified men become available as backstops at each position.

More important, the results are increasingly noticeable to customers. To test the effects of its new sales manpower policies, one leading company engaged an independent research firm to find out how customers rated its sales force. On all counts, the sales force of the innovating company rated higher than those of its competitors and higher than it did in a similar survey made just two years earlier.

Two Basic Remedies

What kinds of specific steps are these companies taking? What seems to distinguish the efforts of the companies with outstanding results in developing sales manpower from those which are not doing an effective job?

Essentially, we have found two basic approaches to the task of upgrading the sales force's manpower capabilities: (1) strengthening individual programs, and (2) mounting a broad-based attack on the entire process of developing sales manpower in the company.

Strengthening Programs

Following the first approach, some leading companies are, after intensive study, improving segments of their development activities.

For example, several companies troubled by a high turnover rate decided to analyze the problem in terms of where all personnel had been hired. It was found that those hired in the field were generally below the standard of those hired at headquarters. Why? Because busy field executives will often settle for the first available candidate simply to fill a territory and get on with the job, and because most managers tend to hire in their own image. Accordingly, since the quality of personnel and hence standards are generally lower in the field than at headquarters, the head office hired better men. The next step was fairly obvious: a decision to centralize all hiring of sales personnel at headquarters. The result has been a marked improvement in the caliber of new men, along with greatly reduced turnover.

Consider these further examples of the positive results accruing from strengthening individual programs:

◖ One major company, in particular, has cut its turnover in half and has also recruited more than 20 M.B.A.'s into its sales force. Through local recruiting, this company formerly had been unable to attract satisfactory numbers of men with bachelor's degrees.

◖ Another company, after studying its sales compensation program, found that its poorer performers were receiving almost as much take-home pay as were its outstanding salesmen. And the pattern was similar for its manager group as well. In fact, pay raises had become almost automatic for everyone in the sales force. In many cases men had to be fired for poor performance only a few months after receiving merit raises. Needless to say, this company has drastically altered the administration of its pay plan for the sales force — with a firm conviction that this will improve the morale and effectiveness of its best performers.

◖ In still another company good men were leaving because advancement took too long. Moreover, the rate of advancement depended more on seniority than ability. In this situation the patient and mediocre employees hung on while the eager and highly motivated men left. After studying this situation, top management completely revised its advancement policy for the sales force. Better men were moved ahead much faster than the others. It became a matter of policy to give the better men exposure to a variety of jobs and to make it explicit that such broadening experience was part of the advancement process.

Once again, the effect of a new, rationalized manpower development policy resulted in discernible improvement. The poorer performers were weeded out faster; the better ones were encouraged and stayed; the sales force took on a new vigor that was reflected not only in the company's image throughout the industry, but, more importantly, in its sales performance. And, incidentally, the grapevine report back to the campus, where the best recruits come from, carried the story, thus facilitating the company's recruiting efforts.

Broad-Based Attack

While these individual steps have produced some very worthwhile and measurable improvements, the top managements of several of the leading companies included in the study have concluded that spot changes could only result in spot improvement.

Moreover, they have realized that only by analyzing the entire process of their sales manpower development and by devising an overall policy can they maximize the benefits they have been achieving in isolated areas. The fact is that changes in one area inevitably have repercussions in another. If hiring standards are raised, top management must at the same time upgrade the training program, compensation levels, and the quality and type of first-level supervision. If high-potential men are hired and given intensive training, management must also provide opportunities for reasonably rapid advancement for the best performers. And top management cannot provide for such advancement unless the organization is sufficiently dynamic and flexible to provide openings, especially at the lower and middle management levels.

Thus, there is an emerging recognition that effective sales manpower development requires that a whole range of activities be linked closely together. In some companies this insight has resulted in a more basic — and effective — attack on the problem than in companies following the individual program approach.

This more fundamental approach — mobilizing all the elements into an integrated program — is what *is* new and exciting in the field of sales manpower development. Because it is new, this approach can be given a new name — the Career Path Concept. The concept grows out of the efforts of a relatively few leader companies that already are achieving major improvements.

Career Path Concept

There are two essential preliminary steps in the approach to the Career Path Concept:

1. An inventory of the current and future manpower needs of the company, including a hard look at the company's current manpower development processes.

2. The formulation and statement of a specific set of policies which grow out of identified problems and are supported by top management.

In the following pages I will discuss both of these preliminary steps to illustrate how — by analyzing the overall process and each of its component elements — top management can successfully deal with the problem of forging an effective and competitive sales organization.

Manpower Audit

The first step — making an audit of all phases of the company's development process — provides top management with a total picture of its sales manpower situation. The purpose is not to effect a revolution overnight, but to provide a starting point for improvement. The value of an audit of this kind is illustrated by the basic insights it has provided companies that have undertaken it — insights into four sources of weakness in existing manpower programs:

- Inherited deficiencies in the current organization.
- Conflicting viewpoints of key executives on basic policies.
- Ineffective administration of manpower assets.
- A piecemeal approach to upgrading the sales force.

Inherited Deficiencies. Many of the manpower problems with which today's top managements struggle are inherited from former administrations. Companies find themselves held back by a serious shortage of effective top-level sales executives and men ready for promotion, in addition to other troubles touched on before — blockade in key jobs held down by men who have no promotion potential; large numbers of men graded as poor performers; and clusters of older men who are hard to motivate and find it extremely difficult to adjust to changing conditions.

The disadvantages of an age-heavy sales organization are implicit in EXHIBIT I, which compares the age profiles of two competing companies in the same industry. As the exhibit shows, almost half of Company A's sales force is over 45, whereas only 9% of Company B's salesmen are in this upper age bracket. These salesmen operate in a very competitive field, where just the physical demands on a man wear him down by the time he is 50. So it is not surprising that Company B has a reputation within the trade for being alert and fast moving, while Company A's image is just the reverse. The effect on sales need not be immediate; indeed, many other factors bear on the sales picture, as any executive knows. But it seems obvious that Company A's age disadvantage must, over a period of time, pull it down unless corrective measures are taken.

It is significant that Company A's aging sales force is the result of inadequate manpower management over a long period of time, and therefore is not likely to be changed overnight by a quick and easy decision — not with several hundred salesmen over the age of 50. But, even

EXHIBIT I. COMPARISON OF PROFILES OF TWO COMPETING SALES FORCES

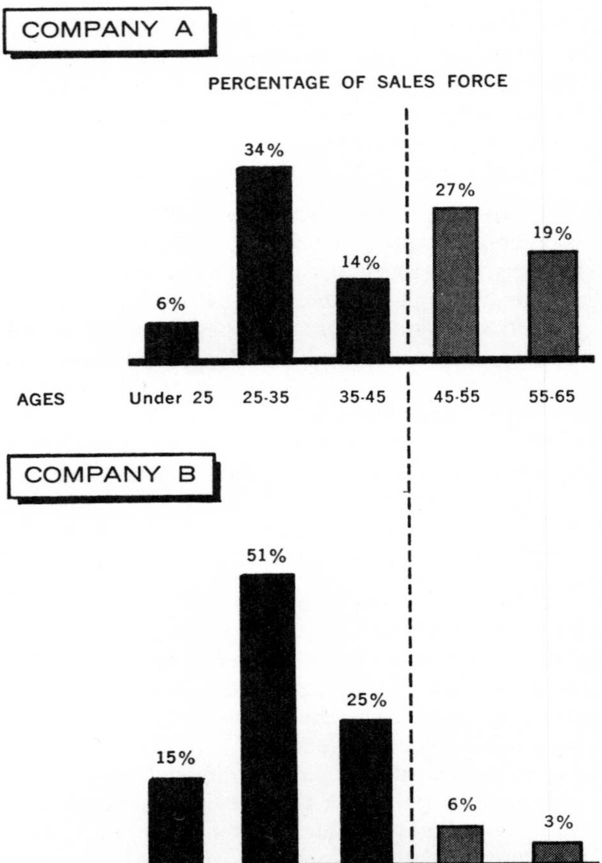

more significant, Company A now has facts to work with; the problem is at least defined, and the executives responsible for sales manpower development are now in a position to formulate concrete steps and policies to correct it.

Executive Conflicts. We have found that the failure of many companies to conduct sales manpower audits is the root cause of many of their development problems. Without facts to guide them, key executives rely on intuition, and policy and action tend to get bogged down in a morass of conflicting opinions.

In such companies there is usually no consensus among executives responsible for sales manpower development on such vital questions as: What kind of men do we need? What, in actual practice, are the best recruiting sources? Where should selection decisions be made? What experience is necessary in order for men to qualify for top sales management jobs? How fast should men move through the organization? What is a sound turnover rate? What should be done about mediocre performance? What priority should be given to development in relation to daily operating tasks?

Recognizing the absence of reliable facts on which to base effective policy on questions such as these, leading companies are beginning to study their manpower needs in a systematic way. The results are eye-opening. For example, to answer the question, "What kind of men do we need?" one company analyzed the academic backgrounds of successful salesmen and sales management candidates who had been with the company for three years. Tabulated in summary form, the results looked like this:

Academic achievement	*Percent of total hires*	*Percent of total promotions*
College degree	61%	84%
Some college	32%	16%
High school only	7%	0%

This analysis demonstrated rather conclusively the superior potential of college men for promotion to supervisory posts in this company's sales organization. The next step, accordingly, was to formulate and implement policy on the basis of the facts on hand.

Encouraged by the results of this study, the company proceeded to analyze its recruiting sources, then its turnover experience in terms of recruiting source. What is emerging, slowly but surely, is a set of recruiting and selection guidelines that this company never had before, despite its size and eminence in its industry.

Ineffective Administration. Companies are finding that it is one thing to hire good men and another thing to keep them. Thus the more progressive companies we investigated are trying to find out why good men are leaving. As suggested earlier, the principal reason is failure to move better men ahead fast enough. In some companies it takes five years or more for a man to get his first real promotion. Moreover, there is a tendency in such companies toward "lock-stepping" — the movement of groups without any real regard for individual performance. Thus ambitious, high-potential men soon realize that they will never get to a position of real responsibility or substantial earnings while they are still young. Consequently, many of them leave.

An example of an unattractive career path is offered by Exhibit II, which shows typical ages at which men are appointed to each level of responsibility and the number of years it takes to move up the ladder in one company. It is little wonder this company is losing recruits at the rate of 50% in the first two years. By way of contrast, another company we studied makes a conscious effort to promote a better performer

Exhibit II. An unattractive career path

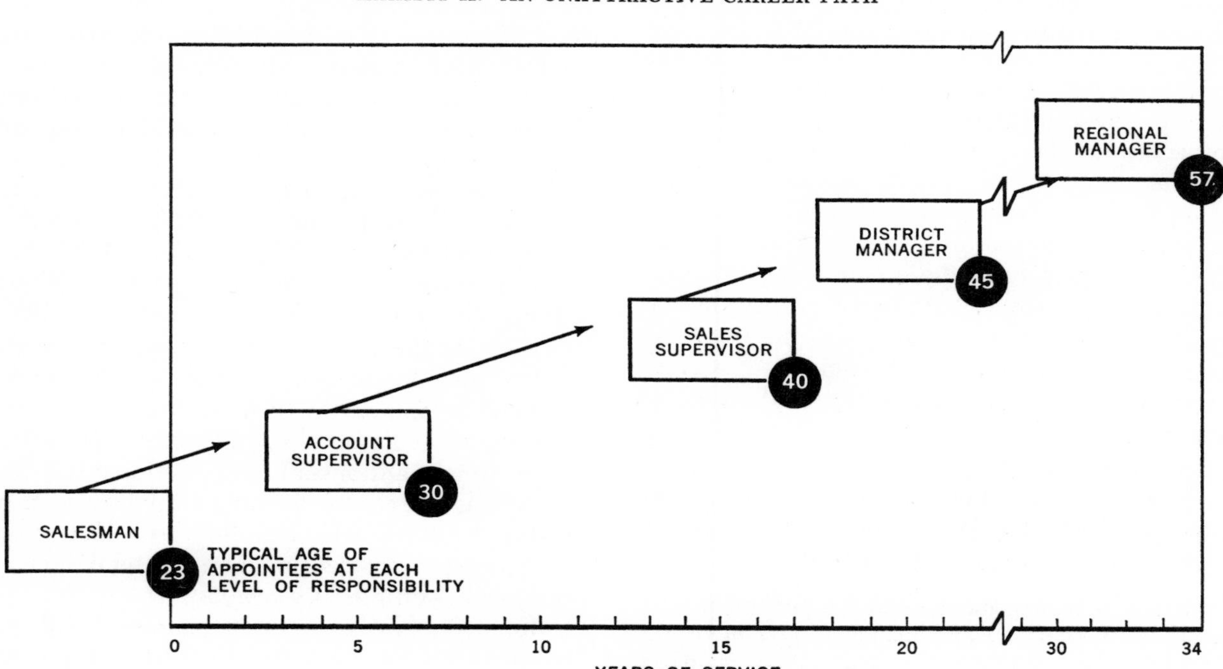

no later than his fourth year in each successive job, until he has had at least two promotions.

Holding good men back is but one aspect of poor administration of manpower assets. Another is that mediocre performers are too often allowed to remain in key jobs. We have found, for example, that after the early weeding out of obvious "mistakes," sales management in a number of companies tends to string along indefinitely with even its poorest salesmen. At the same time, men who do not work out in management jobs continue to hold key positions long after their shortcomings are recognized, thus blocking the path of able and ambitious younger men.

Meanwhile, in many companies development efforts for the large mass of average or above-average personnel are sporadic and uncoordinated. The heaviest emphasis — frequently overriding all of the other activities — tends to be placed on immediate sales results expressed in terms of volume, so that the development of people takes a back seat. Most managers perform day-to-day supervision and coaching in their "spare time," if at all. In many companies the evaluation of performance and specific programs for improving individuals' effectiveness are usually superficial. And when men are promoted, little or no attention is given to helping them adjust or improve their performance at critical career points. This problem is especially pronounced at district manager and regional manager levels, where men are given little or no training for their new responsibilities.

Upgrading. Undoubtedly, as our study disclosed, the critical shortcoming in current approaches to sales manpower development is failure to see it as an overall process. In many companies not even the elements of the process have been analyzed and identified, and in very few companies have these elements been integrated into an organized process. Since there is no apparent method or direction, the usual approach to development is "firefighting" — crash programs to recruit, train, or find ways of motivating the sales force. The total effort is sporadic and piecemeal.

The effects of such practices appear in the crisis that has developed in the sales organization of one company. To illustrate:

Recently management rated the performance of each of its salesmen and managers and made the belated discovery that it had 90 qualified manager candidates — 54 of them with two or more years of service — waiting in line for promotion, with only 14 advancement opportunities due to open up this year and just 12 in 1967. A substantial percentage of these high-potential men will unquestionably be lost, while the slots they might have filled probably will still be occupied by the less qualified men now holding down these jobs.

Surprisingly, these breakdowns in the sales manpower development process are typical and representative. Needless to say, they do not apply with equal force to all companies. But they do illustrate how, by analyzing the overall process and each of its component elements, management may consciously evaluate its own manpower development practices preliminary to setting policies and laying down the track for a manpower development process which will ensure the company a sales organization that is adequate to the demands and pressures which are building.

Policy Formulation

After defining their manpower problems, the companies we studied that are moving ahead in this area are consciously laying down policies as a foundation for manpower building. "Policy" is an operative word here, and for three reasons: (1) it implies top management concern and active involvement; (2) it implies a commitment over an extended period of time to coordinated activity covering a number of specific functions; and (3) it suggests the specification of goals. In these terms *policy* is the antithesis of *program*. At this stage management is not interested in specific programs for recruiting, training, or any of the detailed functions in the development process.

Management *is* interested in seeing to it that manpower development is given real priority. In practical corporate life the immediate day-to-day pressures — for increasing sales volume, getting the customer, nailing down the order, and meeting the quota — are all powerful forces against such long-term considerations as manpower development, which is thus given little more than lip service. Therefore, in order to give weight and meaning to development, the top managements of leading corporations are making it abundantly clear that, as a matter of policy, manpower development is equal in importance to getting sales results.

Moreover, and again as a matter of policy, leading companies are regarding sales manpower development as basically a line management responsibility. Staff groups have a role in the process, of course, but the chief burden is on the field manager, who works directly with upcoming sales personnel and therefore has the most immediate impact in training and identifying top performers. In some companies this responsibility is already explicit. As the sales vice president of one company told us:

"The president of our company never misses a chance to formally say, 'When we consider promoting a man around here, I want to know the names of other men he has developed. And if he can't cite examples of men he has helped bring along, the chances of his getting promoted in this organization are very slim.' "

To give greater practical value to its commitment, the top managements of some companies we studied lay down priorities based on the company's special circumstances. Such factors as its size and growth trends, the relative importance of the sales function, the present level of competence in relation to current sales requirements (an especially important factor in view of changing technology, complexity of products and product lines, and so forth), and the predictable changes in sales requirements within the industry — all these and more are included among the manpower development priorities. Implied in the system of priorities is management's determination to follow an organized approach, recognizing that it takes time, money, and some tough decision making to develop outstanding manpower.

Once top management's commitment is established, policy decisions are made on such vital elements in the process as the kind of men needed, the development stages through which men will pass, how men will be paced as they move through the development stages, performance evaluation and compensation approaches, and the role of training and development activities. Out of these decisions evolves the career path.

Since there are two basic functions in any sales organization — selling and sales management — the career path proceeds along two corresponding lines. Whether recognized explicitly or not, in any sales organization there are bona fide management candidates — that is, those people who are destined to go on to the ranks of sales management and even higher. Similarly, there are those who are best suited to a career as a professional salesman. We will deal first with the management candidate's career path and the six hypothetical stages of his development.

Path: Sales Management

To demonstrate its usefulness, the following pages build up a sample career path based on concepts being successfully applied to sales management by companies we studied. For purposes of illustration, the path starts at the beginning and follows a straight line to the end. In real life, of course, the route is never that simple and direct. No large, established company can start out with a clean slate. In fact, it is part of the realistic attitude underlying the Career Path Concept to begin with the existing manpower situation and, rather than try to effect a revolution overnight, to move clearly in a consistent direction by building, not ruining, morale.

The sample career path that follows points out the way any company can consciously and effectively shape the process by which it develops its sales manpower. It embodies selected policies applied successfully by one or more of the leader companies. But it is not a universal, ready-made plan that can be imposed "as is" on any specific sales organization. Each company shapes its own path in terms of its unique situation and requirements.

Introductory Stage

In this first part of his development (see EXHIBIT III-A) every new salesman begins his work with a productive sales assignment after a prescribed orientation period. In our example we give six months to orientation, but in some industrial situations considerably longer periods of time are necessary to ground a new man adequately in the technical aspects of his job.

Whatever the orientation period required, career path planning dictates that every beginning assignment be productive both in the sense of carrying with it meaningful responsibility for results and of providing an opportunity for evaluation of how well a man does. How long a man stays in this introductory and trial stage is determined by his individual capabilities. In our illustration, within six months the candidate can be promoted to the sales development stage (i.e., when he has been with the company one year). Thus a "fast track" is opened up for the men who get off the mark quickly, while others may stay in this stage up to their third anniversary with the company. At this point, career

EXHIBIT III. SAMPLE BLUEPRINT FOR DEVELOPING SALES MANAGEMENT

CODE TO DEVELOPMENT STAGES

I & T = Introductory and Trial

SD = Sales Development

SS = Sales Supervisory

MO = Marketing Orientation

FMM = Field or Marketing Management

KM = Key Managers

A

INDEX OF COMPENSATION AND RECOGNITION

YEARS OF SERVICE

BEGINS WITH PRODUCTIVE ASSIGNMENT FOLLOWING BRIEF ORIENTATION

PROMOTION OR TERMINATION REQUIRED BY THIRD ANNIVERSARY

I & T

SD

SELLING CAREER

DURATION DETERMINED BY INDIVIDUAL PERFORMANCE

B

INDEX OF COMPENSATION AND RECOGNITION

YEARS OF SERVICE

MINIMUM OF 18 MONTHS' PREVIOUS EXPERIENCE IS FEASIBLE

RESTRICTED TO MEN BETWEEN THEIR SECOND AND SEVENTH ANNIVERSARIES, PROMOTED FROM SALES DEVELOPMENT AND SUPERVISORY STAGES

MO

SS

SD

I & T

SELLING CAREER

NOT A TERMINAL ASSIGNMENT: CANDIDATES MUST WIN PROMOTION OR TRANSFER TO SELLING CAREER BY FIFTH ANNIVERSARY

C

INDEX OF COMPENSATION AND RECOGNITION

YEARS OF SERVICE

MANDATORY EXPERIENCE STEPS

SUPERIOR MEN CAN REACH THIS LEVEL BY THIRD ANNIVERSARY

KM

FMM

2ND LEVEL

1ST LEVEL

MO

SS

SD

I & T

SELLING CAREER

● FORCED DECISIONS ON REASSIGNMENT OR ADVANCEMENT TO HIGHER COMPENSATION LEVELS

NEW APPOINTEES MUST EARN ADVANCEMENT TO NEXT COMPENSATION LEVEL WITHIN 2 YEARS

OPENINGS MUST BE FILLED BY YOUNG, SUCCESSFUL MANAGEMENT CANDIDATES WITH LESS THAN 7 YEARS' SERVICE

SALES MANAGEMENT

path planning dictates an "up or out" decision.

In short, the introductory assignment does not provide a continuing job. It ends with either promotion or termination. Thus, the first action to prevent the growth of an aging, mediocre sales force is initiated, and at the same time the promising individual is given an early indication that his strengths are recognized and his prospects good.

Sales Development

A move to the sales development stage represents a positive vote of confidence in the man. His responsibilities normally are now increasing to include larger and more complex accounts. As we noted earlier, outstanding men can reach this second stage in one year, but everyone has to move up — or out — in three years. A man's career in the sales development stage again has a terminal point. In this hypothetical example we decide that a management candidate must advance beyond this level by his fourth anniversary with the company. Men not qualifying as management candidates automatically move into the career path for salesmen, which will be described later.

In short, we are making a formal early decision on who our most promising management candidates are. Management runs the risk in this way of bypassing the "late bloomer," but companies we studied conclude this is a small price to pay for the advantage of early identification of real talent which can then be intensively groomed, encouraged, and retained. This sales development stage also has a fast track, as shown in the exhibit.

The emphasis so far on fast tracks, formal early decisions, and time limits is not accidental. The Career Path Concept recognizes the importance of moving men through the organization at critical stages fast enough to keep up their motivation, vitality, and spirits, and therefore their productiveness. At the same time, the plan takes into account individual differences, pacing men according to ability and thus avoiding lockstepping or tenure promotions.

Sales Supervisory

As a man assumes his first responsibility for supervising the work of other people, he reaches a critical turning point in his career, as Exhibit III-B indicates. Note that the fast track is kept open so that men can reach this third stage with a minimum of only 18 months' previous experience. Nor is this a terminal assignment for management candidates. They either move up within the prescribed time — that is, by the fifth anniversary — or transfer to a career salesman position as supervisory openings are needed.

These policies recognize that many salesmen do falter when given managerial responsibilities and must be moved out in order to provide the supervisory openings. Keeping a large number of nonpromotable performers at lower level management jobs blocks the advancement opportunities for high-potential men, and this sets the stage for wasteful turnover among the best men.

Naturally, the movement of ineffective managerial candidates back into career selling implies the double risk that once back in the sales force they will still not work out and thus must eventually leave that position as well. In accepting this risk, top management is stating, in effect, that one promotion does not constitute a lifelong commitment to a man, or guarantee him tenure at the lower levels of management. He must meet his challenge at each level if the development process is to work effectively.

Marketing Orientation

As our proven performers emerge, the need for a broadening assignment becomes important. At this fourth stage, those candidates who have demonstrated their ability to handle both selling and sales management responsibilities are brought into headquarters for marketing orientation (as shown in Exhibit III-B). This exposure is intended to provide the necessary experience leading up to a sales or marketing management position.

Only those previously promoted through three levels qualify to participate in this stage. The marketing orientation phase is restricted to men between their second and seventh anniversaries, recognizing again the principle of formal early decisions on management candidates who can move up. Most important, assignments are limited to productive jobs with specific objectives and organized evaluations.

One of the important reasons for bringing a man to headquarters is to size him up. All too often, the only fixes top management has on a young man from the field six months after he has arrived at headquarters are on how pleasant he is to company officers and his general willingness to work late to get odd jobs done. His ability to run a district or region, however, is still uncertain. Beyond this, his ability to think hard about important marketing and sales problems is also unknown.

In order to benefit both the man and the company, this marketing orientation needs to be built around some specific, meaningful projects — ones that the man can come to grips with and thereby demonstrate to everyone concerned his capacity to deal with more complex issues. Companies that have enjoyed the greatest success in broadening their men adhere firmly to this principle of meaningful headquarters assignments.

Field Management

Men who pass through the marketing orientation screen now take over their first broad managerial responsibility in the field (see Exhibit III-C). Note that superior men have moved through the four previous stages by their third anniversary in this hypothetical situation. Thus there is ample opportunity for top-notch performers to move up quite rapidly. (The decision to bring young men into the marketing orientation phase at headquarters also guarantees that field management jobs will be similarly filled with successful management candidates.)

But these new appointees are not out of the woods yet. They must earn advancement to the next compensation level within their second year of the new field assignment to warrant continuation in that job. This is the post-appraisal system in effect again. One company uses this technique to ensure that new district managers are really working out. It establishes a recommended increase in salary which is so large that executives up and down the line must become involved in assessment of the individual before the increase is approved. In this way the young men who are not working out are not allowed to float along indefinitely — a very real problem in too many sales organizations.

Several other companies have a policy of planned geographic changes; key managers are moved into larger districts in order to provide them with the challenge of new customers and salesmen. While this admittedly increases expenses and disrupts some customer relationships, according to these companies it more than pays off in greater motivation and broader exposure of the key managers to the company's sales problems and techniques.

Advanced Level

Finally, our career path moves a man into senior responsibilities (see Exhibit III-C). Even at this advanced level, the plan dictates that a man's development be managed and every effort be made to prevent his drifting through his career. These development efforts are fundamentally carried out in two ways:

(1) Forced decisions on advancement to higher compensation levels or larger districts, which necessarily involve intensive evaluation, are required. Those who do not warrant these top-level responsibilities are prime candidates for reassignment.

(2) Mandatory experience steps for men in these critical leadership posts are part of the program.

At this advanced level, however, no time limit is placed on the candidate's eligibility for promotion to higher jobs. Beyond the fact that the pyramid is narrowing and opportunities are not so readily available, men who are at these positions now normally are receiving the personal satisfactions and compensations that make them less restive.

Path: Professional Selling

The foregoing has described the career path as it applies to sales management. The following is an analysis of the separate and distinct use of the concept being set down for career salesmen by the leading companies that participated in this study.

Perceived Trends

The most significant finding of this study as it relates to professional selling is that advanced companies are beginning to think of active selling as a much shorter career and to plan their sales manpower accordingly. (This is not without precedent; commercial air pilots and military men, for example, retire early.) In other words, while top-notch salesmen are considered for obvious reasons a vital asset, companies are learning from experience to expect a leveling-off of performance even of their best salesmen by the time they reach age 50 or 55.

The career path for professional salesmen, which is illustrated in Exhibit IV, is designed to provide maximum compensation and recognition opportunities for successful salesmen as early in their careers as possible. At the same time, top management is moving toward earlier and earlier retirement ages for salesmen. The practical fact is that the physical demands of most selling jobs, and the inevitable problems of motivation, make it unlikely that most sales-

EXHIBIT IV. SAMPLE BLUEPRINT FOR DEVELOPING FIELD SALES ORGANIZATION

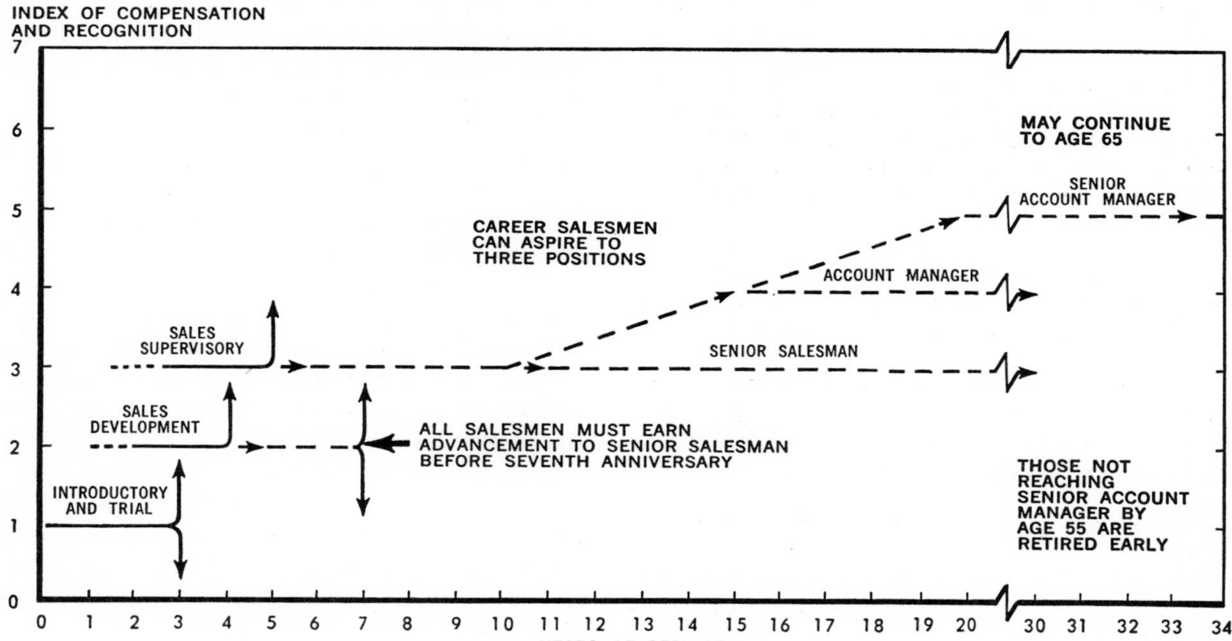

men past their early 50's will continue to be outstanding performers.

Moreover, the tendency for even the best salesmen to level off may occur at any age. Thus the forced checkpoints and decisions that are important in shaping the career path of the sales management candidate are vital in maintaining high standards for career salesmen. These concepts are reflected in the sample blueprint for developing the selling organization shown in the exhibit. Note that the flow of salesmen comes from two manpower sources: (1) those reaching the sales development stage who continue on as career salesmen, and (2) sales supervisors who are more suited to direct selling.

This concept also recognizes that men at the sales development stage must earn advancement to the next higher stage (senior salesman) before their seventh anniversary with the company, or again a forced up-or-out decision is made. (One company has set this hurdle at age 35.) This further ensures the early identification and weeding out of men who are not likely to be productive over the long haul.

Successful career salesmen can then aspire to three recognized promotions: senior salesman, account manager, and senior account manager. Beyond this point, however, senior salesmen and account managers will gradually be phased into an early retirement program. This is simply a recognition of the fact that the selling job is meant for younger men, and that moving older men out of their selling jobs must be factored into the corporate retirement planning machinery.

Early retirement — say, at age 55 — is not as startling as it may seem at first glance. With Social Security benefits expanding and many companies instituting early retirement programs for selected individuals, the basis for this program is already in motion. (In fact, at least one company retires all of its field sales personnel at age 60, even now.) Senior account managers, however, may continue to age 65 before retirement. This is in recognition of their real value as pivotal men in the selling organization.

Conclusion

Abstracting from the experience of companies we studied, we find that the Career Path Concept affords six principal advantages:

- It draws all the interrelated policies and problems involved in manpower development into a cohesive whole, thereby enabling top management to see the overall process, rather than a number of disconnected activities.

- At any given point in time it provides top management with an inventory of sales manpower at each stage of development, and thus a rational basis for evaluating the "people assets" of the sales force.

◖ It gives top management an opportunity to play an active role in the process without becoming enmeshed in the details. With the manpower situation clearly laid out, top management can guide and control the process in terms of the overall needs of the business.

◖ It provides a common language, direction, and unity of purpose to all those in the organization concerned with the development of people.

◖ It forces conscious policy decisions at key points in the process, thus minimizing "drift." With explicit policy to guide them, people are less prone to go off on their own, unrelated ways.

◖ It speeds up the training and development of men, and betters a company's capability for retaining high-potential men whose reason and ambition are both satisfied by the rationality and movement of the career path.

Moreover, the application of the Career Path Concept need not be limited to sales. Although this concept has grown out of our study of sales organizations, it is apparent that it can be adapted and applied to manpower development in any major operating department — production, finance, R & D, and so forth.

Rupert C. Thompson, Chairman of Textron Inc., remarked recently: "The economy has been so strong that it's bailing companies out of a lot of foolish moves." Similarly, our study of sales manpower development leads us to the conclusion that only the strength of the economy has spared many companies the worst consequences of outdated and haphazard methods of developing their sales manpower.

Our study has also disclosed, however, a growing recognition of the inherent dangers of coasting with the men and methods available, and the consequent emergence of new approaches for restoring vitality to the sales organization. These new approaches are characterized by an effort to give integrity to the sales manpower development process. This, in turn, enables top management to see recruiting, selection, training, supervision, performance evaluation, compensation, management development and manpower planning — all these — as aspects of *one* problem, that of forging an effective and competitive sales organization.

In sum, there is a growing tendency to centralize the sales manpower development function, guiding and controlling it with concrete, fact-founded policies, and making it a direct concern of top management. The Career Path Concept described in this article is a composite of these approaches derived from our study of the sales organizations of leading — and thriving — companies.

Derek A. Newton

14 Get the Most Out of Your Sales Force

Foreword

Sales management practice is like Topsy—it just grew. Each sales executive tends to work out his own style of managing from the assortment of principles he inherits from his predecessor, the customs of the industry in which he is operating, his own ideas, the expressed preferences of his corporate superiors, and so on. There has been a signal lack of method in this vital and challenging area of management. The research results presented in this article represent a considerably more scientific approach to the problem. By querying a large sample of companies on their practices and then matching the responses with indicators of high success, the author has derived a useful set of management guidelines for each of the major kinds of selling activity he has considered.

The typical sales executive does a lot of wondering about his sales force, not only about what they are doing "out there," but about his own management practices. Is he deploying his men correctly? How good are the selection and training procedures? Are controls sufficient? Is he paying his men too little or too much? His goals are good performance and low turnover on the selling staff; in order to achieve them he must find the right men and get the most out of them, and obtain their loyalty so that he can keep them. How can he best do this?

Advice for the sales executive in that dilemma has had to be pretty vague up to now. I have recently completed a research project, however, which sheds considerable light on the problem of improving performance and reducing turnover in the sales force. This study was designed to answer four specific questions:

1. How does the selling task to be performed differ for each of the main kinds of selling that are done today; and do these differences call for differences in management approach?
2. What management practices increase performance for each kind of selling?
3. What practices decrease turnover?
4. How are performance and turnover related to one another?

The study reports the responses of 1,029 sales executives to a questionnaire designed to probe management practices and to measure performance and turnover. Of the 1,029 respondents, 75% identified themselves as working at the level of general sales manager or higher. The sample comprised many kinds of manufacturing, wholesaling, and service businesses.

Four kinds of selling

In one sense, the very variety of companies represented in this sample constitutes a stumbling block. A specialized sample, on the other hand, would probably lead only to specialized conclusions. As it happens, pretests of the questionnaire indicated that one can effectively isolate four basic styles of selling that cut across industry boundaries to a large degree, and I shall present the results in this article in the context of these four basic styles:

1. Trade selling.
2. Missionary selling.
3. Technical selling.
4. New-business selling.

Each sales executive queried was asked to specify the primary responsibility of his force—whether it was trade, missionary, technical, or new-business selling. The responses showed that the breakdown of the total sample was fairly even among these four categories.

But before I discuss each of these four kinds of selling in detail, I shall explain the indexes that were used to measure performance and turnover, and present eight findings that apply to the entire sample, regardless of classification.

Measurements

The questionnaire gathered data for the two-year period, 1966-1967. From these data, several quantitative measurements were derived for each of the responding organizations.

Turnover rate: This quantity is the number of salesmen who quit or were discharged from a company divided by the average size of the company's sales force during the two-year period. (This is the same formula as that used by the Bureau of Labor Statistics.) While this formula has some disadvantages, it has the signal advantages of being simple, easily understood, and widely used.

Performance index: This quantity is the rate of growth of sales divided by the rate of growth of sales force. It represents the increase in sales volume per salesman over the two-year period—if you will, the increase in per-man productivity.

The reader may wonder why I did not measure performance directly, by change in sales volume. The reason for this ought to be obvious: factors other than sales force performance bear on changes in sales volume—industry growth rates, mergers and acquisitions, market conditions, management efficiency and marketing efficiency, and so on—and these factors are largely beyond the control of the sales force executive. The executive *does* control the rate of growth of his sales force, however, and I have therefore used this rate as the divisor in the index to counteract the effects of "outside" influences on changes in sales volume. This index reflects the quality of management practices more accurately than mere change in sales volume.

This performance index has its advantages and limitations. For example, while it does reward companies that increase sales faster than they increase manpower, it has the effect of penalizing the company that must temporarily deploy many salesmen to achieve an increase in market coverage. Still, the responses to the questionnaire show that the sales executive judges his own performance along a dimension parallel to this index; that is, the index was high for those companies whose executives thought that their forces were performing well, and the index was low for those companies that thought their forces were performing poorly.

Compensation rates: Compensation rates were tabulated for each company within each of the four sales classifications for the average-, highest-, and lowest-paid salesman. By comparing these data with performance and turnover rates for each company, it was possible to determine how much a salesman working on a given kind of sales force ought to be paid. Conversely, it indicated how high a level of performance and how low a rate of turnover the sales executive ought to expect for paying his men a given amount. The questionnaire also elicited information on methods of compensation—the mixture of straight salary, commission, and bonus that produces the best results in each kind of selling task.

Span of control: This quantity is the average number of salesmen on a force divided by the average number of field supervisors. As we shall see, high performance and low turnover correlate with different spans of control for each of the four sales classifications.

Opportunity rate: The percentage of men transferred out and promoted from the sales force measures advancement opportunity. The specific findings indicate that the sales executive should be careful to see that this rate of opportunity is neither too high nor too low, and the data collected suggest the optimal range for each sales classification.

Earnings opportunity ratio (EOR): This is the ratio of the compensation of the highest-paid salesman on a sales force to that of the average-paid salesman. Extremely high or low ratios correlate with high turnover. For a reason I shall explain later, the executive ought to keep an eye on this quantity as well.

Eight major findings

The digested data from the study exhibit eight strong conclusions that apply to all the sales force classifications alike.

1. *The turnover rate of a sales force does not directly influence its performance index.*

High performance, in other words, is just as likely to be accompanied by high turnover as by low; and the same is true for low performance.

2. *A turnover rate of 10% or more is excessively costly in all classifications, and should be avoided if possible.*

The extra costs associated with turnover, such as interruption of customers' ordering routines, and its less tangible costs, such as the disruption of customer-salesman rapport, are obvious evils. But the executive ought to look beyond these obvious considerations to a much more important one: according to the data, the factor discriminating most strongly between sales forces that are expensive to operate and those that are economical is the level of hiring activity. Hence low turnover is likely to mean a low-cost sales force, and the executive who wants a low-cost force should therefore devote a good deal of his attention to his hiring practices.

3. *The turnover rate is directly influenced by the opportunity rate.*

Sales forces which exhibit opportunity rates in excess of 6% are likely to be plagued by high turnover. I think this fact is explained easily enough: an opportunity rate of 6% or more suggests that the company is using the sales force as a convenient training ground for future marketing managers and supervisory sales personnel, and many applicants will be drawn to such sales forces by the prospect of advancement rather than by the appeal of sales work per se. But selling per se is their main function; and when management becomes aware of any lack of commitment to sales work on the part of its salesmen, it is likely to pass them over, thus inducing them to quit in disgust. In some cases, no doubt, management simply fires them.

4. *Turnover is also directly influenced by compensation level.*

Sales forces that have low average pay scales exhibit high turnover. It is not equally true, on the other hand, that high pay means low turnover. Paying one's best salesman overgenerously is ineffective in reducing turnover (of course, there may be other, valid reasons for tolerating a high EOR). The data show that an EOR greater than 2.0 in any sales force tends to drive up costs without reducing turnover.

5. *The compensation level, however, does not directly influence the performance index, although the method of compensation does.*

Once the executive has satisfied himself that his force's compensation level is on a par with the competition's, he ought to check carefully to see that the balance of fixed salary, commission, and bonus is "right" for the psychological temper of his crew. We shall look into the various payment mixes which are appropriate to each of the sales force classifications later in the article.

6. *The performance index is directly influenced by the character and effectiveness of the reporting system used to control the force.*

The universal characteristic of the high-performance force is that its management *insists* on receiving the frequent and regular reports that are critical to controlling sales force behavior. Because different kinds of reporting are critical to different kinds of forces, and because insistence on excessive reporting boosts the turnover rate rapidly, the sales executive must be extremely careful to identify the truly critical and necessary reports and play down or eliminate all others. The study identifies the specific reports that are critical for success in trade and

Study sample

The survey population comprised companies and corporate divisions that employed 10 or more salesmen as of December 31, 1967. It excluded companies that were primarily engaged in retail selling ("behind the counter") and delivery selling (route selling, for example). It also excluded companies whose businesses were primarily banking, insurance, and real estate. Retailing and delivery forces were excluded because companies engaged in these kinds of selling do not ordinarily compete for the kind of salesmen one ordinarily associates with "outside" selling. Banking, insurance, and real estate companies were excluded because their methods of measuring sales performance and turnover are not easily compared with those of the rest of industry.

Companies that employed fewer than 10 salesmen were not included, because pretests of the questionnaire indicated that such companies are likely to use only limited, *ad hoc* supervisory procedures in their sales force management.

---

technical selling; for the rest, the executive must use his own good judgment.

These six results are augmented by some discoveries about two other key quantities investigated by the questionnaire.

7. *Average chronological age differs among the four sales force classifications, but for each classification there is an optimal average age.*

For example, a "younger" force typically has high turnover, but also has abundant energy. Hence it may perform highly where energy is a major requisite. On the other hand, an "older" force has more maturity and stability, and is likely to perform best where these characteristics are most useful.

8. *Job content is a critical factor affecting performance and turnover.*

The kind of challenge in a particular selling job and the actual work which the salesman is called on to do determine the kind of man the executive ought to hire. This is primary. Once he has the kind of men that he wants, he must then *match his management practice to the men in their jobs.*

Let's take a careful look, now, at each of the four basic kinds of selling jobs that I studied and see (a) what kinds of men are required for each, and (b) how the executive ought to handle his men once he has them.

Trade Selling

The primary responsibility of the trade sales force is to build up the volume of a company's sales to its customers by providing them with *promotional assistance.* This generally amounts to improving the company's distribution channels, or, where the customer is himself a manufacturer, helping him to become a more effective seller. The trade sales force therefore "sells *through,*" rather than "sells *to,*" its customers.

Trade selling is a feature of many industries, but it predominates in food, textiles, apparel, and wholesaling. Products sold in this way tend to be well established; hence a company's selling effort, as such, is often less important than its advertising and promotion efforts. Much of this kind of selling is low-key, and the trade salesman is not as highly pressured from above as are his cousins in new-business sales, for example; but his job can easily become dull and repetitious if he has to do too much shelf-stocking or too much order-taking. The good trade salesman must be helpful and persuasive, and must thoroughly understand how the customer runs his business. Aggressiveness is less important than maturity, and technical competence is often less important than "wearing well" with customers.

Managers of high-performance forces appear to recognize many of the requirements and limitations of this kind of sales activity. For example, the high-performance groups in trade selling are older. *Exhibit I* compares the average ages of salesmen in the four classifications, and shows the average age of the highest- and lowest-performance quintiles in each. Maturity is quite evident in the highest-performance quintile in trade selling, as it is in the highest-performance quintile in new-business sales.

While maturity may be desirable here, seniority is not necessarily so. The study data exhibit no such useful correlation between seniority and turnover, for example. Turnover is largely a phenomenon of the first few years on the job;

Exhibit I. The impact of average age on performance

Age of salesmen	Trade force performance by quintile			Missionary force performance by quintile			Technical force performance by quintile			New-business force performance by quintile			Total-sample average
	Highest	Average	Lowest	Highest	Average	Lowest	Highest	Average	Lowest	Highest	Average	Lowest	
Less than 30 years old	18.8%*	19.7%	23.7%	22.2%	17.8%	13.1%	18.1%	17.8%	13.9%	18.5%	22.1%	22.4%	19.2%
30-39 years old	32.4	35.0	39.6	31.9	34.4	37.9	39.4	37.2	39.4	32.7	34.8	39.9	35.6
40 years old or older	48.8	45.3	36.7	45.9	47.8	49.0	42.5	45.0	46.7	48.8	43.1	37.7	45.2

*Read: salesmen under 30 years of age account for 18.8% of the sales force personnel of firms within the highest-performance quintile, and so on.

in other words, the longer a man has been with a company, the less likely he is to quit or be discharged. But turnover is also a function of chronological age: the younger the force, the higher the turnover. Age and job turnover are in fact so strongly interrelated that observations about the impact of seniority on turnover are pointless.

The kind of comparison made in *Exhibit I*, when applied to other data from the study, provides a number of useful findings. In sketching out the guidelines presented in this article, my general method of analysis has been to find out what is "standard operating procedure" (i.e., average age of existing sales forces, average compensation, standard methods of pay, and so forth) and then to judge what variations in standard procedure conduce to a sales force showing performance in the highest quintile and turnover in the lowest quintile.

Guidelines

Obviously, the trade sales executive should do what he can to improve performance. Also, although turnover does not directly influence performance, it is expensive when it is excessive, and he should do what he can to hold it down. Note that the following recommendations do not involve any trading-off between performance goals and turnover goals; that is, the executive can apply them all without being forced to choose between improving performance and reducing turnover.

To begin with, the executive ought to give considerable thought to job content. Any action he can take to reduce drudgery or the salesman's lurking feeling that he is nothing but a pawn in a giant chess game will improve performance and reduce turnover. Therefore, the executive should:

○ Transfer salesmen among territories as infrequently as possible—except, of course, at their own request.

○ Design the sales-call pattern so that the salesman feels he is making important sales-related calls and not merely putting in appearances for the sake of the company's image. On the average, the salesman should be given three to five chances a day to actually make a sale. Requiring more than five calls a day, even on regular accounts, is associated with high turnover.

○ Avoid asking the salesman to peddle "easy-to-buy" products—it makes him feel like a deliveryman. If a product line requires no persistence to sell it, then it may well not require a salesman at all.

The source of employees has more influence on turnover than the methods used to select applicants. Whereas the number of interviews, tests administered, and so forth do not appear to be associated with performance or turnover, companies that place heavy reliance on employment agencies and advertisements exhibit higher-than-average rates of turnover as well as disproportionately high sales force costs.

Compared with the industry grapevine and company initiative, for example, these methods of procuring applicants tend to be highly impersonal. Hiring applicants "off the street," so to speak, invites turnover trouble—which suggests that executives ought to know more than they do about their salesmen *before* they hire them.

So far as the composition of the sales force is concerned, as I have said, the balance tips in favor of the older salesman. Therefore, the executive should:

○ Use company contacts to seek out and hire salesmen in their forties or late thirties, and avoid placing heavy reliance on advertisements and employment agencies for recruitment.

The *amount* a salesman is paid appears to be an important factor in turnover, and the *method* by which he is paid appears to be an important factor in performance. The desirability of having the trade salesman view himself and his job as important to the company's marketing efforts and the influence of the size of a man's paycheck on his perception of himself indicate that generosity is called for in making compensation decisions about the trade sales force. Therefore, the executive should:

○ Make sure that, unless industry pay scales dictate otherwise, his lowest-paid salesman earns about \$8,000 a year, his average salesman about \$13,000, and his highest-paid salesman between \$20,000 and \$26,000.[1]

Quite surprisingly, the study data bearing on optimal methods of payment show that paying a low ratio of salary to commission works best. The practice of the high-performance, low-turnover forces suggests that the executive should:

○ Pay only about 60% of the average salesman's compensation in the form of fixed salary. (For every other sales force classification this proportion is 80%. That 60% works best here may surprise those executives who believe that, of the four classifications of salesmen, the salesman on the trade force has the least direct influence on sales volume. I was not prepared for this result myself. After all, trade sales volume is very heavily influenced by "outside" factors like promotion and advertising efforts; and it seems to follow that the trade salesman ought to receive a high proportion of his pay in fixed form. But consider the salesman's point of view. If he knows that a larger proportion of his pay is variable, this helps to offset his natural perception that his efforts are unimportant in comparison with his company's promotion and advertising; this increases his job satisfaction and thus improves his performance. Also, if he has the impression that he himself can really influence sales volume, he is less likely to get discouraged and quit. Thus a high proportion of variable pay tends to depress turnover as well.)

Close personal supervision, particularly for experienced salesmen, does little to improve performance and may—as a source of job dissatisfaction—encourage high turnover. Also, many salesmen appear to perceive quotas and paper work as childish or unnecessary. The study data support the conclusion that use of quotas merely boosts turnover and reduces performance. On the other hand, using an intelligent system of reporting to control the critical functions of the sales job improves performance and substitutes for close personal supervision. The data indicate that the executive should:

○ Maintain a ratio of salesmen to field supervisors of around 12 to 1, depending on the proportion of inexperienced men in his sales force. (With a high proportion of experienced men, I would increase this span of control to 16 to 1.)

○ Avoid the use of personal sales quotas for salesmen.

○ Avoid requesting reports from salesmen except for those reports critical to controlling sales force behavior. (In these latter instances, the executive should *insist* on receiving them. For example, the *customer inventory report* is critical in trade sales.)

The company's training programs also significantly affect performance. Hence the executive should:

○ Compare in-house training effects with those of the successful competition. (In my

1. Dollar figures, here and elsewhere in the article, reflect what was reported at the time of the study; hence represent 1967 values.

study, high-performing forces use: less initial training and less classroom training, probably because they seek out better-qualified applicants; more on-the-job training for new men, to make sure of a smooth launching; and less on-the-job training for experienced men, a condition which probably reflects more acute management reporting controls.)

A company that uses the salesman's job as a training ground for marketing management careers may be inviting a turnover problem, as I have already stated. Therefore, the executive should:

○ Refrain from viewing the sales force assignment as a form of purgatory necessary for further advancement in the company. (Specifically, the executive should strive to keep the opportunity rate below 4%, perhaps partly by broadening the supervisory span of control and partly by reducing the number of management levels so as to make the sales organization as "horizontal" as possible.)

The general thrust of these recommendations for trade force management is twofold:

▽ The executive must make the salesman perceive himself as an important element in his company's marketing strategy. To some extent, current trade force practice follows these recommendations. Trade sales executives, compared to executives in the other three classifications, emphasize commission compensation, and tend to design territories for equal earnings opportunities; they play down close personal supervision and opportunities for promotion, and avoid recruiting members of the sales force from agencies.

△ On the other hand, the executive must avoid some current trade force management practice which tends to defeat the goals as they have been stated here (and which, as a matter of fact, accounts for much of the lack of correlation between high performance and low turnover in the sample). This practice—emphasizing use of personal sales quotas, maximizing the number of selling calls per day, and selling the easiest-to-buy items in the line—tends to undercut the importance of the total compensation that the salesman receives.

Following all these recommendations may pose problems for certain sales executives. To begin with, it is not always possible to have salesmen perceive themselves as important elements in the marketing strategy. In many companies, particularly the large, mass-distribution organizations, the salesman just is not very important, and no amount of telling him that he *is* important will offset his observation that advertising and promotion move the merchandise and he merely keeps the shelves stocked. If a company just needs someone to call on the dealers, if marketing management personnel need trade sales experience as training, and if the *real* sales activity must be restricted to a few executive salesmen who call on key customers—well, there may be no justification for making the changes necessary to attract and keep high-caliber trade salesmen.

In other companies, particularly the smaller ones for which the cost of operating the sales force is a significant percentage of the sales dollar, it may be difficult to invest the necessary money in salesman compensation to attract and keep high-caliber salesmen. High costs, however, appear to be more closely associated with high hiring levels than with high compensation levels. Here the small-company executive should pay very serious attention to his applicants.

Missionary selling

The primary responsibility of the missionary force is to increase its company's sales volume by providing its direct customers with *personal selling assistance.* It performs this function by persuading its indirect customers to purchase company products through these direct customers—distribution channels, wholesalers, and so forth. The familiar "medical detail man," who calls on doctors as the representative of a pharmaceutical house, is a typical example of the missionary.

Like trade selling, missionary selling is low-key, but it differs in its primary objective; the missionary force "sells *for*" its direct customers, whereas the trade force "sells *through*" them. Responses to the questionnaire indicate that this type of selling is common in many industry categories—especially so in foods, chemicals, transportation and warehousing, wholesaling, and the utilities.

Good coverage of the market and the ability to make a succinct, yet persuasive, presentation of product benefits is vitally important in missionary sales. One missionary executive refers to his salesmen as "animated direct mail." This term is perhaps a bit harsh. Nevertheless, the missionary salesman tends to be more a communicator and persuader than a problem-solver.

This observation is supported by the relationships between the performance index and (a) the number of calls the missionary makes, (b) the number of calls he must make to produce a sale, and (c) the frequency of territorial transfer. First, the more calls the missionary is required to make, the higher his performance is likely to be. Second, as *Exhibit II* shows, the performance index rises as the number of calls required to make a sale declines. This implies that frequent call-backs are less likely to be productive in missionary selling than fresh calls, underscoring the fact that close customer-salesman relationships are relatively unimportant in this classification. Third, *Exhibit II* shows that the performance index also rises as the number of territorial transfers increases. This indicates that occasional transfers may have a mildly salutary effect on both the customers and the salesmen.

Exhibit II. Average performance index by frequency of transfer and by number of calls to produce an order from a new customer

	Number of companies	Average performance index
Frequency of transfer		
Never	33	102.9
Seldom	105	108.2
Occasionally	54	109.3
Calls required		
One	12	110.3
Two or three	57	108.0
Four or five	56	109.2
Six to ten	27	99.6
Eleven or more	17	105.8

Clearly the situation here is quite different from the trade selling situation, and clearly it calls for a different kind of man.

A basic dilemma

The good missionary salesman, then, is energetic and articulate. He need not be a good "closer," because his primary audience does not buy directly from him. His personality is very important, but the cultivation of long-term customer relationships is less important than it is for the trade sales force. The major drawback in this kind of selling is that the salesman is not challenged intellectually and lacks the opportunity to develop personally satisfying relationships with his customers.

The successful missionary sales force sidesteps these drawbacks by hiring young men with the physical stamina to make a lot of calls and then making them "run like Yellow Dog Dingo," to use Kipling's phrase. (Note the age spreads for this classification in *Exhibit I.*) Little premium is placed on applicants' previous sales experience. Because of their relative youth and inexperience, their compensation package includes a high proportion of fixed salary, and the general level of pay tends to be low. Because the job may not be basically difficult and because the influence of supervision on performance may be hard to detect, the *amounts* of training and supervision are kept at minimum levels, commensurate with getting the job done.

High performance results from keeping the salesman busy; low turnover results from hiring an older sales force. The low-turnover force is relatively well paid; the high-performance sales force is not. The missionary sales executive is thus forced to choose between an older, more stable, higher-paid, relatively low-performing sales force and a younger, more volatile, lower-paid, but relatively high-performing sales force. This dilemma is reflected in the guidelines for missionary sales management that I have drawn from the study.

Guidelines

The missionary sales executive can afford to pay less attention to making the salesman's job activities satisfying, since the impact of this factor on turnover is low. On the other hand, he needs to devote *more* attention to making his men's call routines as efficient as possible, since the impact of this factor on performance is high. Therefore, he should:

○ Deploy salesmen to maximize sales volume at minimum sales force cost.

As I have said, the young sales force outperforms the older, and the need for a high degree of selling skill is not so important, since much of the closing activity is left to resellers. Therefore, the executive should:

○ Seek out and hire inexperienced men in their twenties or early thirties.

○ Avoid judging an applicant by his previous sales experience.

○ As in trade selling, avoid relying on agencies and advertisements for applicants.

Compensation higher than the industry average does little to improve performance, but it does reduce turnover. In addition, a high proportion of fixed earnings is a positive factor in controlling operating costs. Therefore, the executive should:

○ Make sure that, unless industry pay scales dictate otherwise, his lowest-paid salesman earns about $8,000, his average salesman between $11,000 and $12,000, and his highest-paid salesman between $17,000 and $18,000.

○ Use a compensation method whereby at least 80% of the average salesman's earnings comes to him in the form of salary.

To improve sales-call efficiency, the executive can encourage his supervisors to plan more thoroughly to achieve maximum volume at minimum cost. Since the span of control appears to influence performance very little and has a mixed influence on turnover, the average span exhibited by the highest-performance quintile is a good guide. Thus he should:

○ Maintain a ratio of salesmen to supervisors of about 10 to 1.

Although high advancement opportunity may induce costly turnover problems without necessarily improving performance, the executive must permit enough advancement opportunity to attract the energetic young man. The forces in the highest-performance quintile seem to have achieved this balance, and the executive might well be guided by their practice. Accordingly, he should:

○ Keep the opportunity rate below 6%.

Current practice in the missionary sector agrees with many of these guidelines. It emphasizes cold-calling, many calls per day, and many accounts per man; and it plays down call-back and the importance of high compensation. Current practice diverges from these guidelines by emphasizing maturity and previous sales experience as an applicant-selection criterion, and pays excessive attention to close personal supervision. The missionary sales executive can readily check his own practices against these criteria.

Implementing these recommendations poses problems for many companies, particularly the smaller ones that assign a dual role to the sales force. Although missionary selling may be the sales force's primary responsibility, trade, technical, or new-business selling is often an important secondary role, and certain sales management practices better suited to these latter roles conflict with my recommendations for missionary sales management. One possible alternative is to split the sales force, but this action is either impractical or uneconomical for many companies.

If important secondary selling activities require a different kind of selling from the "animated direct mail" function suggested by the data on the missionary sales force, a company may downgrade the total selling capabilities of its current sales force by following these recommendations too closely. If, on the other hand, a careful review of the job content reveals that the sales-force function can be performed by younger, less-experienced, and lower-paid personnel making more calls per day, the increase in per-man productivity may offset the added costs caused by the higher rate of turnover that these procedures will induce.

Technical selling

The primary responsibility of the technical sales force is to increase the company's volume of sales to its existing customers by providing them with technical advice and assistance. The industrial-products salesman who sells to the customer's purchasing agents is a good example of this type. Unlike the trade or missionary salesman, the technical salesman sells directly *to* the user or buyer. The technical sales force is well represented in chemicals, machinery, and the heavy-equipment categories.

In this area, the ability to identify, analyze, and solve customers' problems is vitally important, and in this sense technical selling is very much like professional consulting. As in consulting, both technical competence and personality are important qualities in the salesman—he must be able to penetrate deeply into customers' problems and persuasively present his products' benefits as the partial or complete solution to them. Too much aggressiveness, on the one hand, can undermine this delicate relationship; too little, on the other, will result in lost sales opportunities.

The executive who manages a successful technical sales force provides his men with a good deal of support, especially by emphasizing training and retraining activities and encouraging a close, continuing rapport between salesman and supervisor. The executive selects his men primarily for their ability to achieve technical competence, and then provides them with the assistance they need to master this difficult kind of selling job.

The high-performance sales force is relatively young. This reflects the need for recent education; indeed, the proportion of college graduates is higher in this classification than in any of the others. Pay scales must therefore be high enough to attract the intelligent, educated, and personable young men who are suited for this kind of work.

In the high-performance force, close personal supervision is supplemented by the judicious use of salesmen's reports. The critical report here is the *competitive* or *market information report*. This is just as important to high performance here as the customer inventory report is to high trade sales performance.

Guidelines

The technical sales executive faces the same dilemma as the missionary sales executive: the younger force outperforms the older one, but the younger one exhibits excessive—and hence costly—turnover. In advancing the following recommendations, I am not disregarding this conflict but, rather, am making the assumption that high performance accompanied by a mild degree of turnover is more desirable than low performance accompanied by vitrification of the sales force.

The executive should control those aspects of the work—cold-calling, most notably—that are likely to jar the nerves of the man who has the basic talents and qualities to succeed in technical sales; otherwise, turnover will rise. He must also key his deployment decisions to building up customer-salesman relations, or performance will suffer. These relations are particularly critical in technical sales, where the salesman is frequently responsible for coordinating or supplying customer services, solving customers' problems, and negotiating contracts and the like. Therefore, the executive should:

○ Design sales territories so as to optimize the customer's satisfaction with the sales-call pattern.

○ Avoid requiring excessive cold-call activity, unless the salesman receives very generous compensation for it.

○ Transfer salesmen among territories as infrequently as possible (except, of course, at their own request).

When he makes a hiring decision, the executive should place more emphasis on what a man will bring to his job, as opposed to what he will be able to get out of it for himself. Whatever else, the technical salesman is not in business for himself—he is in business for his company.

In addition, the possession of a college degree, while not associated with high performance, *is* associated with low turnover; this suggests that technical selling provides more satisfaction to the educationally higher-qualified man than any other kind of selling. Therefore, the executive should:

○ Base hiring decisions more on an applicant's technical knowledge than on his desire to make money.

○ Seek out and hire college graduates in their late twenties and early thirties. (For this classification, employment agencies and advertisements are fair sources of applicants.)

For the technical sales force, training can play an important part in improving performance and reducing turnover. In addition, the data shown in *Exhibit III* indicate that the executive who faces major turnover problems might well consider the possibility of lengthening the period of initial training with a view to preparing the trainee more adequately before sending him out to face the company's customers. Therefore, the executive should:

○ Make sure trainees are adequately prepared to handle the selling and technical aspects of the job before assigning them to their territories.

○ Rely heavily on brief, but regular, retraining sessions to achieve the major training objectives.

Unlike the trade sales executive, who should be generous with salesman's pay, and the mission-

Exhibit III. Length of initial training period in technical sales forces by turnover quintiles

Turnover quintile	Average length of period (in days)	Average turnover rate
Very low	125	1.0%
Low	95	4.2
Average	97	7.5
High	62	11.7
Very high	65	24.3

ary sales executive, who can afford to be niggardly, the technical sales executive should ordinarily pay approximately the going industry rate. Because the competition for good technical salesmen is severe, the executive should recognize that he is likely to have to pay a premium for certain of his strategic deployment and selection decisions. Once again, a sensible pay scale appears to be the one suggested by the average of the companies in the highest-performance quintile, and the proportion of variable pay suggested by the average of the companies in the lowest-turnover quintile. Therefore, the executive should:

○ Make sure that, unless industry pay scales dictate otherwise, his lowest-paid salesman earns about $9,000, his average salesman between $12,000 and $13,000, and his highest-paid salesman earns between $20,000 and $26,000.

○ Adjust pay scales upward to compensate for either excessive cold-call activity or a college degree.

The incentive offered by commission and bonus payment may not be as important to the good technical salesman; the executive can follow the practice suggested by the high-performance sales forces here:

○ Pay about 80% of the average salesman's earnings in the form of fixed salary.

Close contact between salesman and supervisor supplements training and provides closer liaison between the home office and the marketplace. A good reporting system conduces to this close contact. The practice of companies in the highest-performance quintile suggests that the sales executive should:

○ Maintain a ratio of salesmen to field supervisors of about 7 to 1.

○ Place heavy emphasis on developing and improving the salesmen's reporting system, with special attention to the market information report.

Once again, a high rate of advancement opportunity, while not necessarily improving performance, contributes to excessive-turnover problems. On the other hand, this kind of environment may be necessary—within reasonable limits—to attract the younger salesmen necessary for achieving high levels of sales force performance. In keeping with practices associated with high-performance technical groups, then, the executive should:

○ Strive to keep the opportunity rate below 6%.

Implementing these recommendations demonstrates to the salesman that his *problem-solving skills are important.* He sees that his supervisor does not insist that he run around drumming up new business; that his job has been organized around the opportunity to provide important services to his customers; that he has been selected for his potential to become technically competent, and that he receives continuous training; that the company is investing above-average amounts in his fixed earnings; that it provides him with management assistance and guidance; and that he is given a fair chance of promotion.

The general thrust of these recommendations is that performance is maximized and turnover minimized when the executive makes the salesman perceive himself as performing an important consulting function for his customers on behalf of his company. Current practice is congruent with most of these recommendations. It emphasizes hiring college graduates, bringing in new salesmen through in-company transfers, training and continuously retraining them (especially in product knowledge), and paying a high proportion of compensation as fixed salary. It plays down cold-calling and calling at random. Other current practices are self-defeating—for example, building a force with a high average age and discounting the importance of the supervisor-salesman relationship.

It is interesting to note that technical sales forces as a whole exhibit a closer association between actual practice and desirable practice than the other three sales force classifications. This phenomenon is perhaps due to the wider recognition—among industrial marketers in particular—that selling has become a professional activity. In many instances, the new generation of products requires a professional to articulate their benefits. More importantly, new attitudes on the part of an increasingly sophisticated generation of purchasers demand a professional who can go beyond the articulation of product benefits and help the customer identify and solve a whole set of problems in which his product may play only a small part.

Using this concept of technical selling may pose problems for certain sales executives. A line may not need—or be able to support—this kind of salesman, especially if it is approaching the "commodity stage" because of customer familiarity and low margins. If it is important to a company that someone merely *calls on* users to keep them reordering, a shift to trade sales tactics may be in order.

Small organizations in which the cost of operating the sales force is a significant percentage of the sales dollar may find it difficult to invest the necessary money in training and supervision. Nevertheless, the increasing competition for both sales and salesmen makes it mandatory for even the small company to field a sales force well equipped to handle the challenges of the new technology.

New-business selling

This kind of selling has been variously called "canvassing," "bird-dogging," and "cold-calling." The primary responsibility of the new-business sales force is to obtain new accounts for its company, and the ability to convert a total stranger into a customer is the critical skill.

The great difficulty in this kind of selling is that the cold-calling it requires keeps the turnover rate high. The good new-business salesman is the rare bird dog who can balance the all-too-frequent exhilaration of "closing the tough one" and the equally frequent deflation that comes with the polite—or sometimes brutal—rejection.

The younger forces perform poorly and the older forces perform well, as the reader can clearly see from the percentages shown in *Exhibit I*. This bears out the conclusion that emotional maturity contributes to success in this area of selling. Younger men frequently find this activity impossibly difficult and burdensome, and tend to quit early in the game. Hence we find that the very young forces not only perform poorly, but are afflicted with excessive turnover.

The study data show that management practices are less important to successful sales operation than finding the right kind of man to begin with—the kind of man, as one executive phrased it, who has "the tough skin and the killer instinct of a shark."

The successful salesman also tends to be rather more independent of supervisory control than salesmen in the other classifications. To some extent, this must be adventitious: this classification showed much the highest rate of sales growth of the forces for the two-year period covered by the questionnaire—and the higher this growth rate, the less attention a company is likely to pay to providing training for its salesmen, presumably because the need for training is less obvious. Partly for this reason, therefore, there are no observable relationships between any training factors and the performance index.

Guidelines

The study makes it clear that applicant sources and selection methods are not correlated with performance levels, although they are correlated with turnover rate. This suggests that although executives have found ways to reduce failure (i.e., quick turnover) through their selection processes, they have not yet found ways to predict success (i.e., high performance). So far as the composition of the force is concerned, the balance turns in favor of the older man. Thus the executive should:

○ Seek out and hire salesmen in their forties and late thirties who enjoy cold-calling and have demonstrated their proficiency at it. (Company initiative is most important here.)

To some extent, the executive can regulate cold-calling where it is troublesome. One method is to restructure working patterns so that each man has enough regular business from established customers to take the sting out of the cold-call routine. The study data indicate that he should:

○ Schedule a salesman for no more than two cold calls a day unless the man is a proven "new-business specialist."

Younger sales forces really need adequate preparation for the cold-calling associated with new-business selling, and it appears worthwhile to spend considerable time and effort to improve initial and on-the-job phases of training. Therefore, the executive should:

○ Make sure that trainees are adequately prepared to cope with the vicissitudes of cold-calling before assigning them to their territories.

○ Rely heavily on on-the-job training for both new and experienced sales personnel.

The executive can be tempted toward generosity in making compensation decisions about the *average* for the new-business sales force, but be restrained in his attitude toward the *highest-paid* salesman. Also, a review of job content and fringe benefits appears worthwhile. The practices of companies in the lowest-turnover quintile suggest sensible guidelines here. The executive should:

○ Make sure that, unless industry pay scales dictate otherwise, his lowest-paid salesman earns about $8,000, his average salesman between $12,000 and $13,000, and his highest-paid salesman earns between $19,000 and $24,000. (*Exhibit IV* summarizes the optimal earnings levels for holding turnover down in the four sales classifications.)

Exhibit IV. Optimal levels of salesmen's earnings for controlling turnover

Sales force classification	Lowest-paid salesman	Average salesman	Highest-paid salesman
Trade	$8,000	$13,000	$20,000-26,000
Missionary	8,000	11,000-12,000	17,000-18,000
Technical	9,000	12,000-13,000	20,000-26,000
New-business	8,000	12,000-13,000	19,000-24,000

○ Adjust pay scales upward to compensate for excessive cold-call activity.

○ After a thorough examination, consider adding new, or making increases in established, fringe benefits.

The optimal proportion of fixed salary to total earnings is just as surprising in this classification as it is in trade sales. The data indicate that it is much higher than I had expected—around 80% for the average new-business salesman.

Many executives would reason that the new-business salesman exerts more direct influence on sales volume than any other kind of salesman, and therefore one ought to spur him on by increasing the proportion of commission and incentive in his total paycheck. But, here again, it is the salesman's point of view that is important. The cold-calling that the new-business salesman must do creates considerable tension for him in his job. Knowing that a large part of his earnings are fixed relieves him of a measure of financial uncertainty and allows him to concentrate better on the vital aspect of his work. Achieving victory in the cold call is difficult enough, it seems, without the salesman feeling that he is playing roulette with his take-home pay as well. Thus the executive should:

○ Pay 80% of the average salesman's earnings in fixed form.

Since the data on new-business sales force supervision and control exhibit very little correlation with data on performance and turnover, the executive is well advised to follow the pattern of the companies in the highest-performance quintile. He should:

○ Maintain a ratio of salesmen to field supervisors of around 10 to 1.

○ Avoid the use of personal sales quotas for salesmen (these are particularly irritating to the older salesmen); improve the reporting system instead.

○ Strive to keep the opportunity rate between 2% and 6%.

Implementing these recommendations would indicate to the salesman that he is a *valued and supported company employee,* not merely a bird dog. Salesmen are continually told this fact, but implementation convinces them: the salesman sees the company investing training time and money in him to ensure his success on the job; he sees the company compensating him in executive fashion; he sees himself protected insofar as possible from the tensions associated with cold-call activity; he feels responsible for his own performance, and is not pressed by an arbitrary quota; and he perceives his job as an important end in itself, not as a proving ground for a better one.

The broad concept here is that to achieve maximum performance and minimum turnover, the executive must hire men temperamentally compatible with cold-calling and then provide them with support and encouragement. In two ways, current practice reflects the trend of these recommendations: *one,* it emphasizes suitable methods of compensation; and *two,* it steers away from employee referrals as a source of applicants.

In a number of other ways, however, current practice is self-defeating. It encourages excessive cold-calling, use of advertisements to attract applicants, hiring on the basis of the applicant's drive to make money, and hiring young men. It also discourages significant training efforts, and plays down the importance of adequate levels of compensation. The executive should check his own practices against this list of trouble spots.

It is interesting to note that current practices in new-business selling diverge more from the study's recommendations than do those of any of the other three classifications. This may be because the new-business sales executive has usually been promoted from the ranks. He is likely to say, "I was a successful salesman, and the job was easy for *me.*" But the job is not an easy one for the average salesman, as the high average turnover rate for this classification indicates.

Giving their salesmen more support may be difficult for some sales executives. Marketing strategy may dictate a great deal of cold-call activity, period. Unless he discovers better methods of selecting salesmen, the executive may have to resign himself to high turnover or pay very high salaries to attract and keep high-caliber people.

Conclusion

To some extent, every sales organization is a hybrid of the four main kinds of sales force, and the executive who wants to take practical advantage of the findings of this study may have to balance his practices to suit the mix of roles he must administrate. If, by chance, he is supervising a selling effort that uses both technical and new-business tactics, he will have to juggle the proportions of younger, better-educated, and highly talented men and older, aggressive, hard-shelled men on his force. As both the pretests of the survey and the survey itself show, however, it is usually easy to identify the main role of any given force easily.

It may be more difficult for the executive to identify the exact goals he wishes to pursue. As we have seen, maximizing performance and minimizing turnover are not always compatible goals; in the prescription for managing the missionary force, for example, the two goals come into direct collision. Each company, or each sales executive, must decide what turnover level is tolerable; once this has been established, the executive can concentrate on specific methods to improve performance.

The study yielded a good many results that could not be included here—for instance, data and conclusions relating to field superintendents, their development, their compensation, and so forth. Also, I could not document the methods of statistical manipulation and interpretation that were used to wash the effects of interacting variables out of the data. I could not even include full statistical evidence for any of the conclusions presented. Still, the working executive will perhaps find these conclusions challenging and thought-provoking, and they may help him make his practices more effective.

Walter J. Semlow

15 How Many Salesmen Do You Need?

For all our progress in developing total marketing concepts and ways of integrating and coordinating the elements of the marketing mix, the practical marketing manager still faces some basic operating problems which are as difficult today as they were twenty years ago. Perhaps one of the most elusive of these management problems is that of deciding how many dollars to spend on the selling effort. Thus your own common sense may indicate that more salesmen are needed in your field organization; determining how many more are required to optimize the volume-expense-profit relationship is quite another matter. Or, conceivably but less probably, the same problem might arise in connection with reducing the size of the sales force.

General selling expense, of course, is made up of many different items of cost. It includes the salesmen's salaries or commissions, the field and home office supervisory and clerical costs, the advertising and sales promotion expenditures, travel outlays, convention expenses, and many other items. Since the direct and indirect cost of maintaining a *field* sales organization is often the major part of total selling expenses, a method of determining the optimum number of salesmen required to develop the most profitable selling effort is most desirable.

From this point on, let us think specifically in terms of increasing the sales force. In getting at the answer to this problem there are certain well-known factors involved with which every marketing manager is familiar. For example:

- *Some* increase in total sales volume results whenever another salesman is added.
- Increasing the number of salesmen by, say, 50% will produce something less than a 50% increase in volume, except in very unusual cases.
- Where a company's sales volume is below its capacity to produce, the profit margin on additional volume is substantial.
- When sales volume approaches plant capacity, a decision must be made by management as to investment in plant expansion. If plant capacity is to be expanded, it will generally be a substantial addition, and increased sales effort and expense will be called for to utilize this new capacity.
- Somewhere there is a point in adding salesmen (and field selling expense) beyond which it is uneconomical to go in the pursuit of volume.

The problem is to evaluate these factors in relation to your own business and to determine exactly how many salesmen you should have and what can be forecast as improvement in operating profit from adding more salesmen, both with and without plant expansion.

New Method

Since this article proposes a method for determining the optimum number of salesmen, it might be well to ask the question: "Optimum in terms of what?" Certainly more than just the highest dollar sales volume. The highest dollar profit? Or the highest profit in percentage on sales volume? Or the highest profit in percentage on investment? The method presented here gives the answer to each of these questions. However, though there might be cases where total dollar profit is more important than percentage of profit on investment, the latter yardstick is the one considered to be controlling in this analysis.

Basic Assumptions

Before discussing the process by which to determine your future needs in number of salesmen, it is necessary to make certain simplifying assumptions:

(1) You are not already obtaining a top-heavy share of the sales volume in your industry.

(2) Your business is one wherein sales manpower face-to-face with customers is a major factor in your selling job compared to advertising and other marketing adjuncts.

(3) A substantial increase in your sales volume would not bring your share of industry volume to a point where unhealthy retaliation by competitors would be incited.

(4) You have, or can develop, market potential data which will tell you what percentage of your total sales volume should come from each geographical area if all areas were to be worked with equal efficiency.

(5) You have a sufficient number of salesmen, at present, to provide a sound background for statistical analysis.

Simple Formula

You are now prepared to begin to develop, through a combination of judgment and mathematics, the exact point at which it will no longer pay you to add another man to your field sales force. The formula for arriving at this answer is simple; the only problem is getting the necessary facts to make it work. Here it is:

$$S(p) - C > 0$$

Where:

S = sales volume that each additional salesman will be expected to produce
p = the expected profit margin on this sales volume
C = the total cost of maintaining this salesman in the field

When the cost of adding the last additional salesman equals the profit on the sales volume he is expected to bring in, you have reached the end of the road. In fact, as the formula indicates, you have passed it. Since there is little sense in just trading dollars, the formula requires the profit to exceed the cost.

Two of the three pieces of factual information required in this formula can be obtained quite readily from accounting records: (a) the operating profit margin on each dollar of added volume, and (b) the total cost of maintaining each additional salesman in the field. This latter item should of course include the increased administrative, supervisory, and clerical costs, not just the direct salary and travel expenses of the salesman.

Practical Dimensions

The sales volume which one additional man might be expected to produce is not so easy to determine, and the method presented hereafter is aimed at assisting in this determination. It is well known that, in general, if two men are put into a territory where only one man worked before, the total volume from that territory will increase. The crucial question, of course, is: How much will it go up? Having the answer to that question we can make a logical approach to determining the best number of salesmen for a company. Of course, putting two men in a territory where there was one man before and increasing manpower 100% is too oversimplified. We must also know what volume to expect from 1% or 10% or 40% more salesmen.

There is no universal answer to this question which will apply in all ways to all companies. The factors involved will differ from company to company. In the illustrative analysis that follows, it is assumed that each present salesman would produce in any given area as much as any other salesman. Of course, this would not be true man-to-man because of variations in individual ability, but since our only purpose in making this assumption is to determine average performance in territories of various sizes, the assumption is sound as long as the present sales force is large enough to provide a reasonable statistical sample. This, of course, was one of our preliminary stipulations.

It is also assumed that each new man added would be, on the average, as good a salesman as the present average man. Now, of course, this will be true only after the new man has been trained and has gained some experience, and only if our standards of selection and training are maintained, but it should be true over a period of years.

As in most analyses of what would happen by changing one element in a complex situation, it is convenient to consider all other elements as fixed. In this case, the variable with which we are concerned is the number of salesmen, so that the fixed elements are the other parts of the sales operation, except only as they may vary directly with the number of salesmen.

Finally, for the sake of simplicity, it has been assumed that the competitive situation is relatively equal in all territories. If, in any particular case this assumption, or any of the above assumptions, is obviously in error, adjustment can be made for such variances by management's seasoned judgment. We must seek first to establish the over-all dimension before adjusting it to the realities of individual situations.

Required Figures

The first step in this analysis is to determine the sales potential for each salesman's territory. (The determination of territory potentials is a vast and varied subject in itself, and it is not intended here to outline or discuss how to determine these potentials; the method will vary with each company and often with each product.) For the purposes of this analysis, territory potential should be expressed in per cent of the total area to be worked. The data on potentials should be broken down by small geographical units, both to permit determination of potentials for present existing territories, and also for any future territories that might be set up.

Having determined the potentials by individual salesmen's territories, the next step is to compile the actual sales performance in each territory in dollars — preferably over a long enough period of time to eliminate abnormal sales situations from year to year. Now divide the dollar sales in each territory by the per cent of potential in each territory. This will give the *dollar sales for each 1% of potential*, which is the key figure in the analysis.

It may be generalized that a large number of salesmen cultivating many small territories will provide a larger total volume than will only a few salesmen covering large territories. This does not mean more profit necessarily; but, at the moment, we are only concerned with determining how much more volume past experience indicates will be produced by adding a certain number of additional salesmen.

The method of application follows naturally. Let us see how it works, using actual figures.

Actual Case

This type of analysis has been made for several companies of varying size, ranging from 12 to 200 men. In general, it has been found that the larger the sales organization, the more accurate the results. The example chosen for presentation here concerns a relatively simple organization of 25 one-man territories.

Plotting the Data

In EXHIBIT 1 these 25 territories have been listed in the order of their percentage of total

EXHIBIT 1. BASIC FACTUAL DATA PERTAINING TO 25 SALESMEN'S TERRITORIES

(In thousands of dollars)

Territory designation	*Size of territory in per cent of total potential*	*Total sales per territory*	*Sales per 1% of potential*
1	11.89%	$351	$ 29
2	9.53	300	31
3	7.68	244	32
4	6.36	179	28
5	6.07	393	65
6	4.78	200	42
7	4.75	192	40
8	4.64	312	67
9	4.58	169	37
10	4.10	187	45
11	3.75	218	58
12	3.42	210	61
13	3.33	151	45
14	3.08	186	60
15	2.65	234	89
16	2.61	235	90
17	2.56	194	76
18	2.50	398	160
19	2.16	208	97
20	1.86	344	185
21	1.83	288	158
22	1.80	140	78
23	1.43	252	177
24	1.39	346	250
25	1.25	257	206
	100.00%		

EXHIBIT II. RELATIONSHIP BETWEEN SALES POTENTIAL PER TERRITORY AND SALES VOLUME PER 1% OF POTENTIAL

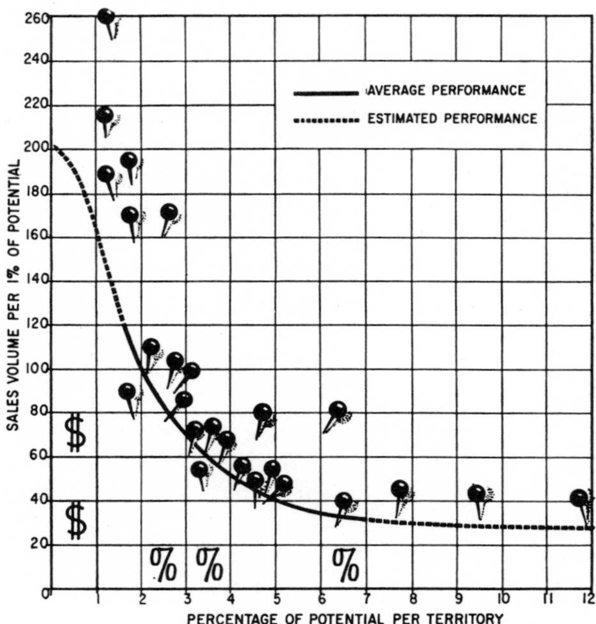

potential. Casual inspection of the exhibit reveals that there is a marked increase in the sales per 1% of potential as the territories decrease in potential. However, this trend is not uniform territory by territory. There are many irregularities. This is natural, for individual salesmen may vary greatly in ability and experience, and some territories may have been worked longer than others.

It is desirable before proceeding further to even out these irregularities, thus producing a smoother average trend of sales volume per 1% of potential for territories of varying size. These irregularities can be smoothed out by statistical methods, but it is probably easier to employ graphic methods. Even if the statistical method is used, it is better to transfer the results to graphic form for further analysis.

Accordingly, the data in EXHIBIT I have been plotted on EXHIBIT II, and an average trend line has been drawn. It will be noted that the trend line has been drawn substantially below the performance data for several of the smaller territories. These have been disregarded since they are known not to be typical for varying reasons. Some of them are located close to the home office and have been cultivated actively for many years. Others are known to have a large part of their potential in a few big accounts which are responsible for a substantial volume. Other territories are covered by unusually experienced and capable salesmen. It is in the interest of conservatism to set aside, so far as possible, such known unusual situations and to draw the trend line to fit the "typical" territories, extending it to very large and very small territories by estimation.

The termini of the curve are estimated on the basis of (a) how much business might be secured if the company had an infinite number of salesmen (zero potential per salesman) and (b) how much business it would do if it had only one salesman. While going to such meticulous extremes may seem pointless, it provides "perspective" in drawing a practical trend line.

Analysis of Potential

From this trend line on EXHIBIT II, sales volume per 1% of potential for varying sizes of territories has been transferred to EXHIBIT III. From this exhibit it is apparent that the company's volume increases with the number of

EXHIBIT III. COMPUTATION OF PROJECTED TOTAL VOLUME WITH VARYING NUMBERS OF SALESMEN
(In thousands of dollars)

Number of salesmen	*Size of territory in per cent of total potential*	*Sales per 1% of potential*	*Total sales volume*	*Sales per average salesman*
200	0.50%	$190	$19,000	$ 95
150	0.67	180	18,000	120
100	1.00	160	16,000	160
80	1.25	141	14,100	176
65	1.54	122	12,200	188
50	2.00	100	10,000	200
40	2.50	80	8,000	200
30	3.33	60	6,000	200
25	4.00	50	5,000	200
20	5.00	40	4,000	200
16	6.25	33	3,300	206
13	7.70	30	3,000	231
10	10.00	27	2,700	270

EXHIBIT IV. DETERMINATION OF OPERATING PROFIT WITH VARYING NUMBERS OF SALESMEN
(In thousands of dollars)

Number of salesmen	*Estimated total company sales volume**	*Operating profit before variable selling cost*	*Variable selling cost*	*Operating profit †*	*Total investment*	*Operating profit on sales volume*	*Operating profit on investment*
200	$19,000	$5,350	$4,000	$1,350	$17,600	7.1%	7.7%
150	18,000	5,000	3,000	2,000	17,200	11.1	11.6
100	16,000	4,500	2,000	2,500	14,400	15.6	17.4
80	14,100	3,835	1,600	2,235	13,640	15.8	16.3
65	12,200	3,470	1,300	2,170	9,880	17.8	22.0
50	10,000	2,700	1,000	1,700	9,000	17.0	18.9
40	8,000	2,200	800	1,400	6,200	17.5	22.5
30	6,000	1,500	600	900	5,400	15.0	16.6
25	5,000	1,150	500	650	5,000	13.0	13.0
20	4,000	800	400	400	4,600	10.0	8.7
16	3,300	555	320	235	4,320	7.1	5.4
13	3,000	450	260	190	4,200	6.3	4.5
10	2,700	345	200	145	4,080	5.4	3.6

* From Exhibit III.
† Column 3 minus Column 4.

salesmen, for the sales volume per 1% of potential increases as the territories get smaller.

It is also apparent that the average salesman will produce about the same volume of business, whether he has a 2% territory or a 5% territory. Of course, if territories are made very large, then the individual salesman's volume will probably increase somewhat as he "skims the cream" from this territory. On the other hand, the salesman has just so much time and energy to put in, and doubling the size of his territory will hardly double his effort. In other words, adding to his territory will not add materially to his personal sales volume unless his present territory is restrictively small and he is transferred to a much larger one.

Varying the Volume

Once the total sales volume that might logically be expected from varying numbers of salesmen is determined, it becomes necessary to compute the profit that can be derived from various sales volumes. This can be estimated from a breakeven chart and study of working capital and estimated plant investment requirements at different volume levels.

It is reasonable to expect that the profit margin will vary with the level of operations, since certain fixed costs concomitant with increases in plant investment are to be expected. In this example, the amounts of fixed costs for various levels of sales volume are estimated thus:

Volume levels	*Fixed cost*
Up to $8,100,000	$ 600,000
$8,100,001–$12,300,000	800,000
$12,300,001–$16,100,000	1,100,000
$16,100,001–$19,000,000	1,300,000

From the breakeven chart it can be figured that the margin available for profit and variable selling expense is 35% of sales volume less the fixed expense incidental to that volume bracket. For example:

> If sales volume were $8,000,000, this margin would be found by finding 35% of the volume ($2,800,000) and subtracting the fixed expense for this volume of $600,000 to yield a $2,200,000 margin. For a $10,000,000 volume, this figure would be $2,700,000.

The dollar profits before the variable sales expenses for a number of possible volume levels are shown in the third column of EXHIBIT IV. It should be noted that these profits increase with sales volume (Column 2), although at a declining rate.

We must now establish the cost of maintaining each salesman in the field, covering not only the salesman's personal income and travel expense, but such other variable expenses as home office staff, advertising literature, technical service, and any other expense increments incidental to adding one more man to the field force. This has been estimated at $20,000.

Profit on Investment

As noted at the beginning, probably the most important yardstick for determining the optimum number of salesmen is the profit return as a per cent of the investment. Total investment at any volume level is considered to consist of plant investment plus working capital requirements.

In this example, we have assumed that the

working capital requirements are 40% of sales volume at all volume levels; that present plant investment is $3,000,000; and that the present plant will service a maximum sales volume of $8,100,000. The additional plant investment required for various volume levels has been estimated as follows:

Volume level	*Incremental investment*
$8,100,000–$12,300,000	$2,000,000
$12,300,001–$16,100,000	3,000,000
Over $16,100,000	2,000,000

We have now established the volume which might be expected from any given number of salesmen; the profit that might be earned from this volume; the total investment required for such volumes; and the cost of maintaining each salesman. From this data, the following must be computed:

- Net dollar profit which will accrue with varying numbers of salesmen.
- Per cent of profit to volume of sales.
- Per cent of profit on the investment.

These figures are presented in Exhibit iv (previous page); and the same data are shown graphically in Exhibits v and vi.

Optimum Number

The exhibits allow us to study the relationships of volume and profit, and to pick the optimum number of salesmen in the light of our goals and objectives. For example:

Exhibit v. Relationship between number of salesmen and total sales volume and total operating profit in dollars

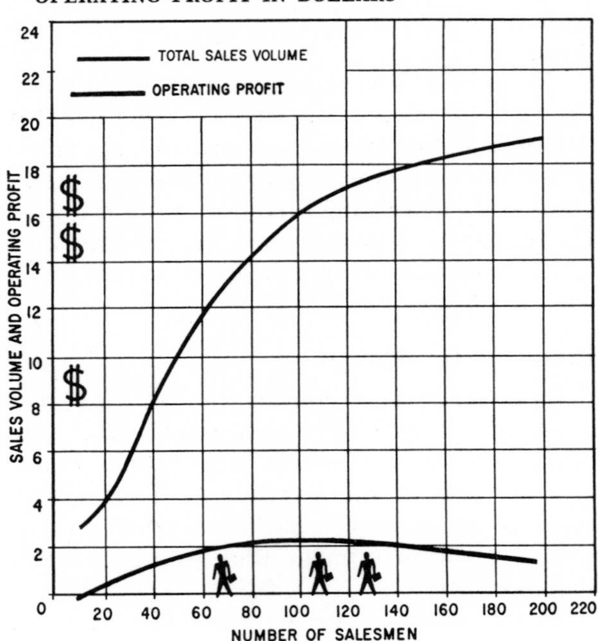

Exhibit vi. Relationship between number of salesmen and percentage of operating profit to sales volume and investment

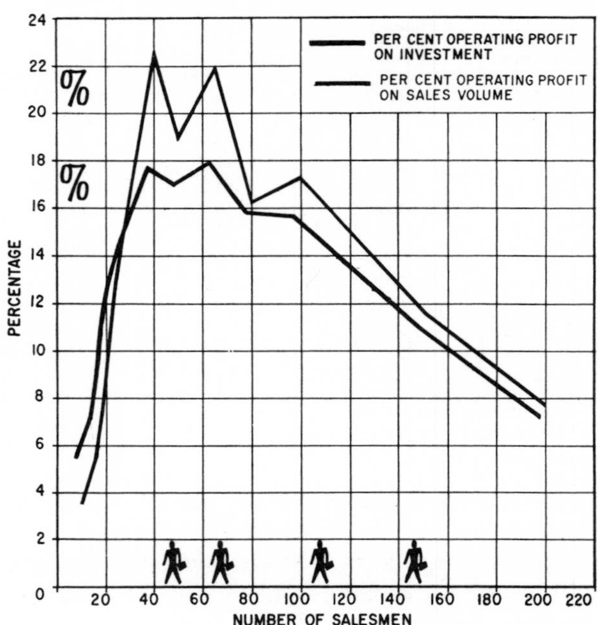

Note: Irregularities in percentage curves are due to increased plant investment and corresponding fixed costs as volume reaches certain points.

◖ If the goal is total dollar profit, the company should have approximately 100 salesmen.

◖ For maximum return on investment or profit on sales volume, the optimum number is shown to be about 65 salesmen.

Now, since the company has 25 salesmen in the field, and with all other factors in the problem remaining constant as in the past, the answer to the problem of how much to increase the sales force becomes 40 salesmen for return on investment (75 salesmen for total dollar profit).

This example has been drawn from an actual situation, in which case the analysis had the happy result of resolving conclusively rather firmly fixed differences of opinion in management regarding the expansion in sales manpower which should be planned. The differences ranged from a conservative 20% to an optimistic 100% — a situation not too unusual in many managements. In this case it was shown that at least doubling the field force definitely was not a fantastic idea.

Lest the reader think that this method does not apply to his business, let me hasten to say that while there are a number of businesses where it would not be applicable, there are also a great many where it has worked and does serve. To illustrate:

◖ The method has been successfully applied in furniture, mill supply, paper converting, stationery, and other lines where the market is diversified, the potentials can be established with reasonable accuracy, and the number of salesmen is sufficient to provide adequate performance data.

◖ It would be most difficult to apply it to companies manufacturing steam turbines, locomotives, defense products on government contracts, or in any case where the direct selling activity is characterized by a few relatively large accounts and only a few salesmen.

Balancing Factors

While, in the example given, it is evident that the company would make the most money on investment with 65 salesmen, it does not follow that it should increase its sales force by 40 men immediately. It must be remembered that it was assumed that each of these 65 men will be as productive as each of the present 25 men. This should be true eventually but will certainly not be true in the first or second, or perhaps even the third or fourth, year of their employment. Therefore, the rate at which the company should move in increasing its sales manpower will depend on how much investment it can afford to make. For example:

If the new salesman can be expected to produce only $50,000 net new volume in the first year, he will provide only $17,500 of profit, and at a cost of $20,000. Thus, the company will have a remaining investment of $2,500 in this man. If he produces $100,000 in the second year, his profit contribution in that year will be $35,000 at a cost of $20,000, or a net profit of $15,000. (This assumes that the addition of this man will not require any new plant investment.)

This question of how fast to reach the desired goal can only be answered by the individual company. In the case of the specific example discussed above, the decision was to add five men per year for the next five years, at which time the situation would be restudied. This decision was based on the time required to hire and train men, as well as the company's financial ability to invest in organization expansion.

Conclusion

It must be re-emphasized, in conclusion, that this method of analysis will not be applicable to companies whose selling programs do not resemble the list of basic assumptions on which the method rests. Moreover, in cases where the assumptions do apply, the method must be adapted to each company's individual situation and used in a realistic and practical awareness of the differences in some territories and in some salesmen.

On the other hand, when used intelligently by marketing management, this way of analyzing the problem does provide a means of coming to grips with the persistent question: How many salesmen do you need? More specifically:

- It provides a way of looking at the problem that takes into account realistic goals of profitability in terms of sales volume and, even more important, investment.
- It relates the objectives of one important part of the marketing mix to the total financial and productive capacity of the firm.
- When applied to the individual case, it gives management both a target and a map of an area in business management that has had pitifully few rules by which to navigate.
- It is simple and direct enough in approach to appeal to practical management men and as such should help them to apply judgment more soundly.

The Development of Sales and Salesmen

Joseph W. Thompson and William W. Evans

16 Behavioral Approach to Industrial Selling

Foreword

Few industrial marketing organizations have conceived as comprehensive a sales training program as Carborundum. Starting with major company objectives of flexibility and interdivisional "systems" selling, corporate marketing people studied the existing body of knowledge on behavioral sciences and incorporated the basic principles into a practical manual of marketing techniques. Then they organized their marketing and related personnel into small, mixed groups that analyzed the techniques and incorporated them into several hundred instructional cases for small group discussion. The results have been received enthusiastically, not only by management and salesmen, but by Carborundum's distributors.

In the marketing of industrial products, where there is a heavy emphasis on technical product features, there is a tendency to overlook some of the newer, more sophisticated concepts which marketers of consumer products find useful. In particular, there is little or no *explicit* application of the behavioral approach in the selling process, though, of course, effective salesmen may employ it intuitively. There are many reasons for this, right or wrong, including the fact that most industrial marketers *think* they know their customers and treat them *as if* they were completely rational and not susceptible to selling techniques beyond the presentation of product features. The fact that there is evidence to the contrary [1] does not alter the fact that most manufacturers of industrial products do act this way—and thus fail to realize their full sales potential.

The Carborundum Company is an exception to this general attitude. As we will describe in this article, the company has made a full-fledged effort to adopt behavioral science concepts for the purpose of creating excellence in its industrial selling.

At the same time we will show how this corporation is utilizing a mix of these same behavioral science concepts to accomplish several other closely related company objectives. These objectives—to strengthen the company's total marketing communication network, to utilize its human resources more effectively, and to develop an organization with marketing flexibility—are related because organizational flexibility is

1. See, for example, Theodore Levitt, *Industrial Purchasing Behavior* (Boston, Harvard Business School, Division of Research, 1965).

best achieved when individuals themselves are flexible and have the capacity to deal with change.

Company background

Carborundum is a producer and marketer of specialized industrial materials and material systems. Its markets are both multinational and multi-industry. Production is integrated from raw materials to final form. Organization is decentralized, with each profit center interrelated with many others. Operating with divisional profit centers that include complete sales forces, the company markets its goods through various types of distributors, and, in many cases, directly to ultimate industrial consumers.

In addition to divisional profit centers, the company has a central marketing organization that provides complete staff assistance to all divisions on a worldwide basis. This covers development of marketing plans, advertising and sales promotion programs including the actual production of these programs, complete public relations and product publicity programs, sales training, and marketing research.

Marketing philosophy

As part of its marketing philosophy, the company has long advocated the selling of systems rather than individual products. Systems frequently cut across divisional and company lines. To sell systems effectively—for example, to sell a cut-off machine produced by one profit center (a division or company) in combination with abrasives produced by another profit center—the groups and individuals need a common understanding of company objectives and policy concerning the marketing of the products. In addition, each group must have a common bond of knowledge and skills to penetrate markets through customer-oriented, team-selling effort.

We sought this bond of knowledge and skills through a behavioral science program based on the key premise—itself drawn from the behavioral sciences—that personal motivation and growth can be generated by the physical and mental involvement of individuals in small group situations.

At random, here are several of the numerous behavioral science concepts involved in Carborundum's behavioral science program: role; self-image; tension binding; perception; empathy; source credibility; readiness; laws of education; projection; physical, social, and psychological proximity; maturity; egocentrism; feedback; verbal and nonverbal cues; and coping behavior.

We shall now describe the details of the program, and demonstrate several behavioral science concepts in action via the case-dialogue method. Then we shall show how the program actually works in market operations, with the participation of distributors and the enlistment of personnel from all parts of the company.

Developing the program

Involvement is crucial. For, if the generation gap is to be bridged (older and newer employees), if a program is to cut across company and divisional lines, if attitudes are to be changed, if knowledge is to be absorbed, and if people-to-people interaction skill is to be developed, then research shows that this may be best accomplished through small group participation techniques. Each individual must get involved; he must expose his thoughts, his feelings, and his behavior patterns in people-to-people situations. He must also get reactions to these factors from other participants. Finally, he must have an opportunity to enact and practice alternative behavior patterns.

Accordingly, the program we developed was designed to provide an environment in which involvement, appraisal, and support could take place.

Groups of 35 to 75 were established at 14 locations in the United States. The program at each location included seven classroom days divided into blocks of three days, two days, and two days. On the average, thirty days elapsed between each block of classroom days.

Participants at each location represented a mix of product specialists, research men, engineers, district sales managers, regional salesmen, and general sales managers, plus (a) salesmen selling such items as machine tools, refractories, electronic components, and specialized carbon products direct to consumers, and (b) salesmen selling abrasives and many related products through distributors and wholesale jobbers. The program also included all marketing staff people throughout the company. The emphasis was on the mix.

Program methodology was a variation of the pure case approach in which a case-dialogue provided the material for discussion at conference table setups. At each of the 14 meeting locations, participants were assigned to conference table groups of 6 men at each table. For instance, 54 men at one location would be divided into 9 conference tables of 6 men each. Each conference table operated as an independent unit; but all tables worked on the same assignments at the same time, coordinated by a program leader. Conference chairmanship at each table was rotated so that each participant had an opportunity to play the role of discussion leader on at least three occasions.

To provide material for the program, a special 18-chapter manual, *The Behavioral Sciences in Industrial Selling*, was prepared and distributed throughout the company, from salesmen to president. (Excerpts from this manual are presented on pages 154–155.) During the program, approximately 250 cases and dialogues were written by program participants, including top executives. (Some 225 turned out to be usable.) The manual and these cases provided basic material for the program; but, more important, they developed motivation by the mental and physical involvement of individuals in small group situations.

The company provided overhead projectors, flipcharts, blackboards, brochures, and the other materials that the salesmen used in their presentations.

Salesman as educator

More and more, industrial salesmen of today are applying the educator's teaching methods and instructional media. What is used will depend on the job to be done: person-to-person selling; salesman before a buying group; selling group to a buying group; or product meeting with other distributors, wholesalers, or retailers. It is not uncommon for salesmen today to contact a customer or a new potential account and find that the person-to-person role evolves into a conference as other individuals are called in to discuss how the salesman's products might be utilized.

While most participants in the program were experienced in person-to-person selling situations, few had had teaching experience, so the conference discussion role was used to relate the idea of person-to-person selling and the role of an educator. Educators agree that the conference discussion leader's role can be enlarged to embrace most educational methods. A conference leader can lecture, discuss, or demonstrate; he can assign participation roles to others. He can use the educator's instructional media, from overhead projectors to blackboards. It doesn't take long for the salesman to see the relationships between person-to-person selling, conference leadership, and the role of an educator.

To understand these roles, the salesman must have an opportunity to practice them in situations comparable to actual field situations, and he must get feedback from others on what he did and how he did it. Role assignments to conference leaders were designed to do this. (Conferees had at least one night and frequently from a week to a month in which to prepare for their assigned roles.) Several of the more representative roles assigned (in this instance to Table No. 2) were:

☐ You are an educator, and you are taking a program involving a new product development to one of your key distributors. Select any product you wish and assume that this distributor has given you just 15 minutes to accomplish your objectives. Actually enact the program at the table. In addition, take 3 minutes to discuss with the conferees at your table the kinds of physical material Carborundum could develop for the program you visualize and what other company resources (mental resources–i.e., people) you might find helpful in actually presenting your program to this key distributor.

☐ Identify, discuss, and illustrate at least five of the behavioral science concepts you would find useful in both group and person-to-person selling. It is recommended that you glance through the glossary, select the behavioral science concepts, and then relate those concepts to group selling.

☐ You are a conference leader discussing role playing. Illustrate how role theory applies to selling. (10 minutes)

☐ Give a 10-minute paper to the entire group (all tables) on the relationship of coolants and grinding wheels. Emphasize problem solving.

☐ Develop a marketing program for your territory. Make any assumptions you wish. (20 minutes)

☐ You are a salesman selling to a buying group of five men from one company. Assume the buying group is composed of an engineer, quality control man, purchasing agent, and two shop superintendents. Describe the company, the men attending the meeting, your relationship with the company, and so on. Assign the above-mentioned roles to the conferees at your table. You have 20 minutes to make your presentation. It is recommended you reread the text chapters on conference leadership and group selling.

□ You are the quarterback (leader) for a group of four (you and three others) involved in team selling. Your group is selling a production systeam of four related products to a buying group from a large manufacturing company. You are to make the role assignments; so select three conferees to be part of your selling team, and five to enact roles as members of the buying group. (For this purpose your table combines with Table No. 6 for a two-table role assignment.) Assign critique roles to the remaining conferees. Make any assumptions you wish.

Each conference leader's role enactment was evaluated by his peers on how well he enacted the role assigned. For instance, did he involve the other participants at his table, did he use questions, did he establish source credibility, did he develop readiness, was he empathetic, and so on?

Concepts in action

In this section three closely related behavioral science concepts—*readiness*, *empathy*, and *source credibility*—are described in relation to the selling function, as they were in the manual. Then, in the next section these concepts will be shown in action via one of the dialogues that took place when a particular case was used.

If there is a workable area called the "behavioral sciences," the concepts must be identified in action; that is why the case-dialogue method is employed. Dialogues reduce certain behavioral science concepts to "sets" and "isolates." A set is a number of specific factors, such as a set of lyrics or a set of motives, grouped so as to make a whole. An isolate is the smallest identifiable element of the set, such as a word. Readiness, empathy, and source credibility are three such sets; let us consider them before turning to see how they show up in a case-dialogue.

Readiness

The first set, readiness, denotes an educational psychology concept that focuses attention on the individual's ability and desire to interact or communicate with another individual. (A term, "double readiness," could be used, meaning that two individuals, say a salesman and a customer, are equally involved in readiness.) In our case, readiness refers to the respondent in the communication situation, and not to the source of the message; yet it fixes the responsibility for the learning process on the source.

A salesman as the *source* of the message *plans* for each call. He wants to affect the potential

customer's desire to interact with him. He does this best when he can present material that is meaningful and can get participation. During the discussion the salesman *appraises* the respondent's ability and desire to communicate about what is presented. The salesman appraises through *nonverbal* and *verbal* feedback, which may be positive, neutral, or negative. According to the feedback, the salesman adjusts if necessary; this is his responsibility. In the adjustment process the salesman *affects* the respondent's willingness to interact by restructuring the discussion process so that it is *meaningful*; he does this by listening and letting the respondent talk.

Empathy

Whereas readiness is largely a mechanical process, empathy—the second set—is almost totally concerned with feelings.

Empathy is defined as an intellectual or imaginative understanding of another's situation or as taking the role of another. By and large, it is a learned quality. To illustrate, just a simple device of a salesman saying to himself, "Now I am Mr. Boss, the purchasing agent in XYZ Company, facing this situation and having to deal with this problem," seems to enhance the salesman's comprehension of the attitude, viewpoint, and overt behavior of Mr. Boss.

Being empathetic means exhibiting a mix of behavior activities (words and actions) that develops a feeling on the part of the respondent in the communication process that the salesman understands the situation. This isn't accomplished by the salesman enthusiastically saying to the respondent, "I understand your situation." Such a statement, especially for openers in the early part of the sales situation, may have an effect just opposite to that desired. It may cause the respondent to doubt what the salesman has said. Instead, the salesman through discussion pinpoints precisely the respondent's business needs as seen by the respondent.

An empathetic salesman is one who will not recommend his product line unless it offers solutions designed to improve the respondent's situation; and the result may be that the respondent views the salesman as one who does indeed understand his situation. Finally, since the way a decision maker feels about a salesman determines to some degree whether he views the salesman's ideas positively, negatively, or neutrally, the concept of empathy overlaps into that of source credibility.

Source credibility

The third set, source credibility, is the trust, confidence, and faith that the respondent has in the salesman's words and actions. In short, is the salesman believed? This is a crucial factor in selling. The salesman represents a company. He sells ideas, products, and/or services. His selling success is in many instances dependent on his credibility as a source. Why? Because the level of credibility that the respondent assigns to the salesman in turn directly affects how he views the salesman's ideas, products, or services. This process has been verified through much research.

Source credibility involves the entire world of verbal and nonverbal communication; yet, for a brief analysis, the factors of trustworthiness, competence, and dynamism can be useful. Research shows that in addition to the cues the viewer gets from the appearance of an individual, certain traits, such as logic, honesty, fairness, reliability, dependability, and openmindedness are associated with trustworthiness. Competence is demonstrated through the salesman's technical knowledge plus application of that knowledge to the user's situation. Dynamism is not forcefulness; it is not so-called extroversion. In selling, it is better associated with positiveness and purposefulness in words and actions. It is associated with energy in the sense of a positive handshake and positive posture, in contrast to a weak handshake and a timid shuffle.

These three factors—trustworthiness, competence, and dynamism—must be in balance. Too much trustworthiness or an overemphasis of competence or dynamism could reduce an individual's credibility. To illustrate, doesn't the so-called extrovert repel as many people as he attracts?

Case-dialogue analysis

Now let us look at how these behavioral science concepts show up in a case-dialogue. This particular case was produced by Tate and Campbell, two company refractory salesmen. It was the first of the 250 cases turned in to the company, and is a relatively simple one.

The essence of this discussion is to demonstrate that behavioral science concepts can be identified via dialogues and can be utilized by a salesman to interact effectively with users and potential users of his product line.

Here is how the case was presented to the participants.

Background

This is the first call to be made by a Carborundum salesman on a newly formed division of Foster Boiler Company that will be making package boilers. Carborundum has, however, done business with other divisions of this company; and Carborundum refractories have been utilized in the past by several boiler manufacturers to circumvent numerous problems, such as space and heat transfer. The objectives of the salesman (Tom Tate) are to make an appointment to see the division's purchasing agent (Mr. Campbell, who has an engineering and design background), to verify what type of equipment will be made, to find out whether there is a new super-refractory need and, if so, who sets the specifications.

Tate (S) has not met Campbell (PA) and was given his name by the receptionist (who, by the way, is very attractive), from whose desk he is telephoning. [The steps in the dialogue—called "marks"—are numbered for easy reference by the participants in the case-dialogue.]

Marks

1. *Salesman*: Mr. Campbell, this is Tom Tate from the Refractories Division of The Carborundum Company; I hope the receptionist has put me in touch with the correct individual for super-refractories.

2. *Purchasing Agent*: Yes, I am the purchasing agent for the design and engineering group, and I'll be handling the refractory items.

3. *S*: That's fine. I'm glad I have the right man because I need your help.

4. *PA*: Well, so does everybody else around here, seemingly.

5. *S:* My understanding is that this division has been established for designing a new package boiler. Am I correct in this assumption?

6. *PA*: Yes, and that's the source of all my headaches at the moment.

7. *S*: May I ask if you are far enough along in design to talk about refractories dealing with temperature problems specifically in combustion-chamber design?

8. *PA*: As a matter of fact, I'm up to my neck in new-boiler problems now.

9. *S*: Mr. Campbell, I'm certain it would be mutually beneficial at this time to discuss the new design of our lightweight super-refractory materials that have proved extremely well suited in the new-type boilers. Experience has proved boilers are tricky, and I might be able to help you hurdle a few of the pitfalls. I had some experience recently with Babcock-Wilcox, and our suggestions saved them considerable time and money in the preliminary stages.

10. *PA*: I probably could, but I'm snowed under with work now. Could you come back at a later date?

11. *S*: Mr. Campbell, there should be no problem with my returning at a later date; in fact, I hope to do so many times. I appreciate the fact that you are busy; however, I firmly believe that now is the time I can be of the greatest value and service to you and possibly eliminate many of the problems that always occur on new design equipment. By taking time now we may well save you considerable production time when it is crucial. What do you think, Mr. Campbell?

12. *PA*: Well, you probably are right, and even though I am busy. . . . Just a moment, Tate, I have another call. (*After a few moments Campbell returns to the phone.*) Tate, something extremely urgent has come up, and I am needed in a meeting right now. Be sure to call me on your next visit. (*Hangs up the phone.*)

Instructions

Question A: Thinking in terms of the background material provided, rewrite Mark 1 as you think a market-manager oriented salesman who understands the concept of readiness would handle the situation. [The "market-manager" orientation, which is developed in the manual, denotes a salesman who capitalizes on market opportunities in his territory by managing his territory according to the principles of planning, organizing, executing, and evaluating.] You may, if you wish, use three or four marks to illustrate your thinking.

Question B: Thinking in terms of the purposes of the call, what did Tate accomplish?

Question C: Mark 11 illustrates that Tate doesn't have an "alternate form of strategy" in mind. Rewrite Mark 11 to show how an adaptable, flexible, thinking salesman would have handled the situation.

Question D: Discuss the above case from the perspective that the salesman of today is a market manager of a territory.

Case analysis

This, excluding editorial corrections, is a verbatim analysis of the Tate-Campbell case as it was presented by the case-analysis leader at one of the conference tables (Table No. 5 with six conferees).

Table No. 5—Chairman Ellis:

We think we've got this case all wrapped up. Here it is. We are supposed to answer Question A and rewrite Mark 1. We don't think we can do justice to our analysis by one mark so we have gone way beyond that. We have developed a dialogue and we are going to read it. First, though, our table doesn't think salesman Tate used the readiness concept, and he wasn't a market manager. As I said, our table has written a dialogue, and we will act it out via a phone conversation. Jim will be the salesman; and Ron, the purchasing agent.

Marks

1. *Salesman*: Mr. Campbell, this is Tom Tate, sales representative of the Refractories Division of Carborundum. Our company. . . .

2. *Purchasing Agent*: Yeah.

3. *S*: We have, Mr. Campbell, been working with Jack Ellis, Master Engineer of Foster Wheel; and recently Mr. Ellis told me you are the engineer to talk to about super-refractories. (*Salesman pauses to let Campbell talk—he does.*)

4. *PA*: Oh, Jack, sure—an old friend. I'm the purchasing agent for the design and engineering groups, and I'll be handling the refractory items.

5. *S*: That's fine. My understanding is that this division has been established for designing a new package boiler. Is this correct, Mr. Campbell?

6. *PA*: You're right, and that's the source of all my headaches at the moment.

7. S: Perhaps we can be of help. Are you far enough along in design to talk about refractories dealing with temperature problems in combustion-chamber design?

8. PA: As a matter of fact, I'm up to my neck in boiler problems now.

9. S: Mr. Campbell, our work in the field has proved these boilers are tricky; and since you are working on temperature and refractories, this could be the time to discuss the design of Carborundum's lightweight super-refractory materials. I should add that they have proved extremely well suited to the new-type boilers. May I come up and see you now?

10. PA: Well, as I said, I'm up to my neck in problems. What are you talking about in time?

11. S: As brief as you want it. I have material, designs, and related facts with me. With your background as an engineer, it shouldn't take long to determine our refractories' use in your situation.

12. PA: OK, I'll send my secretary out to get you!

Chairman Ellis takes over:

You have just seen and heard a great role enactment. Now, this is our analysis of the situation we presented. We think Tate and Campbell have quite a tricky case, and we think Tate was pretty good. But he wasn't a true market manager, and he didn't employ the concept of readiness. According to this case, he didn't plan for his call or he wouldn't have had to use the receptionist as a source of information.

But you can see from our dialogue that we planned for this call. We got information from our company. We got some facts from Jack Ellis, engineer at Foster Wheel. Because of this planning, we can communicate with Campbell if our facts are right. OK, take a look at Mark 3. Mark 3 was read as follows:

Mark 3. We have, Mr. Campbell, been working with Jack Ellis, Master Engineer of Foster Wheel; and recently Mr. Ellis told me you are the engineer to talk to about super-refractories. (*Salesman pauses to let Campbell talk—he does.*)

You can see from this mark that we didn't ask a direct question to verify our information. We just made a logical statement based on our information and Campbell replied. This feedback told us that we were right. At Mark 5 we checked our information but this time with a verification question [one of ten variables in the contact stage studied by company salesmen]. Mark 5 was read as follows:

Mark 5. That's fine. My understanding is that this division has been established for designing a new package boiler. Is this correct, Mr. Campbell?

Now right here at Mark 5 we made the conversation meaningful and would begin to get Campbell's involvement. That's employing the readiness concept. Look, we did this over the phone, but we would do the same thing if we were face-to-face with Campbell; and then it would be easier because you could get nonverbal as well as verbal feedback.

Second step

Other than the fact that Table No. 5 took more than three or four marks to answer Question A, its analysis was accepted by the total conference group as being exceptional. During the discussion of the case, however, a number of the conferees used the terms *empathy* and *source credibility*. To facilitate discussion of these concepts, Table No. 5 was requested to reproduce sufficient copies of its dialogue for all conferees and to discuss the dialogue in terms of empathy and source credibility. On the following day the table presented its discussion:

Ellis: We have divided the analysis into three parts. Jack will discuss readiness; Ron, empathy; and Harvey, source credibility; and me—I'm just going to listen.

Jack: Thanks, Don. The book says empathy is hard to explain but easy to put into effect. Our group quarreled half the night about whether empathy is any different from readiness. We think we sorted it out, though. We believe that the salesman can invoke readiness over the phone and in personal contact as well. We think that neither empathy nor source credibility is fully employed until the salesman is face-to-face with the customer, but the first shades or beginnings of being empathetic and establishing source credibility can take place during a phone conversation; and our discussion is going to proceed on that basis.

Readiness is a mechanical process. We plan to get information about what a company is doing—for example, making new boilers like in the case—so when we contact a man in a company, it is easy to make the conversation meaningful and get his participation. As you can see from this diagram [*Exhibit I*, page 144], readiness is largely restricted to the contact phase of the sale, and it is a process that gets the salesman involved in a meaningful discussion with the potential customer or customers.

Ron: Empathy involves getting an intellectual or imaginative understanding of the other individual's situation. Our group felt that a good way to develop an empathetic relationship was to imagine yourself sitting behind the other fellow's desk and to think of his company and his position in the company. For example, what kind of work is the company doing, say, in the production area? What kind of metals are they working on? What is the quality of the products produced—low, medium, or high? What is the man's position in the company—is it engineer, purchas-

Exhibit I. Stages in making the sale

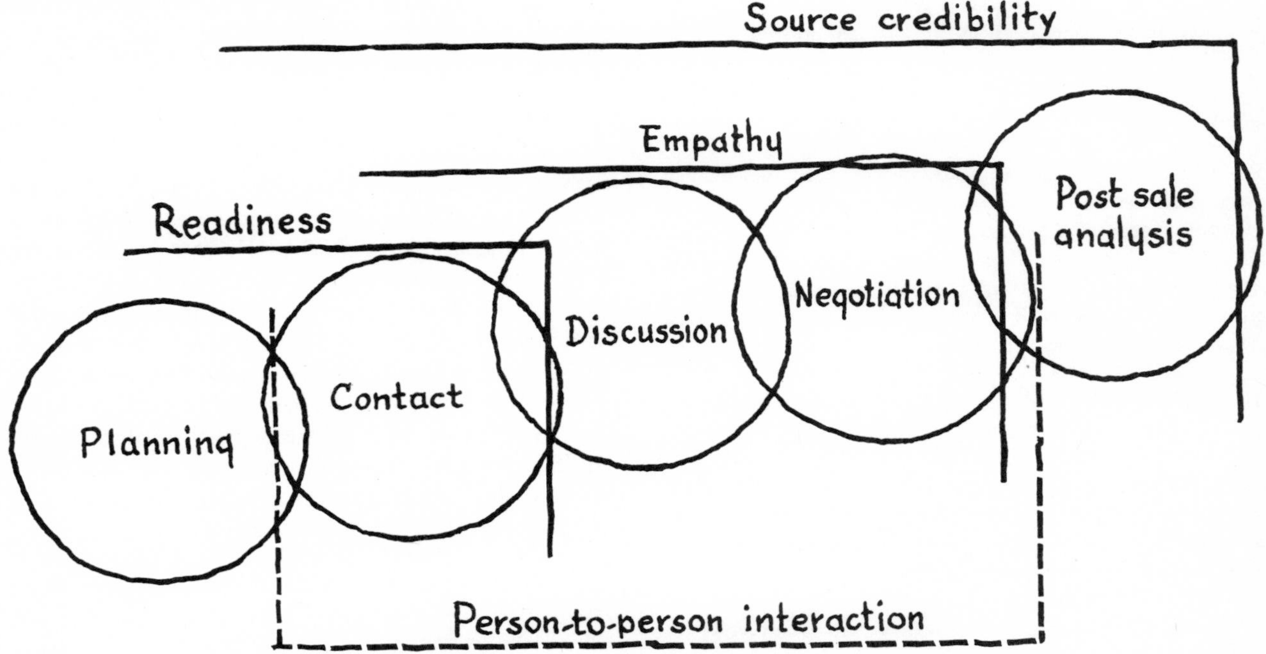

ing agent, machine operator, or president? Also, how important is he to the final decision to buy or not to buy?

We have already quoted the book on empathy; but the book also says that you're empathetic when the customer or potential customer thinks or feels that you understand the situation. We think we can improve on the book, so this idea I'm about to present is copyrighted in Table No. 5's name.

We salesmen spend from 20% to 40% of our time contacting new companies and people, and the rest of our time on our customers. Whenever we are interacting with someone else, that someone *reads* us in terms of what we say and do. Now, it is that reading that gives him a feeling that we understand or don't understand the situation. So if we can do what we are talking about here, the reading a purchasing agent makes will be positive because we will be sensitive to his feelings and will show it by how we talk and act. To sum up, let's go back to our dialogue. Look at Marks 7, 9, and 11. Don't you think that Campbell would feel that Tate understood his situation? Of course you do; so far we are 100% right, aren't we? Now for the last part of our analysis. Harvey, it is all yours.

Harvey: OK, Ron. Since it is known that how the decision maker feels about the salesman determines to some degree whether he views the salesman's ideas or products positively, negatively, or neutrally, the concept of empathy flows into source credibility. We have learned here that source credibility is the trust, confidence, and faith that the respondent has in a salesman's words and actions. In other words, is the salesman believed? Now, the book says that readiness, empathy, and source credibility are all closely related, and that one overlaps the other. The picture we have come up with is something like the diagram Ron just showed you [*Exhibit I*].

We all know that source credibility begins with the company. We represent a fine company, so we have credibility to start with. After we begin to talk with an individual, we are on our own, however. We have been talking positively, but not dogmatically, over the phone. We appear to be competent; but how competent we are, at least in the eyes of the respondent, won't be known until we discuss this situation and offer solutions.

Now, how trustworthy are we? The trustworthiness is sort of a residual effect of the sale. The buyer really won't know this until our product is delivered when it is supposed to be at the right price, does what we claimed it would do, and we check up on the post-sale situation. To borrow from the book, "the final word on source credibility is held by the buyer." In essence, it is a review of the sale by the buyer in terms of the buyer's business and emotional needs. The buyer looks back at the entire process. He looks at the man, the product, and the company—are they believed?

Comments on case

In our opinion, Table No. 5 presented an exceptional explanation of readiness, empathy, and source credibility; and did correctly identify the sections of the dialogue which illustrated those concepts in action. Of course, it is virtually impossible to clearly separate the three concepts; they are closely interrelated. Yet each concept—readiness from education, empathy from social psychology, and source credibility from communication and general psychology—contributes to better understanding of person-to-person selling.

Before leaving the Tate-Campbell case, the reader may wish to test his solution to one of the questions. Take Question C, which calls for rewriting Mark 11 "to show how an adaptable, flexible, thinking salesman would have handled the situation."

One possible solution to this question follows. How does it compare with yours?

From the tenor of the dialogue or discussion between Tate and Campbell, it would seem that Campbell is truly "up to his neck in problems now." After all, Tate did not have an appointment. Why not accept Campbell's statement as fact? Why push farther at this point, when the salesman could achieve the objectives of his call without pushing to see Campbell? The thinking salesman would accept the appointment, establish a time, but would still attempt to get 100% payoff on the call by seeing one of Campbell's designated assistants. Here is how it might look in dialogue.

10. PA: I probably could, but I'm snowed under with work now. Could you come back at a later date?

11. S: Yes, I can, Mr. Campbell. I have my calendar here in front of me and would be able to be back here in three or four days—say, on the twelfth. How does that look to you?

12. PA: Fine. Can you be here at ten o'clock?

13. S: Thank you for the appointment, Mr. Campbell. I would be remiss if I didn't mention to you that I believe now is a time I could be of the greatest value and service to you and possibly eliminate many of the problems that frequently occur in new-design equipment. By taking time now, it may well save considerable production time when it is crucial. This is what I have in mind. If I could now talk to one of your men working on the design areas, I could get the facts I would need so that when I have that appointment with you on the twelfth, I could come prepared with definite suggestions. What do you think, Mr. Campbell?

14. PA: That makes sense. It would probably be best if you would see Henderson or Jones. My secretary will telephone them; and, if they are free, you will be contacted at the reception desk. Better still, hold on a minute, and I'll explain to my secretary what I want done and turn you over to her. She can make the arrangements.

One further comment: Tate's strategy may lead him to conference or to group selling. Tate is hopeful that he will have a conference session with Henderson and Jones because he knows that the conference method is an excellent way to get accurate facts quickly. And when Tate returns for his appointment with Campbell, that return may evolve into a conference situation with Campbell calling Henderson, Jones, and even others into the office for a discussion. Or it may even develop into a salesman-to-group selling presentation. Depending on the information that Tate requires in his discussion with Henderson and Jones, Tate would come prepared for the possibility of a conference or group selling situation.

Another dialogue

The following brief case-dialogue again illustrates how salesmen can learn to apply to their sales approach some of the principles of teaching. Since it introduces two further behavioral concepts, it should give a little better idea of the range and complexity of the rest of the cases.

Background

Ralph Benson is the general manager of the Peer-Martin Company, a manufacturer of canoes, boats, and boating equipment. The company is located on the outskirts of a city of approximately 50,000 in the state of Wisconsin.

Sales are increasing each year, and the company has enjoyed a substantial boom during the 1963-1965 period. The time is now late fall in 1965.

Benson, who has been with the company for approximately 10 years, is a large man, about 6 feet 3 inches tall, weighing about 220 pounds. He is known as a "doer." He is, supposedly, quite dogmatic and the kind of man who doesn't change his mind easily.

Jim Stone, regional salesman of the Diamond Office Furniture Company, has heard of the company's expansion plans and has learned all the above facts in the planning phase of this sales call. After telephoning for an appointment, Stone arrives at Benson's office.

Marks

1. Salesman: Hello, Mr. Benson. I am Jim Stone of the Diamond Office Furniture Company, and I want to thank you for giving me this opportunity to see you.

2. General Manager: Sit down. As I told you, I have a few minutes.

3. S: As my card here indicates (*passing the card to Mr. Benson*), my company is a distributor of six lines

Carborundum sales manual

These two pages give some idea of the scope and depth of Carborundum's manual on sales techniques and their relationship to the principles of behavioral science. HBR selected 3 of the 18 chapters and greatly condensed the material in each chapter to produce these abstracts. (The original manual is copyrighted by Carborundum for internal use by its employees and distributors, but an adaptation of the text has recently been published as a book*).

I. Changing patterns of perception

[Condensed from 18 pages]

The salesman is concerned with perception, for it is in this vortex of human life that the salesman works. Every skilled salesman knows that certain words (such as profit, margin, economy, leadership, effectiveness, volume, and guarantee) mean, at least to some degree, something different to each customer.

How sharply the salesman can, as an instrument of understanding and communication, calibrate these qualitative differences in perception is a true index of his ability to "sell in depth."

A salesman is not expected to change the *basic* experiences, values, or emotions of an individual. These are givens. He operates within the given framework. But it is important that a skilled salesman be able to affect whether or not a particular response will be brought into play at a given moment.

From the principle that "the more familiar a word, the greater will be the individual's 'set' toward its perception," a rule pertaining to selling can be established: "Whenever a salesman describes his proposal or product in terms that the other individual is not ready or set to hear, the salesman may arouse the emotions of frustration." The case is rare where the other individual will stop the salesman and indicate that he does not understand. He will frequently permit the salesman to continue talking, but the main result is negative communication.

These concepts of set explain in part why some individuals or prospects react as they do to salesmen. Over the years, prospects and/or customers have developed a set toward salesmen. Too many salesmen have used tired, worn phrases such as, "I'll only take a few minutes of your time," "You can tell me to leave any time you wish," "I'm not trying to make a sale," "There will be no sale today," or "I just want your advice or opinion." Thus the prospect has a specific set toward a certain problem—the salesmen. Enter Salesman A, Mr. "Average." He uses the canned sales talk, he uses a salesman-oriented sales "pitch," and of course he strikes out. It isn't meaningful.

*J.W. Thompson, *Selling: A Behavioral Science Approach* (New York, McGraw-Hill Book Company, Inc., 1968).

Enter Salesman B, Mr. "Selling in Depth." He has planned his sales program. He is a problem solver. He understands the prospect's situation. He determines his needs, and the prospect becomes receptive. He develops a favorable set.

Why this happens and how the salesman can redirect the prospect's or customer's set is explained by psychologists in terms of perception, set, the structure of stimulus pattern, compromise, redirection of set, stimulus and response, the motivational cycle, needs, identifying motives, needs or wants, and maturity.

II. Motivation

[Condensed from 24 pages]

That status needs are powerful motivational forces is pointed out by psychologist M.S. Hattwick. He tells us in his excellent and fast-reading book, *A New Psychology of Selling* (McGraw-Hill Book Company, Inc., 1960), that individuals have eight basic wants in life, but that one "leads all the rest in importance. One of them, day after day, stands out as probably the most potent of all in selling. That basic want is the customer's desire to be . . . SUPERIOR." Hattwick tells us that "if you understand this basic want better; if you constantly recognize a customer's want to feel important, to feel needed, to be superior; and if you strive to satisfy this want in an honest and straightforward way in making sales calls, you can't fail to make greater sales."

Most people like to receive praise, and most people want to avoid punishment. This belief has made praise and punishment two of the most manipulated incentives in our society and in business today. These concepts are mentioned in most books in psychology, education, communication, selling, human relations, sociology, letter writing, and speech.

In our society, competition and cooperation are important motivational forms. Both stem from the needs of the individual, and they are closely related concepts. But the framework within which the salesman uses each will differ considerably. Some people are motivated in competitive roles; others are best motivated through cooperative roles.

If it were possible to select the one attribute that is most important to sales success, mastery of the concept of feedback, intellectually and in practice, would be considered by many as a key tool. Without the ability, the willingness, and the sensitivity to determine the consequences of one's acts and words, we might be social and/or sales duds.

The salesman plans (gets both personal and impersonal information about the prospect and his company) prior to the initial contact. During the contact stage, he uses verification and permissive questions;

he uses a problem-centered, customer-oriented approach. This approach permits the prospect to "tell" the salesman about his situation and his business problems. It elicits feedback, both verbal and nonverbal, and is designed to appeal to the need of the individual to be recognized, to feel that something is being done, to participate, to have an intellectual approach to a problem. Above all, it is designed to assist the salesman to discover whether or not he is on the right track in his sales interview, and to help him shift if he isn't. The salesman can do this because he can evaluate both verbal and nonverbal prospect feedback and thus evolve a coping behavior according to the needs of the individual. In brief, it is highly flexible.

Concerning needs, Bernard Berelson and Gary A. Steiner in *Human Behavior: An Inventory of Scientific Findings* (Harcourt, Brace & World, Inc., 1964) state: "Various writers have constructed lists of motives ranging from very short and highly general lists to more specific ones containing as many as fifty or sixty social motives. One classical scheme reduced social motives to four basic 'wishes'—for security, recognition, response from others, and new experience."

One of the classifications underlying much current research lists social (psychogenic) "needs" as follows:

Acquisition	To gain possessions.
Conservation	To preserve and protect.
Exposition	To explain, teach, demonstrate.
Order	To be precise, orderly, organized.
Ambition	To achieve power and recognition.
Recognition	To have status, respect, honor.
Exhibition	To excite, amuse, attract.
Pride	To protect reputation
Avoidance	To avoid failure or ridicule.
Defense	To justify one's actions.
Dominance	To lead and control others.
Deference	To serve others.
Empathy	To agree and relate to others.
Autonomy	To attain freedom, privacy.
Contrariance	To be different, unique, unconventional.
Aggression	To hurt or punish others.
Abasement	To comply and surrender.
Blamavoidance	To avoid blame, obey the law.
Friendship	To join, cooperate, love.
Rejection	To be exclusive, aloof, discriminatory.
Nurturance	To nourish, protect, sympathize.
Succorance	To seek help, sympathy, dependence.
Play	To relax, have fun.
Curiosity	To seek knowledge.

The reader may wish to analyze this list and think through what behavior activities on his part would possibly satisfy various needs and what behavior activities on his part would thwart prospect's needs.

III. Role

[Condensed from 19 pages]

A shorthand definition of role perception is "how you see others." The perceptive salesman can, by perceiving the role of another individual as that individual sees it himself, substantially enhance his chances of influencing the other.

Each executive is different. Each may regard his position or role as different. Each may have several different self-images. Nevertheless, the salesman may obtain guidelines to understanding the individual through such cues as the executive's behavior activities, his speech, his comments, obvious status symbols such as lodge, rings, office furniture, plaques, and awards hanging in office.

How we view others is, according to Randall Harrison in "Non-verbal Communication, Explorations into Time, Space, Action, and Object" (*Dimensions in Communication*, edited by James H. Campbell and Hal W. Hepler, Wadsworth Publishing Co., Inc., 1965), exceedingly important. "Interestingly enough," Harrison states, "it has been estimated that in face-to-face communication no more than 35% of the social meaning is carried in a verbal message. Research indicates that these may be some of the key dimensions of source creditability, which in turn is believed to be a vital element of persuasiveness. In short, whether you are persuaded or not may rest on nonverbal cues."

A salesman can and should obtain cues and thereby adjust his role in terms of the needs of the other individual. This means that the salesman must be both perceptive and flexible; he must enact a number of roles; he must have a high threshold of "tension-binding," and he must be an empathetic person.

In sales situations the behavior pattern or actions of the salesman can be described as: (1) information-giver, talker; (2) information-getter, listener; (3) negative, afraid; (4) meek, apologetic; (5) brash, overly positive, overpowering; (6) mature, poised, friendly, positive; (7) joker, glad-hander, overly friendly, overenthusiastic; (8) impulsive; (9) neutral, friendly, goodwill, order-taker.

The roles of prospects can be described as: (1) hostile, recalcitrant, or stubbornly defiant; (2) ego-involved, superior ego, or Mr. "Big"; (3) joker or glad-hander, nothing serious; (4) silent; (5) skeptical or suspicious; (6) slow, methodical; (7) mature, poised, thoughtful executive; (8) Mr. "Average"; (9) impulsive; (10) overly cautious.

An empathetic person can place himself in the other person's situation. He can play the role of the other individual. In a word, he can put himself in the other individual's shoes. Sympathy, on the other hand, is the experience of positive emotion pertaining to the emotional circumstances of another person. But a sympathetic person may or may not be able to place himself in the other person's situation.

Empathy and being able to project this quality to the prospect is one of the most important traits a salesman can have for successful selling. Fortunately, for the most part, empathy is a learned quality.

of office furniture and combines with that a professional service in design color and office flow work. And, of course, Mr. Benson, that is the reason I am here. I was talking to Mr. Black of the Chamber of Commerce, and he told me you were thinking of expanding your plant, office, and display areas. Is my information correct?

4. GM: No, not quite. We do plan on remodeling our display area and on doing some office remodeling as well. But nothing as extensive as you evidently have heard. Perhaps in two or three years we might be working on the plant.

5. S: Thank you for telling me this, Mr. Benson. And, if I may, I would like to ask you a few questions about your remodeling plans.

6. GM: I talked about them at a recent Kiwanis meeting, and I expect that is where Black heard about it. It isn't a secret.

7. S: Yes, he mentioned your talk, Mr. Benson. And in glowing terms as well.

8. GM: Well, that's always good to hear. I think all businessmen should let each other know when they are planning improvements. It shows confidence. But go ahead.

9. S: Mr. Benson, have you, at this point, developed your overall plans on what is to be done?

10. GM: Yes and no. We have plans for space and have done some overall thinking along these lines so far.

11. S: Does that include work on color design, layout, and such ideas?

12. GM: No, not yet. Our staff has been too busy with the regular work to be thinking about that. They will get to it, though.

13. S: I suspect that the work to be done in color design and office work flow is exactly the type of work in which our company specializes. Have you given any thought to having an outside organization work with your people in developing your plans?

14. GM: No, not really. We have some people here who I think can do that work.

15. S: That sounds all to the good, Mr. Benson. However, do you know the specific services that our company offers?

16. GM: Well, in a way. I did gather, from what you said, the type of work you do, but I don't want to get involved in outside consulting services.

17. S: I can understand your viewpoint, Mr. Benson. And I'm sure I would feel the same way if I were you. Nevertheless, may I take a few minutes to illustrate the type of service which we could offer if it were needed?

18. GM: Sure, go ahead. I might as well know a little more about it.

Application of concepts

This dialogue illustrates the application of these educational principles:

The law of effect—Learners will acquire and remember best those responses which lead to satisfying aftereffects.

The law of belonging—When a learner can perceive the relationship of cause and effect, or see familiar elements in a new situation, his speed of learning and permanence of retention will be increased.

Application of the law of effect is seen in a number of ways. Benson's responses are made to positive questions by salesman Stone. Stone does use a "rewarding" or "praise" concept by his statements in Mark 5, "Thank you for telling me this, Mr. Benson," and Mark 7, "And in glowing terms as well." Further, each of Benson's replies could easily be satisfying to him. He is a dominant individual. He is the boss. He is probably quite pleased with the fact that the company has expanded considerably in recent years and is now in the process of remodeling. Benson is giving information, and it is being received tactfully by Stone; therefore, it can be assumed Benson is not having unsatisfactory experiences by replying to Stone's questions.

Referring back to Mark 5, contrast the effect if Stone's reply had been, "I am sorry to hear that," or "I guess my information wasn't too good," or "That's the way business goes," instead of the positive answer, "Thank you for telling me this, Mr. Benson." What is more, assume that at any stage of the situation Stone jumped directly into the sale by telling Benson what he could do for him. Would this be a satisfying experience for Benson?

The law of belonging is working to reinforce the law of effect. It is safe to assume that the discussion between Stone and Benson relates to Benson's business and perhaps to a problem Benson is wrestling with at this moment.

At the beginning and at the end of this talk several applications of the concept of readiness also can be seen again. In the initial stage of the interview Stone is appraising Benson's readiness. And he is building readiness by making the material meaningful and obtaining Benson's participation through questioning. Before long Stone will be discussing such concepts as mental fatigue, physical fatigue, "buoyancy" in colors, work production flow as it relates to the office force, and ways in which sales appeal can be built into the display area. It is safe to assume that Benson is not ready to discuss these concepts. He does not have the background. So Stone will be wise if he utilizes the best dictates of education in handling this educational process with Benson.

Results & appraisal

So far only one of the major themes of this article has been discussed: the relationship of the behavioral sciences to selling. Now we shall explain how this behavioral science program has led or is leading to the development of a company's human resources, greater organizational flexibility, and a market-oriented communication network. We shall do this through discussions of role evaluation, of the seventh day of the program (involving distributors), and of the way the entire program has led to systems selling and companywide communications.

Role and role enactment are two concepts from the behavioral sciences that can be used to identify what the individual—for instance, the salesman—has to do (role) and how he does it (role enactment). How well an individual performs in role enactment provides guides to how well he has acquired skills and knowledge. Research shows that most individuals can expand their role enactment capacity considerably through role practice in small group settings, such as a conference table group. What happened at Carborundum supports that research.

Most of the 477 participants enacted roles of person-to-person selling, group selling, conference leadership, and educator. Most roles were enacted at conference tables, and at no meeting were fewer than five tables involved.

During each phase of the first six days of the program, each role-enacting participant was evaluated (on a scale of from 1 to 10) in terms of his skill in the enactment. He accumulated points for his ability to make his presentation meaningful, to obtain the participation of his five peers at the table, and to use a mix of educator's tools (lecture, discussion, demonstration, and so on) and teaching materials (outlines, cases, films, flipcharts, and so forth).

Each participant was evaluated by a professor and at least one staff executive, and a final point evaluation between professor and executive was made. The final point total was made in terms of the question: "Could the individual take the program under consideration to a distributor organization?" This was identified as Role Z. Here is how 477 role enactors scored:

Group	Score	Percentage	Number
M	0 to 6	15%	72
N	7 to 8	43%	205
O	9 to 10	37%	176
P	10 plus	5%	24

Group M represented those individuals who appeared to be limited in the emotional mix needed to enact more than one role, or had little desire or interest in performing well, or lacked the mental ability or skills needed, or possibly believed that their respective managers did not support the program. In most cases it was a combination of factors. It must be remembered that these roles were enacted with their peers, and most men wanted to perform well before "their own people." This can be called "group-peer pressure"; it is an enormous pressure, but each role enactor also found considerable peer support.

First, each conferee was aware that this kind of a program was approved by the company policy group. And a great deal of empathy was displayed between conferees, for they knew their turn in the spotlight would come. Finally, they knew, too, that this was a group program, not a series of individual presentations; for in its final form in the marketplace, the conferees could be engaged in group selling and in group educational activities with distributors. Thus, it is not surprising that only 9 individuals out of the 72 in Group M performed at levels that were apparently disconcerting to other conferees.

Group N, which numbered 205, was potentially capable of Role Z; but it was believed that these individuals needed more skill development.

Group O represented those individuals who could successfully function as educators with distributor salesmen.

Group P enacted Role Z with a skill beyond the highest standards set for the evaluation. It may be that Group P and the top of Group O represent a pool of future management talent. Time will tell.

Distributor participation

The above analysis suggests that the majority of the program participants could, with their peers, enact the roles of educator, conference leader, salesman appearing before a buying group, or member of a group selling team. And they apparently understood the behavioral science concepts involved in the program. But could they put these roles into action in the marketplace? The seventh day provides the answer.

At each locale of the program, distributor executives and representative salesmen from their organizations were invited to participate in the seventh day of the program. A special program, "Selling in Depth," was assembled for these meetings. It was not about product knowledge or Carborundum, but rather was designed to assist the distributor salesman to sell more effectively all products he handled.

Here is a physical description of the layout for the seventh day of the program:

Situation—Motel, hotel, or university meeting rooms. Round or rectangular tables were used, conference style.
Time—Approximately four hours.
Management—One general conference leader who coordinated all activities.
Organization—Conference tables arranged to handle up to 120 participants; 20 tables with 6 men to a table. The mix at each table was four distributor salesmen and two Carborundum participants. At least one of the two company men at each table was a salesman who worked directly with distributors. The second company participant could be any individual who had completed the previous six days of the program. Distributor executives participated at tables with company managers.

The first hour and a half of meeting time was devoted to a lecture explaining behavioral science concepts. Gradually the meeting was directed to group participation at the various tables. Each conference table was handled as an independent educational unit. Cases and dialogues were analyzed at the tables (the same cases were used at all tables simultaneously). The two company participants at each table worked as a team and functioned as conference leaders and educators. They used a mix of visuals, lecture, discussion, and demonstration, or had distributor salesmen perform roles according to the dictates of the situation.

During approximately two hours of the program, distributor executives walked from table to table and observed the role enactments of their salesmen and the Carborundum salesmen. These executives were asked to analyze the program, to determine whether this was the kind of a program they wanted in their companies, and whether the Carborundum men were the kind of men they wanted to take the program to their organization.

The vast majority of distributor executives wanted the program. Only three of forty-four interviewed indicated they did not. Two of these three distributor executives believed the program was too demanding in time and energy, and they would not subject their men to that kind of a program. The third stated flatly he didn't believe the program would work into his organization. Distributor salesmen who attended the program were not interviewed. Yet their reaction was indicated by their excited participation at the various conference tables, plus the fact that many times during role situations where Carborundum salesmen enacted various selling roles before the entire group, the audience broke into enthusiastic spontaneous applause.

Within six months after the end of the program, more than 50 distributors were participating in a behavioral-science based, personal selling program.

A typical distributor program runs from four to ten meetings spaced over from one to ten months. The written material used in the program is standardized, but the Carborundum salesman managing and teaching the program determines how it is to be presented, and the visuals and cases to be used.

What do the distributors get out of it? In addition to the benefits from the behavioral science selling program, distributor salesmen learn a great deal about combining products they sell into production systems. They learn more about team-selling effort, how to identify market opportunities, and how to feed back this kind of information to the distributor organization. Further, it is entirely possible that a distributor salesman will set up a group selling effort involving, for instance, two of his fellow distributor salesmen specializing in various products with their counterparts at Carborundum. This may take place even though the distributor would not sell the main machine. But the distributor may sell coolants, measuring systems, abrasives, machinery, drills, and many other products which are combined into production systems.

In many cases the program has produced a new and even more harmonious relationship between Carborundum and its distributors than existed in the past. This is especially true of the relationship between the Carborundum salesmen and distributor salesmen.

Companywide effort

These ongoing programs involve a large percentage of the total number of Carborundum salesmen who work with distributors. Perhaps it is even more significant that they also involve many other individuals from all parts of the corporation's marketing areas, including other companies within the Carborundum family who do not work directly with distributors. These men may be invited to participate in a specific distributor program by the salesman or district manager responsible for that distributor.

Here is how that works. A salesman responsible for a specific distributor initiates a request through channels for assistance in a program. The request is granted, probably by phone. The salesman assigns a role to the visiting company man. That role would probably be a duplication or variation of the kinds of roles assigned during the total company program; the topics may change, but the format will not.

There are numerous ways in which the salesman working through various distributors can cooperate. For instance:

Jim Hill sells cut-off machines (for severing metal) produced by a company within the corporate family; cut-off machines are marketed direct to the final users. Don Franklin sells a line of abrasives (there are several divisions producing numerous kinds and types of abrasives), which are marketed through distributors; abrasives are used to remove, shape, and finish metal. These two products, although they are marketed in different ways, can be part of a production system—the severing of metal and the finishing of the metal after the cut.

Assume that Franklin, through channels, says that Hill is needed to make a presentation to his distributor group on the relationship of cut-off machines to abrasives. Assume Hill and Franklin team up and the presentation is made. What are the results? Not only do the two men learn a great deal about each other's product, but also they learn how to work together as a team.

A final word

It is impossible to measure the degree of change brought about by such a program, particularly in the selling process itself. But the fact that the distributors like it is a pretty good indication of effectiveness on this score. Further, it is difficult *not* to believe that there hasn't been some good change inside the company.

Indeed, the entire program may be the next best thing to job rotation. Each participant gets to know a great deal about the individual situation of others in the corporate family. This kind of a program builds a market-oriented communication network. It provides support for individuals and groups. It generates commitment. In terms of corporate objectives, divisional and company lines become less important.

Above all, the program builds corporate flexibility. It gives the policy makers the kind of an organization that may be better equipped to survive in this world of change. Who knows with certainty what the company will be producing and marketing in three years?

Edward C. Bursk

17 View Your Customers as Investments

Most marketing men think in terms of investment — putting money into actions or programs that will pay off *over time.* For example:

- "Let's spend $100,000 to launch this new product."
- "Let's hire five new salesmen to build up that territory."
- "Let's lower our price to increase our share of market from 40% to 50% over the next three years."

The attitude underlying such proposals makes sense — indeed, dollars and cents. For the basic role of marketing is to bring about change — in the market, in consumers' minds, in sales, in market share, in profits. And change takes time, which in turn takes money.

Yet often this kind of investment — expenditures to bring about change in the market that will be to the benefit of the company over time — is intuitive and implicit, rather than carefully reasoned and explicitly calculated. Of course, it is difficult, if not impossible, to pin down precisely either the size of the investment or its prospective payoff. But this makes it all the more imperative to try to think through (and perhaps research) the quantities involved. The chances of making an intelligent decision are just that much better; and if the decisions to be made are crucial and expensive, then it is certainly worthwhile to try to improve them.

Unfortunately, while a number of companies are beginning to follow this reasoned-and-calculated "investment" approach in such marketing activities as new product planning and brand promotion, almost no one is applying it in an area where, if anything, it is more needed and more likely to sharpen decision making. I am referring to the channels of distribution, and particularly to the many situations where wholesaler and/or retailer customers are primarily responsible for the company's sales and profits. As such, these customers represent valuable investments of money, time, and effort.

This concept of customer-investment can be utilized by a manufacturer, particularly if he relies primarily on his wholesale distributors (or retail dealers) to *push* his product through to the consumer, rather than *pulling* it through the channels of distribution by creating consumer demand with advertising. It can be applied even more cogently by a wholesaler, whose chief, if not only, asset is the goodwill and loyalty of his retail customers; or by a retailer, who depends on continuing patronage and store traffic.

In illustrating the use of the concept, I want to focus on its application in the area of wholesale and retail trade, because I have found it particularly helpful to a number of wholesalers and retailers, and also because my own past business experience was in this area.

Real & Valuable

A company's investment in customers can be just as real as its investments in plant and equipment, inventory, working capital, and so forth. And it can be even more valuable in dollars and cents. (As I shall show with a concrete example shortly, it may well be worth two or three times as much in actual dollar value.) But, equally important, it may also be more valuable in the sense that it is more closely related to the company's existence, growth, and profitability over time.

A productive factory or piece of machinery, an efficient warehouse system or fleet of delivery trucks, an attractive store or stock of goods, an ample supply of working capital or credit — all of these are only means to an end. Investment in them is not for its own sake but for the purpose of servicing the company's real investment — its customers — as economically and effectively as possible.

Customer-investment, on the other hand, does not exist to service those other kinds of investment. Moreover, the return on the customer-investment — the gross margin on customers' purchases minus the cost of their being serviced — goes directly to profit.

I am convinced most managers really think this way. No one tries to build a valuable plant or a collection of machinery, and to develop skilled, motivated workers, just for the sake of having them. But managers do strive to build a successful *business*, and this means developing an operating system of customers who will buy its products.

For that matter, the stock market tends to value a company on the basis of its distribution system and share of market, and on the earning power that those represent. Or take the case of a company that is being acquired by another:

> Often the price paid is greater than the book value. In other words, that intangible item, "goodwill," is given more weight than the physical and financial items on the balance sheet. Sometimes goodwill doesn't appear on the balance sheet at all, or it is stated at some nominal, ridiculously conservative figure. But it stands for the value of the market franchise that the company has won — and perhaps also for good relations with its suppliers and employees, which would not exist unless the company had profitable customers in the first place. In short, goodwill stands for the value of the company's customer-investment.

Wholesaler Example

What is more, it is possible to put a specific dollar figure on the investment value of customers. For this purpose, it is useful to consider the return to be the *contribution to profit and overhead*, because this makes a good common denominator for comparing the investment value of different marketing moves. (This assumes, of course, that overhead stays pretty much the same, or changes slowly over time.)

Let me give an example, using rounded figures from a real situation:

> You are the owner, let's say, of a typical wholesale drug company which has $5,000,000 of sales per year on a capital investment (in the usual sense of the word) of $1,500,000. Suppose also that your company has 400 customers, and its gross margin plus cash discounts comes to 15%. Thus you start with 15% of $5,000,000, or $750,000. Now, take off the costs of selling, delivery, a little for postage and telephone and even bad debts — the variable costs associated directly with servicing your customers — which might add up to $350,000. (Consider everything else overhead and profit.) This leaves you with $750,000 minus $350,000, or $400,000 — the *annual contribution* that your customers make to your overhead and profit, or the *return on investment* represented by your customers.
>
> You can translate this into investment per average customer (or even better, as will show up when we look at marketing decisions, into investment in particular sizes or kinds of customers). In this case, if your investment criterion is a 10% return (based on other possible uses for money), then your average customer should be worth $10,000 to you — $400,000 divided by 400, or a $1,000 contribution to overhead and profit, in turn divided by 10%. In other words, you have 400 investments, each worth $10,000, for a total of $4,000,000 — far more than your investment in conventional physical or financial assets ($1,500,000).

Of course, another way to quantify the investment is to add up all the money that has actually gone into it, rather than figuring what it is worth from what it is yielding now. But, in the actual case on which this example has been based, as in most cases, it would be almost impossible to reconstruct what has happened in the past. The company has made many moves in the way of service to its customers — such as improving its delivery service, enlarging its inventory, advising customers to stock up in advance of price rises, and so forth; these are costs which represent money that could have been carried down to profits in the short run. Also, the owners and managers have devoted years of time and effort into promoting good relations with customers — time and effort that could have been devoted to something else that might have made money in the short run.

In any event, the fact is that customers do represent assets built up over time; and, from this point on, costs incurred to improve these assets are like capital expenditures — even though, unlike the usual financial and physical assets, they are not carried on the books as such. Moreover, once customers are recognized as the investments that they are in making action decisions, there is no reason why attempts cannot be made to quantify the money and effort currently being spent on them. In fact, this is the essence of making marketing decisions on the basis of the customer-investment concept, as indicated shortly.

The value figures can be refined further by taking into account such factors as:

1. Normal growth of an average customer over time — say, 5% per year.

2. Mortality of customers through death, bankruptcy, sell out, or transfer to another supplier — say, 20% over ten years.

3. Adjustment for present value of money, using discounted cash flow techniques — say, at 10% for ten years.

If these refinements are applied to the same wholesale situation used in the example above, the investment value of 400 customers comes to about $8,750 each, for a total of $3,500,000, instead of $10,000 and $4,000,000. But such refinements are less important than what can be done with the figures in terms of marketing actions.

Marketing Decisions

The usefulness of the concept is based on the fact that different kinds of marketing action can increase the net value of a company's customer-investment — make it larger in size or improve the rate of return on it. A marketing action that on analysis looks as if it would do this — i.e., add more to the value than the action itself costs — is clearly desirable; one that does not is questionable. And among alternative marketing actions, the one that increases the net value more deserves higher priority.

As a drug wholesaler, again, consider these possible marketing actions:

Adding salesmen to secure more customers. Suppose you have 10 salesmen. If you add a salesman, then perhaps over several years he can secure an additional 40 customers. But will they be worth $10,000 each, which is what your present customers are worth? If, as is usually the case, 25% or 35% of the customers represent 65% or 75% of the business, then you probably have about 100 customers worth up to $30,000 each, and 500 worth down to $3,000 each — all in terms of investment value. And new ones added are likely to be in the down-to-$3,000 range. So you may actually decrease your return on investment as a percentage. For the size of your investment goes up perhaps $200,000 or 5%, but one of your main servicing costs — selling — goes up by at least 10%, and total servicing costs perhaps by 7%.

Maybe this still will bring in more dollars; and dollars are more important than percentages. But *not* if you can do something else that will also maintain or improve your rate of return, because then you will get more dollars and get them year after year.

Improving the effectiveness of your existing salesmen through sales training or closer sales supervision. Perhaps you can utilize your present customers more effectively by getting increased sales out of them, for less than a proportionate increase in cost. If sales training or closer sales supervision costs $10,000 a year but improves sales effectiveness by 10%, sales will be 10% better, but costs will be only about 3% more; your return on your existing investment will be improved. So this is a better alternative than the former one.

Not that it necessarily works this way, but this is how to analyze it and to decide what to do, or not to do, out of whatever alternatives you have.

Helping your customers to improve their operations, so they will be able to buy more. This is another way to increase your rate of return; if your customers become better merchandisers themselves, they will be worth that much more to you. One large drug wholesaler has mounted a very effective program to help his retail drug customers to be better merchants and merchandisers. His payoff is triple: (1) from an increase of sales through better customer performance; (2) from becoming a preferred wholesaler source and increasing his share of the market; and (3) through greater than proportionate responsiveness from those customers who are already more valuable investments — the up-to-$30,000 group.

If in this way sales increase faster or at less cost, you have a still better alternative.

Needless to say, I have only scratched the surface. Other investment increments can be secured by better service, more advertising, and so on — and always there may be a difference in size or type of customer.

Differences in Value

I have worked with other businessmen who have found the concept useful. The differences in investment value are interesting. Compared with $10,000 for the wholesale drug company, average customer-investment for one building materials distributor comes to $5,000; and for one materials handling equipment dealer, to $7,000. For one manufacturer of industrial products whose success in the marketplace is in the hands of the mill supply houses that are his customers, the figure is $15,000. For one savings bank that has to have depositor-customers so it can sell mortgages, it is $500 (interest on deposits must be treated as part of the cost of servicing); and for one magazine that has to have subscriber-customers so it can sell advertising, it is $25.

The specific value depends, of course, on the particular industry and company situation. Some of the significant factors are: (1) the typical size of customers' operations; (2) the proportion that the products in question represent in their total operations; (3) how much of their purchases they tend to concentrate with one supplier; (4) how much service is involved; and so on. Drug retailers are not very large, but they buy a large proportion of their needs from a wholesaler, and do so week after week, if not day after day; in contrast, a road contractor may be a larger operator in terms of his annual sales, but he would only buy sporadically from his equipment dealer, and equipment is only a small part of his expenditures.

The rate of return is also important, and that too can vary. While in most situations 10% seems a reasonable figure to use because the businessman in question should have opportunities of that much potential, I did advocate a figure of 5% for the savings bank, since that represented its current yield on mortgages. Individual businesses will need to choose the rate that best fits their situation.

Retailer Example

By way of nailing down my points, let me conclude with another example, this time from the retail field:

Suppose you are a food retailer whose average customer may buy around $20 of groceries a week, or $1,000 per year. Gross margin of 20%, minus servicing costs of 5% (paper bags, lost shopping carts, pilferage, shelf-filling), leaves 15% as contribution to overhead and profit — $150. At a 10% rate of return, your average customer is worth $1,500. Suppose, further, you have 1,000 customers; in total these would be worth $1,500,000.

Now, if you offer trading stamps that cost you 2¢ per sales dollar, you will be investing an additional $20 per customer per year; and you will want to gain enough sales to keep your investment as productive as before. Actually, sales per average customer will have to rise from $1,000 to $1,154 just to come out even (unless you also mark up prices), according to this calculation, where x stands for sales:

$$(.15x - .02x) \div .10 = \$1{,}500 \text{ (the value at present)}$$
$$x = \$1{,}154$$

But here is another situation where size of customer makes a great deal of difference. Maybe some customers are already buying most of their family's food at your particular store; trading stamps will not increase their purchases at all. However, other customers who split their patronage with another store might be induced to increase their purchases. Just for simplicity, imagine that of your 1,000 customers, 500 do all their buying at your store at the rate of $1,600 annually; 500 do only part of their buying there, at the rate of $400 annually, but could be induced by trading stamps to increase their purchases at your store to, say, $900. Then your "before and after" customer-investment would look like this:

Before Trading Stamps	
500 investments @ (.15 × $1,600) ÷ .10 =	$1,200,000
500 investments @ (.15 × $400) ÷ .10 =	$ 300,000
Total	$1,500,000
After Trading Stamps	
500 investments @ (.13 × $1,600) ÷ .10 =	$1,040,000
500 investments @ (.13 × $900) ÷ .10 =	$ 585,000
Total	$1,625,000

This is not to say that the move would be as productive as indicated. It might, or it might not. If the store's mix of customers is different, it might turn out that the investment has been decreased, rather than increased as above. Or it might be that the same amount of money invested in lower prices or added service, or in a different promotional device, would increase investment value even more. (In most cases, the necessary facts and figures would be available, at least in estimated form, or be readily obtainable through research.)

The point here is only that customer-investment can be a useful concept for analyzing marketing situations of certain kinds, particularly those where marketers depend on continuing patronage. There are various ways of investing money, time, and effort to increase the volume or profitability of that customer patronage; and if the marketer compares them in explicit, quantitative terms, he will be more likely to make intelligent decisions.

Mark R. Greene

18 How to Rationalize Your Marketing Risks

Foreword

Marketing executives often are optimistic when "selling" their ideas to top management, while tending to downgrade the risks involved. This is both shortsighted and self-defeating. A careful analysis of the risks can prevent costly errors in judgment, and even open up unexpected new areas for profitable risk taking. At the very least, knowledge of the risks involved will enable the company to take steps to minimize them. Here the author describes a logical, step-by-step process for measuring risks and evaluating probabilities, and then deciding either not to go ahead or to take preventive action to reduce possible losses.

The risk element is present to some degree in all marketing decisions. Uncertainties pervade every new marketing program, and the unintended and unforeseen may either reduce profits or produce unfortunate financial losses which could have been minimized or prevented with proper planning and analysis.

Yet there seems to be an unmistakable tendency for managers to ignore the risk element in evaluating marketing plans. Planners tend to concentrate mainly on the potential profits. After all, who wants to recognize explicitly the possibility of loss, much less analyze formally how losses may come about? The marketing department may feel that its job is to "sell" itself and its plans to top management, and that emphasis on the negative aspects of a proposed plan might even be interpreted as lack of self-confidence and lead to indecision and delays.

Thus an aura of chronic and often unjustified optimism tends to surround marketing plans. A recent survey of 16 manufacturing companies that introduced a total of 63 new products over the period of 1955-1963 reveals a systematic upward bias in the forecasts made of sales and profits for new products, with a high average error for sales forecasts and an even higher average error—double, in fact—for profit forecasts.[1]

Ignoring or glossing over the risk element in marketing decisions, however, is as shortsighted as it is unnecessary. Just as a good attorney

Author's note: In this article I have developed a range of applications for the concept I described in "Market Risk—An Analytical Framework," *Journal of Marketing*, April 1968, p. 49.

1. Donald S. Tull, "The Relationship of Actual and Predicted Sales and Profits in New Product Introductions," *Journal of Business*, July 1967, p. 233.

Exhibit I. Examples of risk elements in typical marketing decisions

Marketing decision	Risk	Possible loss
Describing market segments	Actual customers not properly identified by given "segment"	Lost advertising and sales effort
Estimating future sales	Actual sales higher or lower than estimated	Investments in plant, advertising, sales, and salaries either too high or too low
Adopting straight commission system of sales compensation	Possibility of high turnover of sales personnel	Wasted sales training; customer ill will
Reducing prices for a product line	Uncertainty over whether demand is elastic or inelastic	Lost sales revenue if demand is inelastic
Granting credit terms to increase sales	Customers overextended	Bad debts; customer ill will accompanying collection efforts

should assess his opponent's likely arguments, and prepare answers for them in advance of the trial, so should a marketing manager analyze and weigh the possible negative results of a given action, as well as its possible positive results. *Exhibit I* provides some examples of the risk elements in typical marketing decisions. And here is an illustration of how risk works in a concrete situation:

If an advertisement is aimed at a given segment of the market, but fails to reach it, a large part of the advertising investment may be lost. The price of pretesting the advertising copy may be viewed as the cost of risk reduction. This cost can then be compared with the potential profit to be expected if the advertising message does reach the market segment for which it is intended. Failure to incur the cost of risk reduction may subject the company to a deteriorating competitive position or unsupportable losses, or both.

This article will discuss ways to analyze formally the risk element in marketing decisions. I do not suggest that, in recognizing the possibility of losses, management should necessarily become more conservative in marketing decisions and take few chances. Rather, my contention is that management can actually be *more* venturesome because a formal evaluation of risk will permit the planner to "touch all bases" and thus make commitments for the future with greater certainty of profits. If risks are brought out in the open, management is in a position to cope with them. A formal evaluation of the possible unknowns also permits management to select opportunities with the greatest possible reward in proportion to the degree of risk and to embark on marketing plans offering such rewards so long as the risks involved are found to meet acceptable levels.

Procedure for analysis

One way of considering systematically the various elements of risk in the marketing decision is to employ a formal procedure general enough to encompass all aspects of marketing risk. The apparatus detailed in *Exhibit II* is designed to provide such a structure; it sets forth a series of steps to be taken in handling marketing risk.

Step 1 of the logic flow chart forces the decision maker to recognize the possibility that losses may occur as a result of the decision to be made—that is, to recognize explicitly the existence of risk. If the manager can be persuaded to give serious attention to this first step, a real psychological hurdle to better decision making will have been overcome. The manager will have then given frank recognition to the fact that the profit coin might come up "tails" rather than "heads," and he will then be more likely to broaden his plans to cope with certain unknown contingencies which may develop in the process of carrying out his marketing program.

Step 2 requires management to make quantitative estimates of the maximum possible losses which could develop if things go wrong. The usual tendency here is to omit the step entirely. The excuse is usually that it is impossible to be definite or precise enough to express the possible loss quantitatively. The fact remains that it is desirable to know how big it is likely to be, and the very act of trying to be explicit about it will produce a better estimate.

Exhibit II. Logic flow chart for marketing risk decisions

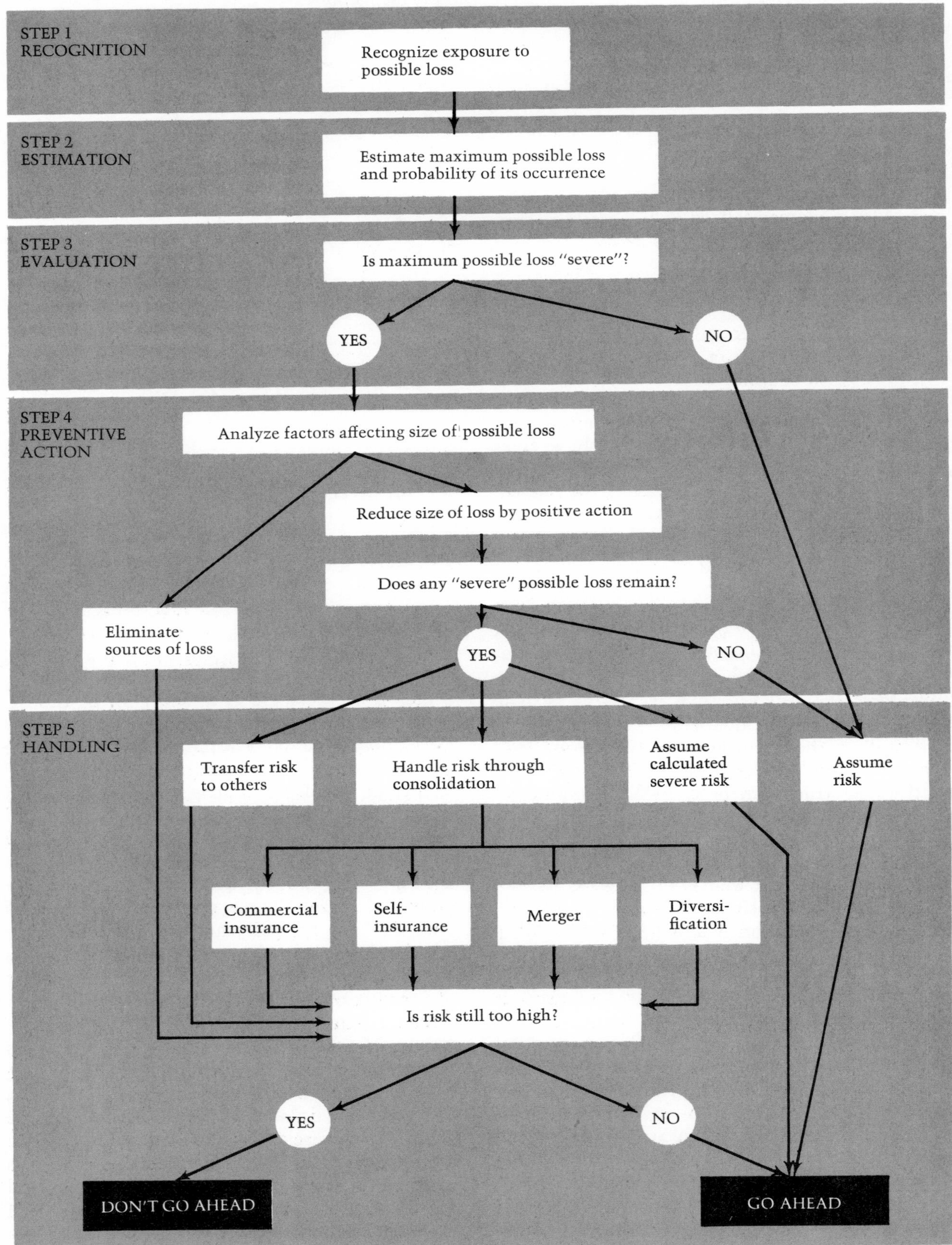

Step 3 is crucial. It asks management to decide whether or not a loss of the expected size (as quantified in Step 2) is or is not "severe." The decision is not an easy one to make. There are obviously many factors to be considered. For one thing, it may not be easy to estimate the maximum possible loss. Even more important, what seems large to one company may be small to another. For example:

A maximum loss of $100,000 may bankrupt a small or undercapitalized company but would hardly be missed by a giant, well-capitalized corporation. The manager of the large company might accept the possibility of a $100,000 maximum loss with relatively modest hoped-for gains, whereas the manager of the small company might not. Yet the latter might still be willing to run the risk of losing $100,000 if the possible profit from the decision is large enough relative to the probability of loss. The mental attitude of the decision maker toward risk is just as important in the decision-making process as is the more objectively determined probability of loss or gain.

Subjective vs. objective

The concept needed to analyze the question of how severe is "severe" is that of *subjective* risk, as contrasted with *objective* risk. This brings us to Step 4, which is a very significant part of the procedure.

Risk itself may be defined as the uncertainty surrounding the occurrence of an event which may cause loss. Objective risk refers to that part of the risk which can be determined by studying facts, usually expressed quantitatively—e.g., in terms of the odds that an event may occur which will cause a loss. Subjective risk refers to that part of the risk that is determined by the judgment and disposition of the manager who makes the decision on whether the risk is to be taken.

For example, suppose that marketing research has established that a proposed advertising program for one of the company's products has, when exposed to a sample of prospective new customers, elicited these responses in terms of buying intentions:

Very favorable	20%
Favorable	40
Neutral	20
Unfavorable	15
Very unfavorable	5
Total	100%

Suppose, further, that past experience has indicated that whenever a program thus tested is launched, "very favorable" usually turns out to lead to an actual purchasing act (which would not have taken place otherwise) on the part of 25% of those responding that way, and "favorable" usually means a new purchase by 10% of those so responding, while only 2.5% of the balance usually buy. This indicates a possible purchase rate of (20% × 25%) plus (40% × 10%) plus (40% × 2.5%), or 10%.

This 10% is known as the "expected value" of the distribution, the "most probable" level of sales that can be estimated in advance. The uncertainty that this estimate will actually be realized can be expressed as a plus or minus range of error around the 10% estimate. This uncertainty, the error range, is measurable and is the objective risk.

Now, suppose further that at 10% the advertising program would pay off—bring in more than enough new sales to pay for itself—but that at 8% it would produce a loss of $100,000, which is the maximum loss acceptable. Here is where subjective risk comes into the picture; it is not a measurement of risk, really, but a response to objective risk as measured or estimated. It answers the question, "Should the risk be taken?" whereas objective risk asks, "How great will the risk be?" And if the manager who must make the decision does not have enough confidence in the research results to feel that actual results will be above 8%, then on the basis of this subjective feeling he will decide not to take the risk and will not go ahead with the program.

Of course, no risk can be measured with complete objectivity; the choice of research techniques and the interpretation of facts and figures inevitably involve subjective judgments. And also, of course, no decision on whether to take a risk is ever wholly subjective; even though it represents an attitude toward risk, at least in part that attitude reflects factual experience in the past. My point remains, however, that it is useful for a manager to try to separate these two aspects of making risk decisions—to try to look at the facts as objectively as possible and then to try to understand how he wants to respond to them.

Explicit expression

Accordingly, in the example just cited, it would be helpful for him to express his subjective risk explicitly—such as, "Whatever the probable occurrence is, I want a safety factor of at least 30% before going ahead." For *his* risk decision-making purposes, the 10% expected purchasing rate would be translated into a range from 10% minus (30% × 10%) to 10% plus (30% × 10%), or 7% to 13%, with the lower limit of course being the crucial one. And since 8% (representing the maximum loss acceptable) falls above that limit, he would decide not to go ahead.

Here the statisticians' "Law of Large Numbers" can be useful. For a given collection of data it indicates what margin of random error

can be expected at various levels of statistical confidence. Thus, a manager can say, for example, "I want 95% confidence that my new product will reach a sales volume of between 40,000 and 50,000 units, or I won't go ahead"; and the statistician can tell him whether or not the data will support that level of risk.

In order for the situation to be expressed this explicitly, however, there has to be a large accumulation of evidence—research from a large sample or analysis of a large body of experiential data. It follows that, if a company wishes its managers to do this kind of decision making, it should try to build such data, and in this way reduce the objective risk. Thus:

One company never launches a new product without testing market reaction in the early days following the introduction. Over time it has accumulated measures of awareness, trial, and repetitive use for various kinds of products; and in the case of a new product that can be compared with previous similar products it is now possible to tell, soon after the product's introduction, how likely it is to succeed. Thus management can quickly modify its budgeted promotional program—decrease it to cut unneeded and therefore wasted expenditures, or increase it to take advantage of unexpected and therefore unrealized opportunities. In other words, the company has deliberately developed the data to create a situation where analysis can be more fruitful.

Management guidelines

Despite what is done to reduce objective risk (and there will always be situations where either the decisions or the data are not conducive to a high degree of statistical analysis), the factor of subjective risk is still strong, if only because the degree of objective risk acceptable in a business situation depends on the mental attitude toward risk of the decision maker, and this can vary greatly with the individual.

Consider, for example, the effects of variations that can exist in subjective risk among executives at different levels of the organization. Suppose $1 million has been found to be the maximum possible loss from a given program for developing a new product. Whether or not the proposition is deemed satisfactory may depend on the relative degree of risk taking—or risk aversion—in the mind of the decision maker. The risk may appear small to the top executive but large to the lower-level executive, who cannot meaningfully interpret the importance and significance of a sum this large. On the other hand, if the marketing manager is more risk-prone than top management, he may recommend proposals involving more risk than top management finds comfortable. There is also the possibility that profitable opportunities for market exploitation may be lost because promising but risky programs are screened out before they reach top management.

These kinds of problems may be resolved by adopting management guidelines following the concepts of risk previously discussed. For example, referring to the marketing decisions outlined in *Exhibit I:*

Management may require those preparing the sales forecast to express the forecast in terms of the degree of confidence that the estimate will be realized, together with the risk that it will not be. The marketing manager would be expected to summarize his report by predicting, "Sales of Product X should be 1,000,000 units, within a range of 5%; the probability that sales will be outside this range is only 10%; and the probability that sales will be less than 900,000 units, or more than 1,100,000 units, is only 3%." Such a procedure would require the marketing manager to give explicit recognition to risk and to produce more careful estimates than would be the case if he were given little or no guidance.

Such requirements would give lower management levels some indication of the subjective risk levels being employed by top management. In other words, there is a possibility of quantification of risk attitudes of top management as a dimension of corporate policy to be followed by all executives, so as to assure consistent decisions in risk-filled situations.

Action steps

In Step 3, if the maximum loss is judged not to be severe, the decision is made to assume the risk and go ahead. If the maximum loss is, however, judged to be severe, then further analysis and activity are called for (Step 4); the procedure does not stop. Perhaps sources of loss can be eliminated. Or possibly the size of the loss can be reduced. What positive action can be taken to do this?

For example, assume that the maximum possible loss in a given marketing plan has been determined, and has been found unacceptable to management (Step 3). Management may either eliminate the given sources of loss or reduce the probability of maximum loss through loss-prevention activity. These actions will vary considerably according to the type of marketing decision.

Referring to *Exhibit I* again, let us look at the marketing decision regarding possible granting of credit terms to increase sales (presumably by raising credit limits or lengthening credit terms):

If the maximum possible loss from such a decision is too high, management may (a) adopt a "cash only" policy for some types of customers or place definite credit limits on given customers (eliminating a source of loss); or (b) grant uniform terms and limits, but step up collection efforts at the first sign of delinquency (action to reduce the maximum possible loss).

Does any severe loss remain? If not, assume the risk and go ahead. If some does remain, what further can be done? This brings us to Step 5 in the logic flow chart, which illustrates various ways of handling risk.

If, after the preceding steps are taken, some severe sources of loss still remain, there are three kinds of additional action which can be taken in Step 5: (1) transfer unacceptable risk to others (e.g., by selling the accounts receivables to a factor or to a bank without recourse); (2) handle through consolidation (e.g., commercial credit insurance or dispersion of risk through diversification of products or customers, and mergers); or (3) simply accept the remaining risk if the potential gain in additional sales is worth it.

Applications of flow chart

I can now illustrate how the logic flow chart may be used as a guideline in making decisions. Three typical marketing problems which may be viewed in a risk framework are presented in ascending order of complexity.

Compensation & training

The manner in which salesmen are compensated and the investment is made in their training involves important elements of risk. There are several possible approaches.

A straight commission system reduces financial risk to the company in the sense that if the salesmen fail to sell, no commission or other payment is due. If a sale occurs, the revenue from the sale covers the cost of the commission. But the straight commission system may result in larger personnel turnover, which could cause customer ill will, loss of sales, and loss of the money spent on training. The straight commission may be viewed as a *risk transfer* device, transferring the financial risk to the salesman, who must bear the expenses and loss of his time if he fails to sell. The cost of transfer is the potential loss due to possible ill will of customers and the training costs.

Hiring a salesman already trained by someone else may be seen as a *risk avoidance* device (eliminating the source of loss), since, if the salesman is inadequate or if he leaves, the employer does not lose the sum invested in training. On the other hand, if the company invests money in training, this sum can be viewed as a *loss prevention* activity (reducing the size of the possible loss), since this investment presumably increases the likelihood of good customer relations and reduces the probability of lost sales due to inadequate field representation.

When the salesman is paid on straight commission and is not given any training, certain sources of loss can be eliminated by establishing "house accounts" where large or important customers are handled by specially trained individuals rather than the general run of salesmen. Another way of eliminating the source of loss is to combine straight commission and salary compensation in a plan designed to reduce sales turnover and provide certain nonselling services to customers to retain good will.

Following the logic flow chart, the decision maker may first make an estimate of the maximum possible loss from using the straight commission system without providing much training, as opposed to using a salary-plus-commission system and providing training. In many companies, this maximum loss may be unacceptable, since a straight commission system may produce the type of sales force which places undue stress on the making of sales and insufficient emphasis on service.

For example, say the estimate is that 10% of the company's customers will be lost with the straight commission system, compared to only 5% with an alternative system. The differential can be reduced to dollar figures so that management is able to evaluate the risk. If the maximum loss is unacceptable, the risk may be reduced by one or more of the steps in the logic flow chart. For instance, in undercapitalized companies, the sales function might even be transferred to an independent agency with salaried salesmen for a set fee known in advance. In this way the risk is transferred without the danger of loss of customers from a straight commission system.

Forecasting for a new territory

Let us assume that a company has had sufficient experience in introducing new products to make a reasonable estimate of the number of units of a certain product that can be sold under given conditions in a given territory. Perhaps the product is a household item which has been successfully introduced in other territories, or it is a new product which is expected to follow the sales pattern established by other, similar products in the new territory. It may be that the estimate of potential sales can be further refined by market testing or consumer surveys.

The marketing manager estimates the probable expected sales to be 1,000 units, and he knows that the break-even level of sales is 800 units. On the basis of analysis of the data thus available, it is further estimated that there is 68% confidence that sales will be between 900 and 1,100; 95% confidence that they will be between 800 and 1,200; and 99% confidence that they will be between 700 and 1,300.

Now, assume that the marketing manager wishes to have 99% confidence that sales will not fall below 800, the break-even level. On the basis of *objective* measurement and analysis, sales cannot be counted on to reach 800 with 99% confidence, which expresses the degree of *subjective* risk he is willing to assume. While there is a small chance that they may reach 1,300, there is also a small chance that they may reach only 700. So on the basis of his stated criteria the manager will not go ahead.

The chance of sales falling below 800 is, however, *very* small. (The statistician could, from the same probability distribution he used to supply the figures already cited, show the manager that there would be only a 3% to 4% chance of sales falling below 800 even at the 99% level of confidence.) So, of course, the marketing manager could alter his statement of risk to conform to reality.

There are more positive ways of handling the situation, however, than changing the statement of attitudes toward risk. Following *Exhibit II*, the logic flow chart, the marketing manager may use one or more of these actions to bring the range of risks down to acceptable levels:

☐ A careful study may lead to a segmentation of the market into given income or social classes within the territory; this may save the company from wasting its marketing efforts on marginal customers [2] and lead to concentration on the market segments with greatest potential (elimination of a source of loss).

☐ Certain parts of the new territory may be eliminated; this may avoid a possible loss due to inadequate sales (elimination of a source of loss).

☐ Special product demonstrations may be undertaken within the stores, or special studies may be made of competitors' products, psychological attitudes of consumers toward the product, or advertising media; this will help to ensure product acceptance (loss reduction).

☐ Sales of the product may be turned over to a subagent; this simply gets the company out from under the risk of investment in distribution channels, advertising, and so forth (risk transfer).

☐ Another company with more experience in producing and selling similar products may be acquired, and the new product assigned to this

2. For a detailed analysis of one method of treating this problem, see Roger A. Layton, "Controlling Risk and Return in the Management of a Sales Team," *Journal of Marketing Research*, August 1968, pp. 277-282.

company for handling; this increases the chance of the product's success (consolidation through merger and diversification).

Choosing optimum store size

In this situation, risk is measured by a different method from the one used previously. Here risk measurement is based not on mathematical probability distributions but on estimates of probability ranges made from market studies.

Exhibit III. Long-term average net rates of return on investment

Sales level	Size of store	Price line level High	Medium	Low
High	Large	20%	15%	10%
	Small	12%	10%	6%
Medium	Large	12%	8%	10%
	Small	15%	12%	5%
Low	Large	−5%	−2%	0%
	Small	3%	5%	2%

As an illustration, let us consider the problem of determining the optimum size of a retail shoe store in a new shopping center. The objective is to obtain the largest rate of return with the least risk. Market studies have been made of possible sales levels for each of three possible price lines. The fixed costs of operating stores of two different sizes have been determined. The marketing manager may now study the problem in terms of possible rates of return on the investment with varying combinations of sales levels and price lines. The possible returns are shown in *Exhibit III.*

Let us examine first the results if a high price line is chosen. The marketing manager determines by direct observation that if sales are high, he can obtain a 20% return on investment in a large store but only 12% if the store is small. If sales turn out to be at a medium level, his rate of return is larger in a small store (15%) than in a large store (12%). If sales turn out to be low and his store is large, he may expect losses of 5%. Intuitively, the marketing manager may see that if he chooses a high price level for his shoe line, his risk is less with a small store—no matter what the sales level may be—because he will not experience losses, and he may actually experience a higher return with a small store than with the large store if sales are at a medium level.

But he can be more precise. For example, he may make estimates (which may be subjective or based on marketing research) of the probability that sales will be high, medium, or low. Suppose he assigns probabilities of 30%, 50%, and 20%, respectively, to the three sales levels (high, medium, and low). The expected rate of return and the degree of risk for the high price line level is given in *Exhibit IV*. Not only is the risk lower for the small store, but, in addition, the total expected return for the three possible sales levels is larger for it. However, if the marketing manager is very willing to assume more risk, he may still choose a large store size, which makes possible a 20% return on investment. Regardless of the decision, the marketing manager can now choose his store size in full cognizance of the risks he is taking.

Expenditures on marketing research to determine better estimates of possible sales levels may be viewed as the price of risk reduction. The value of the marketing research corresponds to the possible gain in the rate of return on the investment.

For example, suppose that the total investment, in the case of the high price line, is $100,-000 in a small store and $200,000 in a large store. The value of marketing research here depends

Exhibit IV. Expected rates of risk and return for high price line

(a) Size of store	(b) Sales level	(c) Probability assessment of sales level	(d) Conditional rates of return*	(e) Expected returns (c×d)
Large	High	30%	20%	6%
	Medium	50%	12%	6%
	Low	20%	−5%	−1%
				11%

Risk = (Expected return − lowest possible gain) ÷ expected return
= [11% − (−5%)] ÷ 11%
= 145%

(a) Size of store	(b) Sales level	(c) Probability assessment of sales level	(d) Conditional rates of return*	(e) Expected returns (c×d)
Small	High	30%	12%	3.6%
	Medium	50%	15%	7.5%
	Low	20%	3%	0.6%
				11.7%

Risk = (11.7% − 3%) ÷ 11.7%
= 74%

*From *Exhibit III.*

Exhibit V. Possible value of marketing research expenditures for determining actual sales levels, high price line

(a) Sales level	(b) Best store size*	(c) Excess of investment, large vs. small	(d) Excess of investment return, best store size vs. alternative size†	(e) Annual saving by choosing best store size (c×d)	(f) Present value of annual savings‡
High	Large	$100,000	8%	$8,000	$99,680
Medium	Small	$100,000	3%	$3,000	$37,380
Low	Small	$100,000	8%	$8,000	$99,680

*From *Exhibit III*.
†For example, if sales are high and the price line is high, the rate of return for the best store size is 20%, and the rate of return for the alternate store size is 12%. The net advantage in profit return for choosing the best store size is therefore 8%.
‡Figures are calculated on a 20-year basis at 3% annually.

on the difference in investment in the two possible store sizes, under appropriate assumptions as to the length of time to be used in judging the investment. Suppose, further, that the investment is to be amortized over a 20-year period and that a conservative interest rate of 3% is to be used. The theoretical maximum value of marketing research expenditures to determine the true sales level is given in Column (f) of *Exhibit V*.

Since the research expenditure will never reduce the risk entirely, the values in Column (f) of *Exhibit V* might be discounted according to the extent to which the marketing manager wants to depend on the research. Thus:

▽ A marketing manager who is risk-prone might view $50,000 as the top price he would pay for risk reduction. He may reason that he has at least a 50-50 chance of choosing the right store size anyway, even without incurring the risk reduction expense. So he would discount the values in Column (f) by 50%. Or he might take the figure for the medium sales level, and consider the maximum value of risk reduction expense, $37,380, as the most realistic value of the research.

△ The risk-averting marketing manager, on the other hand, may be willing to invest up to $99,680 in marketing research in order to obtain as nearly perfect information as possible.

Risk-return trade-off: By a process identical to that used in developing *Exhibit IV*, which shows expected return and risk levels for the high price line case, we may develop expected return and risk levels for the medium and low price lines. The results for all three price levels are shown in *Exhibit VI*. The marketing manager is now in a position to examine the increase, if any, in the risk involved in a given increase in expected return. He may make an orderly examination of all the possible combinations.

Examination of *Exhibit VI* shows that the highest expected return (11.7%) is for a small store selling high price lines. The risk level of this solution is 75%. Investing in a large store selling high price lines would lower the expected return slightly, but would nearly double the risk level. The marketing manager could move to a medium price line with a small store. This reduces his expected return from 11.7% to 10%, but it also lowers his risk from 75% to 50%. The relative reduction in risk is twice the relative reduction in expected return. Accordingly, if the marketing manager is a risk averter, he may prefer a small store with medium price lines to a small store with high price lines. However, it is not likely that he would accept a small store with low price lines, since he thereby obtains less than half the expected return from a medium price line (4.7% vs. 10.0%) and suffers an increase in the attendant risk (57% vs. 50%).

The marketing manager may narrow his field of choices by arbitrarily deciding to eliminate any risk level exceeding 100%. When risk exceeds this level, there is a possibility of a net

Exhibit VI. Expected risk and return for three price levels

	Price level		
	High	Medium	Low
Large store size			
Expected risk	145%	125%	100%
Expected return	11.0%	8.1%	8.0%
Small store size			
Expected risk	75%	50%	57%
Expected return	11.7%	10.0%	4.7%

loss on the investment. (It is of course possible to construct other definitions of risk and other decision rules, such as indexes of regret.)

Conclusion

To emphasize a point made earlier, risk analysis should not necessarily lead marketing management to be more conservative. Rather, the aim is to bring risks out in the open where executives can deal with them more effectively.

It is true that marketing—at least, adventurous marketing—cannot be made completely into a "science"; there will always be a strong element of "art" in it. Yet how often it seems to be the case that the company which avoids the analytical approach altogether is the one which either makes costly marketing blunders or consistently avoids venturesome projects, preferring instead to follow courses tested first by competitors and to make marketing decisions without establishing independently any other explicit criteria. One is reminded of a famous *New Yorker* cartoon showing a chairman of the board addressing his directors in these words: "What we need is a completely brand-new idea that has been thoroughly tested."

Perhaps companies following the play-it-safe approach could not be blamed if their one and only alternative was to plunge blindly into risk taking. But today their choice is broader. Risks can be taken intelligently, and the more intelligence that is brought to bear on them, the greater the risks that can reasonably be assumed.

Of course, it is not just intelligence that is needed. When risks are made explicit in decision making, it generally becomes apparent that the managers involved take varying attitudes toward risk, with some being highly risk-prone, others highly risk-averse, and the rest in the middle. Once such conflicts become apparent, pressures will develop to resolve the differences one way or the other. Will the conservatives triumph over the liberals, or vice versa—or will some sort of compromise be worked out which may end up pleasing no one?

Top marketing executives should lead in developing *desired* attitudes toward risk—attitudes which are consistent with the company's overall strategy and planning. Ideas can be worked out as to what is a tolerable amount of uncertainty and what is not; what is "too big" a chance to take and what is not; and what the conditions are under which certain risks can be taken. Indeed, it may turn out that the greatest value of risk analysis is its tendency to force marketing leaders to resolve such questions.

Theodore Levitt

19 The New Markets—Think Before You Leap

Foreword

There can be a need, but no market; or a market, but no customer; or a customer, but no salesman. For instance, there is a great need for massive pollution control, but not really a market at present. And there is a market for new technology in education, but no customer really large enough to buy the products. Market forecasters who fail to understand these concepts have made spectacular miscalculations about the apparent opportunities in these and other fields, such as housing and leisure products. A growing host of analysts and fortune tellers are flooding top management with glowing technologically based forecasts. But computer extrapolations are not enough. Market plans must be tempered with common sense.

The easiest kind of expert to be is the specialist who predicts the future. It takes only two things: imagination and a good command of the active verb. Predicting is obviously a lot different from implementing. It is felicitously free of risk. This accounts for the existence of so many futurologists—specialists on the subject of the future. They live in a wonderful world. The greater the supply of futurologists, the greater

Author's note: This article is adapted from my forthcoming book, *The Marketing Mode—Pathways to Corporate Growth* (McGraw-Hill Book Company, Inc., 1969).

and more eager becomes the demand for their services. It is curious how little some things change. In this age of sophisticated science and technology, the gypsy fortune teller and oracular tea-leaf reader thrive magnificently. Only their clothes and artifacts are different from those of their Central European brethren.

Man's greatest continuing preoccupation is with the unknown. As his condition becomes ever more pervasively characterized by change rather than convention, he increasingly draws that much closer to those who claim some sort of comforting prescience. Predicting the future has become an industry all its own, indeed one of our more thriving growth industries. Its most avid customers are corporate executives charged with the tantalizing but awful responsibility of responding to and capitalizing on the future.

Yet many predictions served up to them in such splendidly expensive packages are either banal or fatuous. All are, of course, carefully staged to be properly provocative. Some are solemnly inspirational. But few are actionable. They stimulate, if not always thought, at least adrenaline. This has some virtue, but generally lasts about as long as it takes to get back to the pressing problems at the office.

To be told that in the year 2000 at least 30% of our food supply will be harvested in the ocean does of course alert us to the possibilities of marine biology and the competition to surface food sources. It may even suggest a possible course of action for the International Harvester Company, for Ralston Purina, for the Bath Iron Works, for Bolt, Beranek & Newman, and for anybody else who seeks growth opportunities. The prediction has its uses, especially if it is grounded in some imminent truths about science and life.

Yet it is precisely this grounding which is so often weak. The sea may harbor a huge food supply, but the consuming public is not likely to embrace any great fondness for strange new foods. Food habits are among the most difficult of all to change, even in the face of extraordinary privation. No better and no more discouraging examples are the singular disappointments suffered in recent years by companies that have created new, low-priced, high-protein foods for consumption by undernourished masses in South America and India.[1]

Clearly, a prediction about the future of the ocean's contribution to our lives may be misleading if it is based solely on scientific or technological possibilities but without regard to how people live, what they value, and how they change their accustomed habits. Thousands of wretched people starve daily in India amidst the world's largest roving supply of edible cattle. The capabilities of technology form perhaps the least realistic basis for predicting what we will consume or how we will live.

Market, but no customer

There can be a need, but no market; or a market, but no customer. When Pittsburgh's steel mills shut out the sun at high noon 30 years ago, the need for pollution control was obvious. But there was no market then; nobody thought of doing anything about the smog, even though techniques for controlling it were available. And today there is a huge market for water pollution control; but, as we shall see later in this article, not always a customer for it.

Thinking ahead must not be a simple exercise in linear extrapolation. It requires a creative synthesis. When that synthesis is absent, the result can be catastrophic. In recent years one of the most illuminating examples of such a bitter harvest has been the experience of the industries associated with residential construction.

The extravagantly optimistic extrapolations of the mid-1950's regarding the imminent boom in family formation and babies proved almost totally false, even though the young people who were to produce this boom already existed. A huge national industry spent billions developing products and productive capacity that stood wastefully idle as the eagerly anticipated housing boom refused to materialize.

What went wrong? Retrospective wisdom reveals the pitfalls of extrapolation and illustrates what we mean by creative synthesis. A complex series of changes knocked historic trends off their optimistic course. For one thing, people married later than expected. Marriages were postponed partially because of the new tendency for people to go on to college and partially because they stayed there longer. Birth control became easier and more legitimate, greatly lengthening the period between marriage and parenthood. The college boom itself was facilitated by three interrelated things:

1. The sheer abundance of so many young people competing for jobs gave those with superior educational credentials access to better jobs.

2. Hence the accepted formula for personal

1. See Ray A. Goldberg, "Agribusiness for Developing Countries," HBR September-October 1966, p. 81.

career success shifted from personal energy to formal knowledge.

3. Society became willing to tax itself far beyond any previous levels to provide itself with more higher education at lower prices.

More education and more birth control resulted not only in postponing childbearing, but also in giving young people greater access to a wider labor market. Suddenly jobs beckoned not just in the old home town but out there in the entire nation. A childless couple could more easily travel and avail itself of more distant opportunities. With better transportation—the speed of the airplane and the privacy of the automobile—uprooting and moving ceased to be the logistical trauma of the past. Gone too was the psychological trauma of departing from the folks at home. They themselves had reasonably secure

jobs, assured pensions, telephones for long-distance conversational visits, and fast airplanes for weekend access to the grandchildren. Besides, leaving home was not a solitary adventure. Everybody was doing it.

With booming times and all this access to a national labor market, young couples were doubly encouraged to preserve their career mobility as long as possible early in their working lives. The result was a life style totally different from that of the young couples of the period immediately after World War II. The war veterans, reared in depression and dispersed into the peripatetic uncertainty of a terrible war, eagerly returned to the solid stability of a home of their own in their familiar home towns. Their children of the 1960's sought the opposite—the freedom to pull up stakes, to explore their own world, and to live their own independent experimental lives. And they preferred the mobility of apartments to restrictions of home ownership. The result was the creation of sick and enormously chastened residential construction and construction-materials industries.

A general rule can be laid down about predictions regarding the shape of distant business conditions. Beware of the fluent expert. The answer man is always inspirational, owing his success to the same wonder-working evangelical talents as the itinerant soul-saver in a tent. But inspirational answers are seldom prescriptive answers.

Instead of filling the air further with Buck Rogers futurism or fast extrapolations, let us look at some aspects of the future in a reasonably responsible marketing-oriented fashion. The future does not occur de novo, arriving prophetically on some bright spring morning to the inspirational accompaniment of Beethoven's "Ode to Joy." Inescapably it emerges slowly out of today. We will in this article take no quantum jumps, no prophetic leaps to the great centennial divide of 2000 A.D., not even to some magical decadal extension like 1980. We will merely move onward from where we are today. And our purpose will be less to see what lies ahead than to suggest ways of thinking about the future within the context of concrete conditions now before us.

The slippery public market

Nothing today excites the business community more than the prospect of a huge new market in what has typically been called the "public sector"—education, pollution control, mass urban transportation, medical care. And nothing is more likely to produce the frightful disappointments that have already begun.

General Electric and Time organized the General Learning Corporation in 1965 with elaborate fanfare. The newly resigned U.S. Commissioner of Education was put at the helm of an enterprise funded with $10 million in cash, lots of electronic equipment from GE, a huge library of educational materials from Time, and with an enormously talented and energetic staff. Two years later General Learning was a shambles. It had to be fully reorganized, its strategy entirely repositioned, its targets severely lowered, its staff ruthlessly cut. General Learning's only comfort was that many of its similarly optimistic competitors suffered a similar ignominy.

The reason for these massive failures is not

that the forecasters were wrong. There is indeed a huge education market. But the existence of a market does not assure the automatic existence of a customer. The point is that there are no customers large enough to buy very much of the elaborate new educational technology visualized by scientists and educationists. This is the vital distinction that the soothsayers have missed—the distinction between the existence of a vast number of eager prospects (the market) and the nonexistence within these ranks of any solvent customers.

The reason companies such as Raytheon and General Electric covet the education market with such acquisitive anticipation is that they correctly recognize the enormous pedagogical power of technology in education—equipment for language labs, equipment for instruction in reading skills, in mathematics, and in a huge range of subjects that have been taught since their origin in the undeviatingly inadequate face-to-face fashion of the ancient little red schoolhouse. This, coupled with the obvious need to find more efficient educational methods in the face of manpower shortages, makes the new technology a hard prospect to resist. But in spite of the palpable presence of an expanding education market, it remains a market that is devoid of customers for the new technology that would solve the manpower problem.

There is no customer because the product that is most sensible to produce is also too costly to produce and hence too costly to buy. With no customer large enough to buy it, the product does not get produced. It took dozens of educators and scientists in Harvard University's Project Physics over five years to produce a brand new, one-year basic high school physics course. The course employed sophisticated modern technology, not just for classroom laboratories but also for transmitting the material to the student and for feeding his work back to the source for correction, modification, and reinforcement. It required extensive teacher training.

The development bill was over $12 million. This compares with the $30,000 or so that it costs a publisher now to produce a conventional physics book. In the latter case, however, most of the development cost is hidden. It is borne by the author, who takes it "out of his hide" working weekends and evenings. But there are not enough weekends in a hundred thousand lifetimes to produce and test an electronically sophisticated basic physics course such as the one Harvard produced. It takes a large group of dedicated specialists who must be financed directly with real money, not just with moonlighting personal commitment.

No school system big enough

The New York school system is the nation's largest, with approximately 470,000 high school students. Yet it is too small either to underwrite the creation of a basic physics course or to encourage private companies to do it. Its ironclad promise to use and annually pay for the use of such a new course for the next 20 years, even without modifications in the course to include new knowledge during all that time, would not be sufficiently enticing to produce even a second sales call from the company eager to be its developer. Within any reasonable range of annual costs, no single school system is big enough to amortize the development cost.

Perhaps only all the combined public school systems of the entire state of California are really large enough for a promise to use a truly sophisticated, high-technology, new course to encourage a private company to develop and produce it. But no state's public schools operate in this manner. And no private company is large enough, or has yet reached a sufficiently charitable state of public-service mindedness to produce such a course on speculation the way textbooks are produced. Moreover, if a combined California system could afford the program, it would still have to build special classrooms, build special labs, buy enormously expensive equipment, and train hundreds of teachers.

This explains why the constant refrain of companies such as Raytheon at education conferences is, "We can do it; just give us the money." They will not develop the basic courses or the needed equipment on speculation. And it is not really that the cost is too high—they have spent more than that on other fragile speculations. It is that there is no customer. The school systems simply cannot afford the product. Even if they could, it would take years for inertia and resistance finally to yield to its use. The world will beat no path to this mousetrap. As a consequence, Dean Theodore R. Sizer of Harvard's Graduate School of Education in his 1968 *Annual Report* declared that major industrial organizations which had hoped to make educational technology a new area of activity and profits had already begun to scale down their expectations and budgets.

Until there is massive public support for developing such courses—on the order of the federal government's \$1.8 billion contribution to the \$2 billion supersonic transport—the brave new world of electronic education is unlikely to materialize. Only one customer can cause the product to be produced, and that is the most unpopular and suspected of all U.S. customers, Uncle Sam.

The school systems cannot do it, not for lack of money, but because they will not join together to create the size needed to encourage the developers. The school systems will not get together because their entire reason for existence is that they be separate. There are over 19,000 school districts in the United States. There are more than 25 in the Chicago metropolitan area alone. Each, in effect, was created in order to be autonomous from every other one. Each represents the efforts of some town or suburb to have a self-controlled system of its very own, uncontaminated by the standards and tax bases of surrounding towns and cities. The long struggles for school system consolidation by educators and money-wise politicians have produced an unblemished record of total failure.

No support for pollution control

The same absence of a customer exists in air and water pollution. While individual companies can be compelled to scrub their air and water effluence, there is nobody to compel the towns themselves to do it. Nor will the towns really fully compel the factories on their tax rosters to do a complete and, it will turn out, highly costly job.

Who will underwrite cleaning up the shamefully contaminated Charles River in Massachusetts that looks so beautiful and smells so awful to the Harvard-Radcliffe lovers on its banks? It is abutted by Cambridge, Watertown, a half-dozen Newtons, Allston, Brighton, Waltham, West Roxbury, Dedham, Dover, and several other independent towns. It deposits its unseemly float into hapless Boston—a city with a real estate tax already stratospheric beyond redemption. All the abutting communities suffer the river's beautiful but terrible presence. Yet not one of them can by itself afford to clean it. Not one town, even if it could afford to do the job, could in fact get it done. It is an area problem, not a town problem.

As long as each community exists to escape the problems and taxes of every other community, the job simply will not get done. There is no customer for the obviously compelling need to clean the Charles River. None of the abutting communities will, on this matter, join forces to create a single financially viable and workable customer. Indeed, many years ago the abutting communities thought they had actually created the administrative machinery to solve the problem. They created the Metropolitan District Commission, a super, area-wide governmental unit with, among other things, responsibility for the care and management of the Charles River over its entire course. But the MDC is wasting away. The communities refuse to pay the taxes the MDC needs to do its job. Each community is convinced the others are most culpable for the river's contamination. None wants to pay any more than it already does.

Significantly, however, these same communities have effectively joined forces on one major matter of mutual concern—urban transportation. Just as New York created the Port Authority, so eastern Massachusetts has created the Massachusetts Bay Transit Authority. It operates a gigantic, reasonably efficient, and highly convenient network of buses, streetcars, and subways. With enormous efficiency and dispatch, the MBTA brings Wellesley's stockbrokers to their austere State Street offices in Boston each morning, and swiftly returns them each afternoon to comfortable, settled domestic surroundings characterized by handsome and progressive public schools and excellent snow removal.

Wellesley, Newton, Lexington, Beverly, Marblehead, and all the other polished suburbs agreed eagerly to the good sense of cooperation and sharing with Boston in the creation and support of this single customer, the MBTA. The stockbrokers, professors, and razor-blade executives need each day to get into the city in a hurry, and out of it even faster. What could have made better sense than do the civic thing, to cooperate in providing appropriate facilities?

Unfortunately, pollution control and educational innovation are not viewed as being equally compelling. The result is that obvious needs go unfulfilled. There is no viably solvent customer for a visibly huge market. The suburban self-interests which have so thoroughly fragmented metropolitan-area government in every U.S. city prevent the solution of problems which this fragmentation is largely designed to escape. And attitudes are getting worse, not better, even at the official level. Thus William F. Haddad, a member of the New York City Board of Education, recently argued for a further fragmentation of the city's metropolitan public school system into even more separate and autonomous enclaves. Said he:

"If we had local control of the schools on the West Side of Manhattan [where he lives], I'd feel a lot better about putting my kids in the schools here because . . . I'd go down there and I'd damn well make that school function for my child."[2]

Federal help needed

Private enterprise will not properly benefit from the huge public market represented by education, area-wide pollution control, and other major public problems until there is a viable customer. Because of the strong and probably irremediably parochial interests of the numerous small governments that prevail so powerfully in the urban areas of the nation, it is unlikely that they will willingly reconstitute themselves into viable customers.

The magnitude of the problem of creating a viable customer for any number of public projects that require massive areawide effort is illustrated by the fact that in the greater Chicago metropolitan area there are 1,060 different and not necessarily cooperating local governmental units.

But federal involvement is precisely what the business community has generally rejected almost as an article of faith. Washington is almost automatically viewed as bad and to be resisted. The only reason its pervasively monopsonistic powers have not been resisted in national defense is because national defense is aimed at external threats. Internal threats are not generally viewed by the business community as warranting any similar suspension of customary opposition to the expansion of Washington's activities.

Yet perhaps, with a more realistic appreciation of what is possible, the needed changes may be achieved more readily than now appears possible. The fact is that Washington's activities in these areas can be greatly expanded without an equal expansion in its powers. This is not generally recognized, even where it has already happened.

Thus we have a national system of unemployment insurance that is purely states-rights in character and administration. It is the result of a highly instructive federal innovation. To get all states to institute the system, and to obtain some sort of national uniformity and minimum standards, the Unemployment Compensation Act provided for a federal tax on payrolls. But 90% was rebatable to the states on condition that they establish and operate an unemployment compensation program of a clearly stipulated character. The administration was to be, and still is today, by the states. The incentives for establishing a proper system were obvious. Every state quickly did its duty.

The same principle also operates in a variety of other areas, and it has merit for education and area pollution control. Whatever merit there may be to the old arguments about states rights and local autonomy, the necessities imposed by modern times require new views about how to accommodate these necessities. Until the very men who live in the Wellesleys, the Upper Montclairs, the Wilmettes, and the Santa Monicas recognize the compelling need for federal customer-creating machinery for the achievement in the twentieth century of what modern technology and knowledge both demand and make achievable, these men will not achieve for

their businesses the thriving benefits from the public market that they now so optimistically covet.

Thus, before business can profit from a new technology in education on the massive scale it entertained in the mid-1960's, it must support the creation of a customer who is now even less likely to materialize than in those optimistic

2. *The New York Times*, September 1, 1968.

days. As Dean Sizer observed in his 1968 *Annual Report*:

"A national government, faced with an angered minority of poor, both black and white, and even an armed insurrection, has found it easy to postpone educational reform.... Plans to strengthen the police and the National Guard are now more in the Federal rhetoric than those to strengthen the school. Education takes too long, it seems."

If business wants to apply its organizing and technological skills to education to the full extent of its powers, it must first solve the customer problem. That requires a major change in its way of looking at Washington. It must begin, even more than it has already started, to view the national state not as the traditional enemy that is to be resisted and fought at every turn, but as a possible instrument for national betterment—an agency which, properly directed, advised, and supported, can be an instrument to expand the potentials and liberties of man, and derivatively the profits of business as well.

The illusory leisure market

Few things in recent years have been more confidently hailed than the magnificent opportunities offered by the so-called leisure market. To repeat the ecstatic hyperboles would be to commit a major redundancy.

It is true that sales of skis, boats, and Coleman heaters are in unprecedented ascendance. Whether this is the fallout of leisure rather than of affluence is another question. It is a highly relevant question. Its attribution to leisure is generally accompanied by expansive forecasts of expanding leisure for our population. More leisure (defined as time uncommitted to regular work) is generally assumed to mean more free time, and more free time means bigger markets. Yet the facts are contradictory.

In 1967 the U.S. population actually had substantially *less* leisure than in 1940, and even less free time. In 1939 the average U.S. factory worker spent 37.7 hours at his job each week. In 1967 he spent 40.6 hours. Yet, in 1939 we skied less, boated less, camped less, drank less, and went to fewer football games. In 1939 we were still in a deep depression, with nearly 12 million willing and able men walking the streets searching for nonexistent jobs. Those with jobs clung to their meager savings against the possibility they would have no job next week. In 1967 they had jobs; and instead of working a partial week, they worked overtime. They had less leisure, but they spent more money and more time on leisure activities.

More leisure does not automatically mean more free time. The 40-hour week of 1969 actually leaves less time than the 40-hour week of 1940. Where in the bad old days it took a steelworker 5 minutes to walk to work, or 15 minutes on a streetcar, it now takes him a half hour on a clear day driving a late model car. Even with freeways to speed him along his urban path, for the next ten years any reduction in the work week is likely to be more than consumed by the lengthening of the commuting time.

Even when there is more leisure and a briefer commute, whether there will in the foreseeable future be more time is sufficiently questionable to require serious attention. What counts is not absolute time, but discretionary time. The relevant question is: How much time will be left over to consume all the splendidly expanding artifacts of business's fertile imagination?

The answer requires a look at how man becomes acculturated. When in his less affluent years he bought a bottle of whiskey on rare ceremonial occasions such as New Year's Eve or weddings, a Saturday night blast was a special indulgence. When he finally reached the stage of buying a bottle cyclically every Saturday night, the weekday drink became the indulgence. When the weekday before-supper drink finally became a regularity, it became viewed as a civilized necessity. Drinking ceased to be discretionary. It was obligatory—a routine style of life, like three meals a day. New styles of life tend quickly to become habitual. Consumption patterns that at first seem indulgent and discretionary tend to become routine and necessary. Once certain patterns develop and commitments are made, the so-called leisure (nonworking) hours to which they are committed are no longer so easily part of the available time.

More so-called leisure-time products and services will indeed be demanded in the years ahead; but it is affluence, not leisure, that will produce most of the demand. Yet the extent of affluence is itself a weak predictor of the style of leisure life.

Income levels deceptive

Consider today's autoworker in Detroit who earns $8,500 a year and whose working wife brings home another $5,000. This family income of $13,500 is well above that of the new M.I.T. graduate with an M.S. degree in electrical engineering. The traditional taxonomy places both families in the upper middle class. But in operative, consuming terms, the taxonomy fails to fit.

The Detroit family actually belongs in a new and perhaps anomolous category: the overprivileged working class. Its income qualifies it for inclusion in *Look* magazine's exclusive list of one million "Top Spot" subscribers—America's economic aristocracy. Yet this family's consumption style hardly makes it an attractive audience for *Look*'s Mercedes-Benz advertisements. In its buying habits it will be more like other $8,500 Detroit auto worker families than like young $13,500 Bloomfield Hills auto executive families. It will spend less on gin and more on bread, more on bowling and less on entertaining, less on clothing and more on credit. Yet, according to the National Industrial Conference Board, half of the U.S. families with $10,000-to-$15,000 income owe their status to working wives.

Just as income is not a functional guide to the pattern of consumption, so any reduction in the length of enforced on-the-premises work-time is not a functional guide to the availability of discretionary time. As man gets more liberated from on-the-job obligations, he creates for himself new off-the-job obligations. For instance, one reason for the reduction in the formal work-week is improved productivity, based on increased knowledge, but to keep up with the advancing knowledge a man must spend increasing time in off-the-job study.

Thus it is probable that the demands on his off-the-job time will accelerate more rapidly than the expansion of the time itself. Time that is not consumed by the necessities of study and of keeping up with the new uses of knowledge will rapidly be consumed by commitments modern man makes to other patterns of time usage, such as new recreation patterns and social service programs. What remains for discretionary distribution among other goods and services is not likely to produce some of the magnitudinous leisure-time consumption booms that are so confidently predicted.

Special qualities of leisure

I have suggested here that money has been more important than time in helping produce leisure-products demand, that in the future there may be less discretionary time than superficially optimistic forecasts now suggest. But money itself is an incomplete explanation for the obvious boom in certain leisure products. Why, for example, do people spend it on skis, golf, sailboats, camping equipment, sports cars, do-it-yourself workshops, oil paintings, Hawaiian vacations, and trips to Europe? Why not more on better home furnishings, tithing to the church, or dinner parties at home?

A clue to the answer lies in looking at the specific human character of those booming leisure-time activities. They have one thing in common: they are activities possessed of a highly individualistic, personal, nongroup character. The skier, the golfer, and the painter are each engaged in a solitary activity whose credit for mastery will be uncontestably his own, unshared by others and not lost deep in the bowels of some cooperating task force or team. The husband who produces a lamp in his basement workshop will have engaged in an act of creation that is unquestionably his own personal achievement, just as the wife with her cookbooks, herbs, and condiments produces a gourmet meal that is her own personal output, not that of some factory kitchen in Minneapolis.

Today's discretionary market is selectively engaged in activities that may be characterized as representing a silent revolt against, or at least an escape from, the organized, structured, mass-production quality of modern life. It is an act of self-assertion in a world of group assertiveness, of trying to find personal distinction in a homogenized environment, of testing and demonstrating one's own private powers of mastery in a visible way in order to offset the dissatisfactions of a life where one's personal contributions are never fully measured and are generally hidden deep inside some committee, task force, assembly line, laboratory, or other essentially group effort.

Everywhere modern man turns, he is the captive of rules, clocks, schedules, traffic lights, confining customs, and rigid routines of other people's seemingly demonic making. Not even the president of a large corporation or nation can escape; perhaps he especially cannot.

Yet the modern adult is not all that imprisoned. As his life gets more regimented and homogenized, and as his own personal contribution to getting things done in this world is increasingly less identifiable in a world where things are increasingly done by groups, he has found ways to assert his own personal worth. Leisure-time activities of a highly personal character are his "out." They are his ersatz freedom.

To appreciate the point, one needs only to look at how few of the leisure activities in which he so actively engages are team activities or are passive in character. They are personal and active, not group and passive. He is not playing basketball on a local church team, not organizing a neighborhood adult hockey league. He is engaged in solitary activities where his own personal contribution is highly visible and unambiguous. When he does join a team, it is something like bowling, where his personal contribution is absolutely clear and not dependent on the help or contribution of his teammates.

Similarly, the growing emphasis on product options and product tailoring to specific customers will create new opportunities for companies emphasizing extremely narrow lines of standardized products, as the Volkswagen has so successfully demonstrated in the automobile business.

The persistent proletariat

There is another kind of missing customer.

A more fundamental analysis of the psychology of our society can also bring to commercial attention what is now so widely visible on the social front. This is the existence of what may be called the persistent proletariat. The United States, in spite of its felicitous economics and its educational democratization, is a polarized economy. Consider:

When all the figures about affluence are finally sifted, averaged, and adjusted for tax deductions, the results are startling. In March 1967 the average weekly spendable earnings of a U.S. worker with three dependents (a wife and two children) were $88.75. That comes to $4,615 a year—not even half of what is needed for the U.S. Bureau of Labor Statistics' calculation of a decent cityworker's family budget: in autumn 1966 this modest budget for an urban family of four came to $9,200. No wonder there are working wives and moonlighters! What is more, in 1967 nearly 12 million U.S. adults had less than a sixth-grade education; about 2.7 million never went to school at all; and about 23 million never completed grade school.

This is indeed a persistent proletariat. Only a fraction of it is in the so-called overprivileged class. A great deal of it is in the underprivileged and exploited class. Not everybody is affluent. Not everybody has Westchester tastes. Many of those outside the benign and narrow circle of affluence have the resources needed to pull themselves into it. But a great many of them don't. They persist in almost paralyzing poverty.

It takes a special kind of heartlessness to cite these figures for the purpose of helping businessmen to focus on their commercial possibilities. Nevertheless, the future is likely to be characterized by social turmoil and demands for equality and reform in proportions larger than the liberating advances in technology that are commonly predicted. These speculations are almost invariably exercises in lyrical optimism. Yet the future that ought to occupy U.S. business more is not the technological breakthroughs which seem likely or the surging affluence of the affluent classes, but the considerably less edifying subject of the reactions to all this unevenness of those who seem so fated to lag behind.

It is a future of which the death-dealing urban riots of 1967 are a harbinger, if not of more riots, certainly of more social change; a future in which the tantalizing television advertisements that are so widely presumed to grease the wheels of commerce will increasingly play the powerful revolutionary role of creating dissatisfaction and unrest among those whose appetites are whetted by the televised standard of living, but whose means never come within reach. The more effective the advertisements, the greater the discontent.

It is not a happy outlook. It suggests that, in looking ahead, U.S. business may be best advised to look not so much to the improvement of business conditions as to the improvement of the society within which business must function. The old trickle-down theory obviously does not work as well as it has always been assumed to work. It is now clear that good business, prosperity, and economic growth do not automatically produce the good life for everybody, or even necessarily for a majority.

Customer, but no salesman

There can be a need, but no market; or a market, but no customer; or a customer—that is, a prospective customer—but no salesman.

Few operating problems in business command so much continuing attention or produce so much anguish as "the salesman problem"—where to get salesmen, how to evaluate and improve their performance, how to keep them from quitting. Psychological tests, seminars, and incentive systems proliferate. The future is viewed with a combination of apprehension and hope—always hope that things can be improved if we only work at it more imaginatively and energetically.

Yet realistically it seems unlikely that anything of the kind that is done or contemplated will solve the so-called "salesman problem." Indeed, it will not be solved any more than it has ever been solved. It is the oldest malignancy known to business. Not even when 12 million desperate men walked the streets in the awful depths of the Great Depression was business satisfied with the supply and quality of its salesmen. Why? Let us try to understand the reasons for this dismal condition. Understanding will not solve the problem, but it may alleviate the stress.

The sales manager's dissatisfaction with his salesmen arises in part from the same reason that the president is dissatisfied with the sales organization. The primal reason, to which every other consideration is totally subordinate, is the natural and understandable presumption that sales can be improved simply because "up" is infinite, and therefore it is to be expected that more can be done. No such logic applies suitably to any other function in the business enterprise. There are presumed to be limits below which costs cannot be reduced, above which machines can produce no more parts. Only sales are presumed to be without reasonable limit.

A second source of dissatisfaction with salesmen arises less from their performance than from their uncontrollability. The selling task is solitary and never fully under the eye of its manager. Salesmen travel, or they work in isolated corners of the store. They are on their own, not constantly under the scrutiny of a boss in the next office. The man who thinks himself a boss or manager understandably chafes at his resulting impotence. He is nominally in charge, but in fact finds it difficult to exercise his apparent power. He is unable to manage subordinates on whom is bestowed the right to operate independently away from his constant view. That is why sales managers feel so much better when they go out into the field; not because their presence yields more sales, but because it makes them feel more in control, more like honest managers. Salesmen are not only hard to direct and control, but are also likely to set their own sales and earnings levels. When they have got enough, they go to the ball game—preferably on the expense account with a cooperating prospect.

Finally, selling is hard work, even when you are selling dollar bills for fifty cents. The prospect is always skeptical, especially when the proposition looks *that* good. It takes a lot of work, patience, good cheer, perception, and persistence. Few people can take the pressure, frustration, and, worst of all, the suspicion and hostility of the prospect. That is why so few are interested. More pay would help, but not really enough.

Eliminate the salesman

There is no solution. There are only placebos. The closest thing to a solution is to escape—not to improve the salesman, but to eliminate him. That is what the vending machine has done. Technology has replaced man. A great deal more could be done if companies just thought about it more systematically. The self-service retailer has done it in some fashion. The meat counter at the supermarket finally did it through functional prepackaging of cut meats. The mail-order house is doing it. And it can be done under more difficult circumstances. Take the retail gasoline station:

□ In the United States the gasoline station provides employment to several million men who do today exactly the same thing their great grandfathers did on the first day of the automobile's creation: they insert a tube into a receptacle to transfer gasoline from the vendor to the motorist. The poverty of imagination this stagnation represents is the more forcefully emphasized when we consider (a) how much everything else about the industry has changed during these many years, and (b) the persistent plaint of petroleum companies about the accelerating shortage of service station dealers and attendants.

For many reasons, self-service is not a promising solution. Other possibilities are different kinds of fuels that require less frequent purchasing or power systems that require no special stop at all. One ridiculously simple possibility is merely to furnish cars with significantly larger gasoline tanks. It seems entirely reasonable that the combined efforts of the nation's major petroleum companies might have some persuasive effect on Detroit.

But if our guide is the total elimination of the station attendant, the technology exists today to do it. Gasoline tanks could be designed for automated bottom filling—loaded from underneath through a nozzle that electrically finds and inserts itself into a compatible self-opening and self-sealing orifice in the tank after the car is driven onto a set of self-locking runners on the service station driveway. The runners would unlock only after a credit card is inserted into the meter to record and debit the sale to the customer's account.

Such a device would of course cost the auto companies a great deal more than the petroleum companies, while saving them nothing as opposed to great savings for the petroleum companies. But a cooperative development program between the two industries, and indeed some sharing of subsequent expenses, would not be their maiden exercise in cooperation. It would, however, go far beyond the Mickey Mouse dancing on the periphery to which their mutual ventures have accustomed them.

Simplify the sales job

Job simplification is another promising possibility for easing the salesman problem. It holds more promise in some areas than others.

Sales jobs can be simplified by extending to the face-to-face encounter between prospect and salesman a principle that is so successfully employed in selling situations where seller and buyer are not now in close personal contact. We may call this the *principle of the controlled proposition.* That is what media advertising is all about: a carefully rehearsed, fully controlled, and infallibly executed and standardized proposition. This controlled or standardized advertising proposition tends greatly to simplify the job of the salesman who serves the customer who has seen the ad. The salesman needs to do less work because the advertising proposition has done part of it for him. This principle of the controlled proposition can be extended directly to many face-to-face selling situations.

For instance, the salesman can place on his prospect's desk an attaché-case-sized rear projector, to run off movies or slides that go into the details of what is being offered with great care and professional effectiveness. The proposition is thus controlled, and can vary in detail and sophistication according to the needs of the situation. Similarly, telephones could be used in a store to enable a customer to plug into a taped explanation of the item that interests him. Already selling has been done with cathode-ray tubes for product display and demonstration and direct ordering through communications consoles on the customer's premises. All these cases, actual or potential, represent steps in the elimination of the salesman via job simplification through technology.

The computer is a powerful facilitating mechanism, both in console purchasing and in direct mail. In direct mail it greatly facilitates the continuous refinement of prospect lists. This makes it easier to pinpoint and evaluate prospects of a given profession, age, income, family size, and purchase history. And it applies for industrial as well as for consumer prospects. The result is that all of us will get more sales propositions through the mail, but increasingly less of this will be "junk" mail—unsolicited offers to sell us things in which we have no conceivable interest. We will get more mail, but it will be more relevant because it will be mail that the computer tells the seller is relevant to our lives. The father of three grammar school children will get different mail from the father of three high school children; golfers will be differentiated from beer drinkers, and symphony fanciers from ballet fanciers.

Finally, through specialization of the sales force according to the industry and size of accounts, a salesman will be spread less thin, and will become an expert in the business of one or two industries. He will serve each prospect better, and feel better for being able to do a better job.

All these practices boil down to the same thing —job simplification. While improved methods of salesman training continue to improve the old malignancy from which the field selling organization has suffered, they will help even more when the sales job is simplified. That is what the future will bring because that is what is already happening; and it is happening because the technology is available precisely at the time when the need becomes urgent and society is ready to accept the necessary changes.

The 'verglomerate' market

Even as the salesman's role changes, there is destined to be a new kind of complexity in the marketplace. It is increasingly likely that large corporate customers will seek to capitalize on their size in their procurement activities. This will then tend to produce more conglomerates and more vertically integrated firms. The next phase in conglomeracy will then become the vertically integrated conglomerate—what I call the "verglomerate."

The twin ideas of leverage and synergy are very much on the minds of today's corporate empire builders. It is only a matter of time before these ideas penetrate down to the empire operators—the men who must make the conglomerate systems work once they are put together. They will see soon enough that size gives them purchasing power vis-à-vis their suppliers. This realization will ultimately force the creation of a new kind of corporate customer. It will be a customer who pays as much attention to his purchasing activities as he now pays to his selling activities.

Indeed, at least one famous conglomerate originated as a vehicle to give its conglomerated member companies purchasing leverage over their suppliers. Gulf & Western Industries, in its reincarnation under Charles G. Bluhdorn, was developed as a chain of automotive aftermarket distributors specifically consolidated to achieve major purchasing strengths. Manufacturing companies can benefit similarly when they recognize that (according to the 1964 Census of Manufactures), on the average, 57% of their value of shipments represents purchased materials and services. This means that a $50-million company with a 40% operating margin would need a sales increase of over 12% to match the increased profits produced by only a 5% cut in purchasing costs. This is a relationship that is hard to ignore.

The increased recognition of this road to profits promises to produce pressures for major changes in the way large companies operate. Take one actual example:

□ Hooker Chemical Corporation had sales in 1967 of over $300 million. Early that year it reorganized and centralized its fragmented purchasing organizations. Hooker established written procurement strategies and created corporatewide purchasing specialists in such areas as equipment and capital goods, basic materials, and containers. Field and plant purchasing were centralized under a single corporate manager. A corporate purchasing function was created to study vendor performance and to continuously audit Hooker's own purchasing operations.

The outcome was a thorough professionalization of purchasing that put new demands on vendors and new muscle into Hooker's buying activities. By coordinating and, where possible, consolidating procurement activities, Hooker achieved purchasing benefits that only its consolidated size could produce.

What Hooker did represents more than meets the casual eye. Centralization not only produced purchasing strength, but also greatly changed the things suppliers could and needed to do in order to deal with Hooker.

While the large supplier ends up making more concessions to this kind of centralized purchaser than to a fragmented purchaser, centralized purchasing can also produce unexpected benefits for that supplier. For example, the very fact that the supplier may be more easily persuaded to carry the customer's raw material and parts inventories and make deliveries on a more exacting schedule also makes it that much easier to persuade the customer to accept purchase contracts. Concessions which require the supplier to integrate his operations closely into those of the buyer in turn require the buyer to get binding supplier assurances in order to guarantee the smoothness of his own operations. Purchase contracts create the form of this assurance. But they also guarantee the seller a stipulated demand for a stipulated period of time.

There are very good reasons why large industrial buyers will increasingly favor purchase contracts in the years ahead. And the result may very well be a better overall deal from the supplier.

Perhaps the most compelling reason stems from the rising sophistication of sales forecasting and production scheduling. Just as better forecasting creates the possibility of more effective production scheduling, so better production scheduling creates the possibility of more effective scheduling of acquisition of materials and purchased parts. In-shipments of raw materials and parts can be more carefully programmed to coincide with the buyer's carefully timed need for them. And if the buyer can find a supplier who can deliver according to such a carefully timed schedule, he can afford to allow this supplier to be intimately locked into his productive and inventory plans through a long-term purchase contract. For the end result will be lower inventories, less space tied up by inventory backup stock, and a consequent reduction in cost—thus contributing to a better deal.

New forms of purchase contract

The inducements to both sides are obvious. But increasingly the process of entering such contracts will involve more than a simple negotiation. Centralized purchasing, though seemingly in conflict with the idea of divisional autonomy and independent profit centers, can have such powerful cost-saving appeals that it will almost necessarily force a modification of traditional ideas. In the process it seems equally likely that the old ideas about contract negotiations between major seller and major supplier will be modified.

As the seller's operations get more tightly integrated into the buyer's production schedule, the buyer becomes more firmly dependent on the performance of his supplier. The result will be that both sides will make entirely new kinds of concessions to each other. Price will, of course, be one of these concessions. But instead of concessions being made in the old-fashioned atmosphere of personal bargaining, they will occur in a tight process of businesslike, sophisticated bidding.

In fact, what will make the process sophisticated is that bid proposals will have to stipulate a great deal more than price itself. Increasingly the process will follow the pattern set in defense and aerospace contracting. Price will be an enormously important consideration, but it will hardly exhaust the proposition. Ability to perform the logistics of tightly scheduled delivery will become fully as salient an issue as price. Thus, as the inevitable problems of performance rear their heads, as they have in military procurement, industrial bid evaluation will place increasing emphasis on the indicated capability of the vendor to accomplish the required scheduling, logistical, and service jobs. This will be the most elaborate component of the bid proposal because it is this performance that will be so critical for the buyer.

As a consequence, purchase contracts will result in the formalization of many things that are now generally left to good faith. Exactly how products are to be shipped and delivered will be formally stipulated. Customer services, now viewed as being merely incidental to the product and rendered on a call or on a vendor-initiative basis, will be carefully spelled out and committed by the vendor. Contracts will enumerate and describe in detail the exact character of stipulated services and related activities. The result will be a de facto legal recognition of the fact that the thing people and companies buy is not just a tangible product, but a whole cluster of related benefits, services, and values. I have elsewhere referred to this notion of what the customer buys as the "augmented product." [3]

These contracts will become more frequent as purchasing becomes more centralized or simply just more tightly coordinated by a central corporate source. This will of course occur predominantly in the large, multidivision, multicompany corporations. Computers, value analysis, cost-benefit analysis, life-cycle cost analysis, as well as the less fashionable old-fashioned analytical devices—all these will increasingly revolutionize corporate purchasing. Centralization will be the organizational outcome, and purchase contracts the operational consequence.

What can the seller do?

Vendors will not generally welcome these eventualities. But they must guard against a self-defeating opposition to them. In fact, one company has already taken strong steps to prevent exactly that by actually promoting centralized purchasing to its customers:

□ The Carborundum Company, which anticipates the early inevitability of these developments, is doing some extraordinary things to benefit from them. It has over the years been highly aggressive and successful in practicing the "augmented product" concept. It views the coming growth of centralized purchasing, bidding, and contract selling as leading to a reemphasis on price in selling that will parallel the simultaneous intensification of the competitive struggle around the expansion of customer services.

Carborundum believes that increasingly the buyer will take a hand in defining the content of the product's "augmented" features. Hence, it believes that vendors who on their own create these features will eventually cease getting the automatic jump on their competitors that they got in the past. Their expanded services to the buyer will merely suggest to him what he should be asking other vendors to include in their bid packages.

To strengthen its position with existing and prospective customers, Carborundum is therefore developing a program to teach large multicompany and multidivision corporations how to organize and operate a centralized purchasing function and how to do bid purchasing. Carborundum's strategy is that by participating with these companies in developing centralized procedures, it will learn better than its competitors exactly how these companies will be operating, how they will be thinking, and how they will be making vendor-selection decisions. This

3. See my forthcoming book, *The Marketing Mode—Pathways to Corporate Growth* (New York, McGraw-Hill Book Company, Inc., 1969).

would give Carborundum an edge in shaping its bids and proposals.[4]

Two-way integration

The complete verglomerate will be the conglomerate whose separate corporate entities are themselves vertically integrated—such as a steel company with its own ore, own railroad to ship it, own fabricating plants, and own warehousing system. The vertical segments will be important customers of and suppliers to each other. The horizontal entities will, in turn, become joint contributors to the creation of product and service systems that they jointly sell and install. The impact on marketing practice can become profound. A verglomerate has already shown the way:

□ Litton Industries acquired the A. Kimball Company, whose unit ticket control cards in retailing expand and complement the "product" of its Monroe-Sweda cash register and accounting machines; and it has acquired Streater Industries, Inc., which makes retail display showcases. The net result, still in process of completion, will be a vertically integrated series of companies selling a complete retailing facilities system to department stores.

In the process, the stores, in order to capitalize on the system that is being offered, will have to plan their facilities purchases in a highly unaccustomed manner. Gone will be the separation of purchasing decisions for accounting machines, cash registers, display cases, and merchandise price-marking devices. Everything will be a tightly integrated part of everything else. The new product will have altered the purchasing practices of the customer.

These changes will not come easily or quickly, or without bitter resistance in companies wedded to the idea of autonomous profit centers. Many will resist for a long time. The price of pride and ancient preferences will certainly be higher costs.

The new verglomerates will, in operations (though certainly not in spirit), become the U.S. equivalent of the old-fashioned European industrial complexes—famous for their highly centralized control by hard-faced men of ancient lineage working anonymously out of the deepest recesses of distant headquarters offices. It is no accident that these offices have been so frequently located in and closely associated with banks. As in today's conglomerates, headquarters performs what is largely a banking function, passing on budget requests, setting performance standards, and collecting and consolidating the profits.

The merits of this system are easily overlooked when we justifiably criticize the somewhat shortsighted fiscal orientations of the old-world industrial empires. But centralization does not inevitably sentence a company to such narrow orientations.

A case in point is Japan. The Japanese today function in the stealthy fiscal manner of their European predecessors, but with the seminal distinction that they are solidly oriented toward the production of what the market will take rather than toward the production of things that serve a pseudo-commercial, inner-directed, and sometimes highly political purpose. It need not be supposed that all error flows simply from organizational structure, or therefore that changing the structure changes the results. Few ideas in business are more appealing and less serviceable than those that promise by organizational reconstruction to solve problems of ancient and human lineage.

Forces already at work suggest that the conglomerate view of fiscal leverage will, I believe, through the influence of purchasing and marketing considerations, increasingly produce acquisitions whose purpose is to enhance marketing synergy. The new corporate form that will emerge will be the verglomerate, a new U.S. operating version of an old old-world structural form.

Conclusion

Man generalizes in order to make life tolerable, even possible. Otherwise, each problem he faces, each task that demands action, requires him to start all over again. Every generation would have to learn from the beginning and by itself all that it needs to know for its effective survival and progress. Such a style would be disastrous; it would have prevented man from ever descending from the trees.

Thus there is an immense attraction to principles and formulas that appear to represent the learning of the past. This is why management textbooks sell so well, as do management development seminars that promise to provide instant

4. For another aspect of Carborundum's marketing effort see Joseph W. Thompson and William W. Evans, "Behavioral Approach to Industrial Selling," HBR March-April 1969, p. 137.—*The Editors*

answers, liberating check lists, and other spurious shortcuts.

But today, as never before, businessmen live in a world of fast change and new environments. Decisions of great magnitude must be made at an increasing rate and under conditions of considerable uncertainty. The guidelines of the past may not fit the future.

The danger is obvious. We must learn from the past in order to make any progress at all. Yet as we learn from and progress beyond the past, we run the risk of employing obsolete dogmas for new times. The issue is not whether knowledge and know-how are transferable. It is whether they are applicable.

This means that now, even more than in the past, the essential managerial skill is not a good memory for principles, as is so often the case in law and medicine, but the ability to determine what the problem really is. It is the ability to do that which distinguishes the chief executive from the janitor. Understanding is more important than dogma.

Aubrey Menen once pointed out that a soldier does not have to know right from wrong. As long as he knows right from left, he'll do fine. His commander, however, must know what the soldier need not know. And just as right and wrong have no absolute moral content, neither do business rules or principles. In the end there are no rules or principles. The commander must struggle alone to decide what is right for the situation that he must analyze for himself. The burden is on his capacity to open up his pores for all the subtle inputs that characterize "the situation," and then to think alone what is appropriate to the objectives on which he has decided.

The management of a large organization is far more difficult than most men who manage are themselves aware. Few in fact are managers. They are custodians. Somehow the enterprise keeps going at an acceptable rate, but usually only because its competitors are no better. Most managers unfortunately do very little thinking in the course of their work. They are entirely unaware of how much they manage by formula, by dogma, by principles, textbook maxims, and resounding cliches; and of how much, in the process, they are forfeiting the one distinction by which we tell man from animal. Their resort to easy generalization is explained by the heavy burdens of their job. But to explain it is not to condone it.

When you reach some stage of your maturity, you want to look into the mirror and be sure *you* are there. You want to know that it is you and not the ventriloquist for some ancient soothsayer who is really running things. There comes a time in the life of every business when you have to abandon old formulas and do what's right for new times.

Index